B.A.Young

G000059662

Volume 1

State Trials

By the same author

A Long Time Burning: The history of literary censorship in England

Points of Contact: A collection of poems 1958–1961

Volume I

State Trials

Treason and Libel

Edited by

Donald Thomas

Routledge & Kegan Paul

London and Boston

First published 1972
by Routledge & Kegan Paul Ltd
Broadway House, 68–74 Carter Lane,
London EC4V 5EL and
9 Park Street
Boston, Mass. 02108, U.S.A.
Printed in Great Britain by
Butler & Tanner Ltd, Frome and London
© *Donald Thomas 1972*

No part of this book may be reproduced in
any form without permission from the
publisher, except for the quotation of brief
passages in criticism

Library of Congress Catalog Card Number: 72-81447

ISBN 0 7100 7325 9

For My Father

Contents

Illustrations

Preface

Throughout much of its length, *State Trials* is less remarkable as a work of legal erudition than as one of the most vivid social and historical documents illustrating English life between the reign of Henry II and the early nineteenth century. Indeed, to a lawyer in search of precedents or decisions there could hardly be a less convenient place for them to lie than in thirty-three volumes consisting largely of partisan, first-hand narratives of political conspiracy; faith and martyrdom; the scandals of English prisons; marriages and liaisons; murder and its detection; the glories of battle and the iniquities of conquest.

The voices of *State Trials* which impress us most are not usually those of judges or counsel, except perhaps in the cases of such men as Judge Jeffreys or Lord Mansfield, but those of ordinary English men and women, or, no less important, those whose countries had come under English government. The voices range from the serene wit of Sir Thomas More facing the scaffold, or the Irish dignity of Wolfe Tone, to the facetious quibbling of the Wexford peasantry, or the tear-jerking clichés of the Duchess of Kingston as she tried to blind the eyes of the House of Lords to her notorious past.

Most of the remaining copies of the Cobbett and Howell edition of *State Trials* in thirty-three volumes lie gathering dust in library stacks. It might be hard to justify reprinting the contents in their entirety, yet they hardly seem to deserve such neglect as a source of information for English social history. In the four volumes of this edition I have chosen what seem to me to be the best trials from the point of view of documentary literature and historical narrative. The first two volumes contain cases illustrating public or political issues, while the third and fourth volumes are devoted to the crimes of private life.

Fortunately, most of the trials in the selection are not too long to be reprinted in their entirety, though with the improvement of shorthand towards the end of the eighteenth century some later transcripts became very long indeed. Where I have had to reduce the length of a report, I have generally tried to leave as much of the witnesses' narrative as possible and cut the length of speeches by judges and counsel. Such cuts are either indicated by a note in the text or marked by a set of asterisks. Until the later eighteenth century many speeches by judges and counsel were little more than a summary of evidence for the benefit of the jury.

I am extremely grateful to Mr E. H. Jones, the Reference Librarian of Cardiff Central Library, who provided me with a number of volumes of the Cobbett and Howell edition of *State Trials*. I also owe a debt of gratitude to Mr David Young who put me in touch with what must have been the only bookshop in Britain with a complete set of the Cobbett and Howell edition on its shelves. Having acquired the texts, the mass of material which they yielded would have been quite intractable without the assistance of my wife, who managed on the one hand to keep relevant subject-matter in its due place and, on the other, to see cross-references which gave cohesiveness to such a variety of documents.

Text Note

The text of the trials in this selection is based on that of the Cobbett and Howell *Complete Collection of State Trials* published in 1809–26. Unless otherwise specified, all references to *State Trials* in the notes to the present selection are to the Cobbett and Howell edition. I have modernized spellings and punctuation where necessary. Yet since the slightly old-fashioned punctuating of *State Trials* probably represents quite accurately the manner of speech of the participants, I have interfered as little as possible in this respect.

In order to preserve the Cobbett and Howell footnotes, they have been included in the text at the appropriate place, in square brackets and roman type. Any additional notes will be found at the end of each volume and are in numerical sequence for each trial. I have preserved almost all the Cobbett and Howell footnotes and, in a few cases, expanded the description of sources to which they refer. In the extract from Clarendon, which forms the first Cobbett and Howell footnote to Penruddock's trial, I have followed the W. Dunn Macray edition of the *History of the Rebellion*, which differs slightly from that used in *State Trials* but has now become the authoritative text.

Material in round brackets belongs to the Cobbett and Howell edition, my own summaries, interpolations, or corrections appear in italic in square brackets. Where descriptions of gesture or action occur within what is principally a passage of dialogue I have put such descriptions into italics, and also into brackets if they occur within a line of dialogue.

Where there is a blank in the Cobbett and Howell text, I have let it stand. Such gaps are rare and are the consequence of a reporter having failed to get a word or name for the original publication which was later to be incorporated in *State Trials*.

Introduction

'I feel some touch of sympathy for those simple-minded readers who avowedly prefer the police reports to any other kind of literature,'[1] wrote Leslie Stephen with genial condescension in 1892. As practical proof of his sympathy he gave his essay on the *State Trials* a place in *Hours in a Library* alongside other pieces on the novels of Fielding or George Eliot, the poetry of Crabbe or Shelley, and the plays of Massinger. The processes of law and order were not to be quite so evidently the subject-matter of literature again until the appearance of such documentary accounts as Norman Mailer's *Armies of the Night* in the 1960s.

Stephen's sympathy reflects his view that literature is the manifestation of its historical period, rather than a set of varying achievements in terms of disembodied or ideal aesthetic forms. To separate the study of literature from the study of history, or indeed the study of ethics, was to impoverish the study of all three. In the earlier twentieth century such criteria were generally replaced by the evaluation of poetry or fiction without undue emphasis on the historical circumstances in which it happened to be written. Yet the past decade has shown some return to the attitude which Stephen represents. A growing suspicion of artificiality, and even of art, has fostered both a historical interest and a critical egalitarianism which would regard the autobiographies of thieves and prostitutes in Henry Mayhew's *London Labour and the London Poor* as being as much a part of literature as *Oliver Twist*, let alone Ouida's *Moths*. Indeed, it is often the extreme of imaginative literature which may have to be defended against charges of fantasy or escapism.

If the distinction between the study of literature and the study of history grows harder to maintain in many areas, there could hardly be a more apt appeal to the later twentieth century than Stephen's apology for *State Trials*.[2]

There are times when we feel that we would rather have
the actual sounds, the downright utterance of an agonised
human being, than the far-away echo of passion set up in
the artistic brain. We prefer the roar of the tempest to the
squeaking of the Aeolian harp. We tire of the skilfully
prepared sentiment, the pretty fancies, the unreal
imaginations, and long for the harsh, crude, substantial
fact, the actual utterance of men struggling in the dire
grasp of unmitigated realities. We want to see Nature itself,
not to look at the distorted images presented in the
magical mirror of a Shakespeare. . . . If this theory of art
be sound, is not the most realistic historian the only
artist? Nay, since every historian is more or less a
sophisticator, should we not go back to the materials from
which histories are made?

The last question seems to go straight to the sympathies of our
own time with its growing preference for education by the
materials rather than by the sophisticators of history. Nor does
Stephen find it a happy compromise for the historian to
incorporate a mass of the materials in his own narrative. As
Stephen remarks in his essay on Macaulay, the consequence of
so clogged a style is merely to make the reader long for a fire
in the State Paper room. Moreover, even the depth of knowledge
and narrative genius of Macaulay could hardly produce a
portrait of, say, Judge Jeffreys to rival the contemporary
transcription of Jeffreys's outbursts at the trial of Richard
Baxter in 1685.

Stephen makes a persuasive apologist for history as documentary literature but the vogue for *State Trials*, particularly
in the Victorian period, was far more than a taste for the texture
of life in the seventeenth or eighteenth centuries. *State Trials*
had often been an instrument of political debate and social
inquiry, never more so than when the definitive Cobbett and
Howell edition began to appear in 1809. In its eighteenth-
century origins the *State Trials* collection had been a weapon
of party politics, while to the late Victorians it remained a classic
of political education by example.

Without questioning the usefulness of *State Trials* to the study of law, two non-legal motives appear to have determined the form of its appearance at various times.

In the first place, it is indisputable that some of the material in *State Trials* was published in response to that public curiosity over cases of 'horrid murder' or sexual scandal which has been the support of broadsheets, ballads, and, in the twentieth century, of the mass-circulation Sunday newspapers. One might argue that such cases were never the principal feature of *State Trials* but since the Cobbett and Howell edition contained 705 cases in thirty-three volumes, even a small proportion of these might still amount to a considerable number of cases. Certainly, the preoccupation with prosecutions for murder was less apparent than in a twentieth-century collection like the *Notable British Trials* series, but the more sensational cases were there, including the trials of that aristocratic young duellist, Lord Mohun, reviled by Swift and Thackeray; the prosecution of Spencer Cowper, grandfather of the poet William Cowper, in one of the earliest cases to be decided largely on medical evidence; and that most pathetic of all murder trials at which, in 1752, Mary Blandy was accused of poisoning her father at the instigation of her gallant but unscrupulous lover. The verdicts were by no means a matter of course, and it is easy to appreciate in such cases how the ritual, revelation, and suspense combined to produce the folk *genre* of the murder trial. It is a truism, but an apt one, that the murder trial and the detective novel share something of the same formality and popular appeal, acting in certain respects as mirror images of one another. In a less appealing guise, the seventeenth- and eighteenth-century taste for trial literature of this sort had less to do with the later cult of the detective novel than with the contemporary enthusiasm for public executions.

Murder trials, whether scandalous, bloodcurdling, or pathetic, shared the public's curiosity with those other cases in *State Trials* which detailed, for instance, the trial and execution of the Earl of Castlehaven for rape and sodomy; the divorce of the Duke and Duchess of Norfolk, or the prosecution of the Duchess of Kingston, formerly the notorious Elizabeth Chudleigh, for bigamy. It may seem remarkable that no expurgation of such cases took place in the Cobbett and Howell edition of 1809 to

1826, since it appeared during the very years when the Society for the Suppression of Vice was becoming celebrated for its prosecution of indecent literature, while Thomas Bowdler's excising mind was at work on literature as a whole. Presumably, the official-sounding title of the collection and the daunting prospect of combing its thirty-three volumes, double column, for indictable material would have deterred all but the most resolute vice suppressor. Others who specialized in reporting scandalous cases were certainly not immune from prosecution, as Alexander Hogg discovered in 1802, when he was convicted of obscene libel in the Court of King's Bench for publishing *A New and Compleat Collection of the Most Remarkable Trials for Adultery: or, A General History of Modern Gallantry and Divorces.*

The Norfolk divorce case might sell more copies than the martyrdom of Sir Thomas More: the names of men and women executed for witchcraft at Salem or Bury St Edmunds might mean nothing beside the fame of Mary Blandy or the Duchess of Kingston. Yet the apparent and dominant motive for the publication of *State Trials* collections has been a desire, however partisan, for political improvement and social reform. There is no better evidence than the preface which Thomas Salmon wrote for the first edition of all, which he published in 1719.[3]

> Since 'tis observable that the best and bravest of mankind are far from being exempted from Criminal Prosecutions, and that potent malice, or prevailing faction, have too often attempted the most consummate merit; that Learning which shows how life, honour, and innocence are to be defended, when they shall happen to be injuriously attacked, will not, 'tis presumed, be thought inferior to that, which instructs us how to defend our less important rights.

In that same year, Salmon issued a supplementary volume, containing the case of John Hampden who had refused to pay ship-money to Charles I. Salmon, who was anything but a supporter of Walpole in 1719, used the case to make this point obliquely by way of a special preface. 'It is of the greatest concernment and importance for a Prince to have about him Faithful Counsellors,' he concluded, adding, 'It is an undoubted truth, that Princes see with others' eyes, and hear with others' ears.'[4]

Far from being exclusively a record of distant history, editions of *State Trials* in the eighteeenth and early nineteenth centuries were involved in contemporary issues. The Cobbett and Howell edition includes three volumes of cases which occurred after the edition itself had begun to appear. When the final volume was issued in 1826, it included the trials of five men for treason in 1820, following the so-called Cato Street conspiracy. In the view of the radicals it was the publication of the cases which afforded the best evidence for their accusation that one of the conspirators, Edwards, a government spy, had been deliberately planted by the administration as *agent provocateur*, to involve radical leaders in a treasonable conspiracy. Far from being an academic echo of the past, the trials were published when the principal target of the alleged assassination plot, Lord Liverpool, was still prime minister.

The political vogue for *State Trials* continued throughout the Victorian period, though the most tangible evidence of it came at the end of the nineteenth century. The Cobbett and Howell edition was supplemented by eight volumes of *State Trials: New Series*, edited by Sir John Macdonell and published between 1888 and 1898. Macdonell was later to compile his own narrative collection of *Historical Trials*, ranging from the trial of Socrates to the European witch trials of the sixteenth and seventeenth centuries. However, the new series of *State Trials* included major political prosecutions of the early Victorian period. There was a market, too, for abridged selections from the original Cobbett and Howell edition, as in Sir Henry Lushington Stephen's *State Trials: Political and Social*, which appeared in four volumes in 1899–1902.

In another form, *State Trials* were used in the late Victorian period as the raw material for more popular, narrative accounts of their proceedings, geared for the most part to illustrate Macaulay's proposition that 'the history of our country during the last hundred and sixty years is eminently the history of physical, of moral, and of intellectual improvement'.[5] So in the 1870s and the 1880s, to the greater glory of parliamentary democracy, trial by jury, and a free press, appeared such works as J. W. Willis-Bund's *Selection of Cases from the State Trials*, a

narrative of political trials for treason, or G. Lathom Browne's
Narratives of State Trials in the Nineteenth Century (1882). 'It is
proposed, in these volumes,' wrote Lathom Browne, 'to present
in a popular form the incidents of such of the State Trials during
the first thirty years of the present century as appear most clearly
to exhibit the political and social phases of that period.'[6]
Like Thomas Salmon in 1719, Lathom Browne is concerned
with civil liberty, though in the late Victorian glow of Democracy Triumphant it is no longer liberty in peril but liberty
achieved. And, of course, unlike Salmon, Lathom Browne writes
not for the enfranchised few but for the newly-literate mass.
Historical documents are abandoned in favour of an engaging
narrative, 'in the hope that the information and instruction to
be drawn from these trials will thus be more widely diffused.[7]

Leslie Stephen's tastes were not to be vindicated. The new
readers preferred the 'sophisticators' of history to its 'materials',
even in the new editions of *State Trials*. That most admirable
aspect of late-Victorian culture, the will to educate for democracy, was undertaken through the work of Macaulay or
Buckle, or in less academic histories like James Routledge's
*Chapters in the History of Popular Progress: Chiefly in Relation to the
Freedom of the Press and Trial by Jury* (1876), rather than through
the thirty-three volumes of Cobbett and Howell. Yet the vogue
for such trials, even in narrative form, and the style of some
historical writing owed much to that aspect of English history
enshrined in *State Trials*, and specifically in the Cobbett and
Howell edition.

Collections of trials, judges' reports, and legal decisions were
by no means a novelty when Thomas Salmon published his
four volume edition in 1719 as a *Complete Collection of State Trials
for High Treason, and other Crimes and Misdemeanours*. Thomas
Salmon (1679–1767) was the author of a number of historical
and geographical works. Though possessed of no formal
academic qualifications, he had what the antiquarian William
Cole described as 'no small turn for writing, as his many
productions show, most of which were written when he resided
at Cambridge, where at last he kept a coffee house but not
having sufficient custom, removed to London'.[8] Apart from
his published criticisms of Whig historians like Burnet, Salmon

gained a reputation as a geographer from such works as *The Modern Gazetteer: Or, A Short View of the Several Nations of the World*, and was one of those who accompanied Anson in his voyage round the world in 1739–40.

Salmon's 'turn for writing' and penchant for political argument gave *State Trials* an enduring appeal which had, for instance, eluded the work of Lord Chief Justice Scroggs who survived the threat of impeachment after the 'Popish Plot' scare and turned retirement to profit by editing the trials of innocent men whom he had condemned. Of course, Salmon had a wider scope and in his first collection he chose trials which had occurred as far apart as the reign of Richard II and the reign of Queen Anne. Neither he nor his successors defined clearly the distinction between a 'state trial' and any other trial. The term was generally used to indicate a case which had been of major political significance, though it was never so strictly defined as to exclude the more notorious cases of divorce, bigamy, or abduction. The primary aim of such collections, however, seemed to be a demonstration that legality and justice were far from being identical on every occasion.

In the year of the first edition, Salmon added a fifth volume, in which he included the proceedings in the case of John Hampden's refusal to pay ship-money to Charles I. Apart from its political interest, Hampden's was one of the earliest of the cases to be documented in great detail. Yet even while Salmon's edition of Stuart trials was appearing, his own contemporaries were being prosecuted and condemned by their political enemies, and these proceedings were to be included in later editions of *State Trials*. The political significance of Salmon's collection was not hard to appreciate in a period which saw, for instance, the impeachment of the Earl of Oxford for treason in 1717; the trial and execution of the young printer John Matthews, in 1719, for printing a comparatively mild Jacobite tract, or the proceedings in 1723 against Francis Atterbury, Bishop of Rochester, and others for treasonable conspiracy.

Salmon, like Cobbett, was no impartial observer of political events. Still using the subject-matter of *State Trials*, he expressed his opinions more openly in 1720 in his *Critical Review of the State Trials*. He spoke kindly of the House of Stuart and was regarded as an enemy to the Glorious Revolution of 1689 and all its consequences. Francis Hargrave, a later editor of *State Trials*, made a belated attempt to unmask Salmon's prejudices in 1775.[9]

As we have had occasion to take notice of Mr. Salmon's *Critical Review*, and some readers may not be apprized of his character as an author, it may be of use to observe that however indebted to him the public may be for his industry in first forming a *Collection of State Trials*, and in afterwards abridging them, there is little obligation to him for some of his remarks upon them. In his political principles apparently an inveterate enemy to the Revolution, he is frequently betrayed by an intemperate zeal into a false notion of characters and opinions, and too often disguises both when the demon of party demands a sacrifice.

In 1730, when Sollum Emlyn published a second edition of *State Trials* in four volumes, adding two more supplementary volumes that year, political prosecutions were as much in evidence as ever. At this period they took the form of a series of press prosecutions brought against Tory publishers by Walpole's administration. The years 1729–38 were the time when major prosecutions were brought against *The Country Journal: or, The Craftsman*, which was often the voice of Bolingbroke or Pulteney, and five cases were begun in an attempt to suppress the political satire of Jonathan Swift. As Emlyn remarked in his own introduction, a collection of *State Trials* 'must appear at first sight very beneficial to all studious inquirers into the Laws of this nation, especially into that principal branch of them, which concerns the Life and Liberty of the Subject'.[10] Those to whom he addressed this claim may well have shown practical sympathy, since Emlyn was able to boast that 'The favourable reception which the First Impression of this Work has met with from the Public, is a sufficient recommendation of it in general.'[11] He added a seventh and an eighth volume to the set in 1735.

With the disintegration of Walpole's administration, the time was ripe for yet another adjustment of the perspectives of political history, and in 1742 a third edition of *State Trials* was issued in six volumes, with four supplementary volumes in

1766. Trials such as those of Matthews, the printer, for treason in 1719 were included, and that of Franklin, the printer of the *Craftsman*, for seditious libel in 1731, reflecting party warfare during the long years of Whig rule. More recent cases were added, including the trials of the Jacobite lords in 1746–7, and the case of James Annesley, the 'missing heir', in 1743, one of the longest trials and most remarkable stories which had ever come before a British court.

The last edition of *State Trials* to appear in the eighteenth century was published in eleven volumes by Francis Hargrave in 1776–81, the work of a lawyer and antiquarian. Hargrave extended the period covered by the trials to 1776 and attempted to add material for earlier historical periods. In an age when antiquarianism had become an intellectual fashion, Hargrave turned to the British Museum as well as to the courts for his sources of material.[12]

In the course of my enquiries for new Trials, I resorted to the British Museum, in hopes that the immense Collection of Manuscripts in that repository of learning and science would supply me with some new materials of importance; and I was particularly encouraged in this expectation by the promising Titles of various Articles in the Catalogue of Harleian Manuscripts. But I was wholly disappointed; for on examination, the few Trials I met with proved either too meagre and insignificant to be made use of, or nothing more than mere transcripts from some of our old printed Chronicles. And here I take great pleasure in bearing testimony of the exemplary conduct of those Gentlemen, who by their offices have the superintendence of the Manuscripts and printed Books in the British Museum. Though I have had frequent occasion to give several of those gentlemen much trouble, yet I have ever found them uniformly studious to render the access to the valuable Collections entrusted to them easy and agreeable. I have also had the full opportunity of noticing that their deportment and attentions to others are of the same obliging kind. So honourable a discharge of their duty well entitles them to some rewards beyond the small emoluments of their respective offices.

The truth is that Francis Hargrave had been spoilt by having so many of the trials of his own time available in every word, thanks to the shorthand transcriptions which were increasingly made by men like Gurney. To turn to trials of the medieval and Tudor periods is to find them succinctly reported with comparatively little direct quotation. Indeed, it was sometimes impossible to offer any account of a trial except by gathering a number of short descriptions or references from various general histories of the period.

The last and greatest of the major editions of *State Trials* had its origin in the enthusiasm of William Cobbett for republishing documentary material on a scale which would almost have done credit to a twentieth-century reprint corporation. The character of the edition also owes something to Cobbett's very distant supervision of the first ten volumes, which bear his name on their title-pages, but its real debt is to the unremitting industry of a hired editor, Thomas Bayly Howell, and his son, Thomas Jones Howell, who, unlike Cobbett, were lawyers. Cobbett's own experience of the law, other than of being prosecuted under its provisions, was brief. He recalls in his *Life and Adventures of Peter Porcupine* how in 1783, at twenty years old, he was employed by Holland, an attorney, who, 'happening to want an understrapping quill driver, did me the honour to take me into his service, and the next day saw me perched upon a great high stool, in an obscure chamber in Gray's Inn, endeavouring to decipher the crabbed thoughts of my employer'.[13] By comparison with the political drama of a trial for treason, or the agreeable indignation of fighting against abuses of power, the mundane work of the law seemed a profession of mind-blunting tedium.[14]

> No part of my life has been totally unattended with pleasure, except the eight or nine months I passed in Gray's Inn. The office (for so the dungeon where I wrote was called) was so dark that, on cloudy days, we were obliged to burn candle. I worked like a galley-slave from five in the morning till eight or nine at night, and sometimes all night long. How many quarrels have I assisted to foment and perpetuate between those poor innocent fellows, John Doe and Richard Roe! How many

times (God forgive me!) have I set them to assault each other with guns, swords, staves and pitchforks, and then brought them to answer for their misdeeds before our Sovereign Lord the King, seated in his Court of Westminster! . . . Gracious heaven! If I am doomed to be wretched, bury me beneath Iceland snows and let me feed on blubber; stretch me under the burning line, and deny me thy propitious dews; nay, if it be thy will, suffocate me with the infected and pestilential air of a democratic club-room; but save me from the desk of an attorney!

Cobbett was later to revise his opinions of the 'democratic club-room', in the light of his conversion to the cause of radical reform, but he showed no enthusiasm again for the practice of the law.

Cobbett's publishing partnership with John Morgan, at the sign of the Crown and Mitre in Pall Mall, lasted from 1801 until 1803. It saw the first publication of *Cobbett's Political Register* which appeared in 1802 and survived Cobbett's own lifetime, ending three years after his death in 1838. Among other major ventures was *The Works of Peter Porcupine*, published in twelve volumes in 1801.

When the partnership with Morgan ended, Cobbett began to move towards that radicalism which characterized his actions and publications for the rest of his life. It was the economic theory of the radicals, according to which the labouring class was increasingly exploited by landowners and merchants, which won his allegiance in the first place. Propagation of radical opinions became the policy of his next partnership, with his friend John Wright, in the years 1804–12. In his initial eagerness, Cobbett made plans for issuing works of daunting size. *Cobbett's Spirit of the Public Journals*, a compilation of contemporary periodical literature, was short-lived, but *Cobbett's Parliamentary Debates* survived until it was sold to its printer, T. C. Hansard. In 1806 appeared the first volumes of *Cobbett's Parliamentary History*, which was eventually to cover the proceedings of Parliament from the Norman Conquest until the beginning of the nineteenth century. Three years later, in 1809, came the first four volumes of what was to be the *Complete Collection of State Trials* in thirty-three volumes of about a million words each. In addition to these undertakings, the political and financial demands of the *Political Register* involved Cobbett's first attention. His association with *State Trials* was, in a literal sense, nominal. Despite his disenchantment with the profession of the law, Cobbett accepted as editor Thomas Bayly Howell (1768–1815), who was a barrister but also a Fellow of the Royal Society and a Fellow of the Society of Antiquaries.

It was the *Political Register* which was at once the most significant and the most menacing of publications so far as the partnership of Cobbett and Wright was concerned. The first omens of financial trouble had come in 1804, in the wake of certain articles, signed 'Juverna', which had appeared in the *Political Register* in 1803 and had attacked the government of Ireland. Cobbett was sued for libel by Lord Hardwicke, Lord-Lieutenant of Ireland, and others. The cases were heard in 1804 and duly recorded in volume XXIX of the Cobbett and Howell edition of *State Trials*. Damages were awarded against Cobbett but he was never called upon to pay, since he disclosed to the plaintiffs the identity of 'Juverna'. The articles had been written by the Hon. Robert Johnson, Judge of the Court of Common Pleas in Ireland, but though proceedings were taken against him, these were dropped in 1806.

Of more immediate consequence for *State Trials* and the other Cobbett projects was a seditious libel prosecution brought in respect of an article in the *Political Register* of 1 July 1809. At Ely, members of the local militia discovered that the cost of their knapsacks was to be deducted from their pay. The men surrounded their officers and demanded that this money should be paid to them. General Auckland arrived with a force of German mercenaries, who suppressed the 'mutiny' and kept order while the five leading mutineers were awarded 500 lashes each. Cobbett reprinted the account of this from the pro-government newspaper the *Courier*, and then attacked the ministry with furious irony.

> See the motto English Reader! See the motto and then
> do pray recollect all that has been said about the way in
> which Buonaparte raises his soldiers—well done, Lord
> Castlereagh! This is just what it was thought your plan

would produce. Well said, Mr. Huskisson! It really was not without reason that you dwelt with so much earnestness upon the great utility of the foreign troops whom Mr Wardle appeared to think of no utility at all, poor Gentleman! He little imagined how a great genius might find useful employment for such troops. He little imagined that they might be made the means of compelling Englishmen to submit to that sort of discipline which is so conducive to the producing in them a disposition to defend the country at the risk of their lives.

When Cobbett was indicted, the whole article was quoted in the indictment but if one passage, more than any other, was unforgiveable in the eyes of the government, at a time when news of the disasters of the Walcheren expedition seemed rivalled only by fears for the tenuously established position of Wellesley's army in the Peninsula, it was the concluding lines, in which Cobbett compared the British army's code of discipline unfavourably with Napoleon's.

On 9 July 1810 Cobbett was tried in the Court of King's Bench before Lord Ellenborough and a special jury. He was found guilty, sentenced to be fined £1,000, to be imprisoned for two years, and to find sureties totalling £5,000 for his good behaviour for the next seven years. In the world of radical politics he became a hero. On his release from prison, Sir Francis Burdett presided over a dinner given in London for 600 supporters, to celebrate the occasion. When Cobbett returned home to Hampshire, the church bells rang for him and there was another dinner at Winchester. On 25 July 1812, his own account of the trial and imprisonment was published in the *Political Register*.

So far as the radical cause was concerned, Cobbett emerged with triumph from his ordeal, but the finances of his publishing partnership with John Wright were in a state of desperate confusion. He had suffered obvious and considerable losses through the fine and imprisonment, but he and Wright had always assumed that the commercial success of *State Trials*, *Parliamentary Debates*, and the *Parliamentary History* was an established fact. They had hardly bothered to consult the accounts. A brief investigation showed the comfortless truth, as

Cobbett recalled. 'I was engaged in the publication of two works, called *The State Trials* and *The Parliamentary History*. There had been a great outlay for these works; several thousands of pounds were due to the paper-maker and the printer. These works were, as far as regarded me, ruined.'[15] In the case of *State Trials*, its editor, T. B. Howell, was to have been rewarded by a share of the profits once the sale exceeded 800 copies. The ten volumes which appeared by 1811 had never reached such a figure, so Wright had paid Howell the sum of £1,400 during Cobbett's imprisonment. An attorney was brought in to disentangle the complexities of the financial failure and to apportion the obligations of the two partners. He concluded that Wright owed Cobbett £6,500, which, of course, Wright was in no position to pay but which was discharged by Wright surrendering his share of the partnership to Cobbett.

Though the internal debts of the partnership were settled, Cobbett still owed money to others, particularly to his printer, Thomas Curson Hansard. T. C. Hansard, the eldest son of the famous Luke Hansard, had been the printer of all three series, and also of the *Political Register*, which had earned him three months in prison at the time of Cobbett's conviction for seditious libel. As a last resort, Cobbett sold the three series to Hansard in order to clear his debts. From then onwards, the *Parliamentary Debates* became *Hansard's Parliamentary Debates*, while the edition of *State Trials*, which had carried Cobbett's name on its first ten volumes, now assumed the name of its editor, T. B. Howell, instead.

Without Cobbett's initial enthusiasm there might have been no major edition of *State Trials* in the nineteenth century but, ironically, the series made much better progress once he was no longer associated with it. Between 1811 and 1814, eleven volumes appeared under the editorship of T. B. Howell, bringing the collection down as far as the prosecution of William Shipley, Dean of St Asaph, for seditious libel in 1783–4. Howell had undertaken much of the work on the later volumes when his health was deteriorating and he had relied heavily on the assistance of his son, Thomas Jones Howell. When T. B. Howell died in 1815, a series of twenty-one volumes was complete, covering as long a period as any earlier edition but illustrated by a greater quantity and variety of documentary material.

In the light of previous financial experience of the series, it might conceivably have been left as it remained at the death of T. B. Howell.

For three years, no more volumes were issued but it would have taken a phlegmatic publisher to have ignored the possibility of a continuation in the political circumstances of 1817. The false security of international peace in 1815 seemed to many contemporaries to have become a discarded illusion as the government of Lord Liverpool and the militant radicals prepared for their final combat. 1817 produced the trial and acquittal of Dr James Watson and three other defendants on charges of treason, which arose from a riot that seemed to have certain parallels to the insurrection in Paris on 14 July 1789. Jeremiah Brandreth, 'The Nottingham Captain', and other defendants were convicted and executed for treason. There was no need to search historical documents for a continuation of *State Trials* when contemporary events offered such subject-matter. Eighteen seditious libel prosecutions were begun, though the personal advocacy of William Hone in his own three trials of December 1817 brought this attack on the radical press to a temporary halt. Men like Hone issued *verbatim* reports of their trials, reports which served as political propaganda since they publicized the disruption of the courts by defendants who had turned Guildhall into a political arena. The reputation of such proceedings lived long after them. John Henry Newman, for instance, had acquired an edition of Hone's trial in 1818 and recalled such proceedings to his mid-Victorian audience in his *Lectures on the Present Position of Catholics in England*.

It was in 1817 that the first volume of the 'continuation' of *State Trials* appeared. An announcement was inserted by the publisher to the effect that T. J. Howell, who had long been his father's close collaborator in earlier volumes, would edit the continuation. Hansard himself considered the continuation necessary, being 'fully impressed with the importance that the State Prosecutions of the interesting and eventful era, at which the Work is now arrived, should be recorded in such a manner as to preserve to the *State Trials* that high reputation which they now enjoy as a Book of legal and historical authority.'[16] During the next two years, five more volumes were issued, completing the trials of the eighteenth century with those cases of treason and seditious libel in the 1790s which seemed so close a parallel to the cases of 1817–20. A further five volumes in 1820–3 covered the period of the Napoleonic wars, and the final two volumes of 1824 and 1826 completed the continuation by dealing with the events of 1817 to 1820. The whole work was then classified in an index compiled by David Jardine and published in 1828. Hansard still retained the proprietorship, and though the index acknowledges the work of the Howells, father and son, Cobbett's association with the project is ignored.

In terms of historical periods, the Cobbett and Howell edition of *State Trials* begins with the proceedings against St Thomas à Becket in 1163 and ends with the trial of the Cato Street conspirators in 1820. Brief though some of the reports may be, the earlier cases sound almost like an anthology from the works of Elizabethan dramatists. The proceedings against Piers Gaveston and, subsequently, Edward II, are followed by those against Mortimer for treason and Berkeley for the King's murder. The impeachment of the Duke of Gloucester in the reign of Richard II is a prelude to the proceedings against Richard himself under the rule of Henry IV. In the reign of Edward IV, the schemes of the future Richard III are reflected in the condemnation and murder of Edward's brother, George, Duke of Clarence.

The majority of cases in *State Trials* until the end of the Tudor period are, predictably, trials for treason. It is not until the development of the conflict between Charles I and Parliament that those cases which involve freedom of the press become significantly frequent. Even after that, treason trials remain a feature of the collection from the Restoration until the accession of George IV, though they appear less as a continuing series than as groups of cases, corresponding to the Popish Plot scare; the Jacobite rising of 1745; the fear of France in 1794, or the threat of an English revolution in 1817–20.

From the reign of Charles I until the early nineteenth century there appears a second sequence of cases, concerned specifically with the freedom of the press. There were some prosecutions against those responsible for Puritan or Catholic literature in the reign of Elizabeth but, with the cases of Roger Manwaring in 1621; Alexander Leighton in 1630; William Prynne in 1632, and Prynne, Bastwick, and Burton in

1637, continuing press prosecutions became a second principal feature of political history amply illustrated in *State Trials*. The Cobbett and Howell edition is particularly well supplied with documentation of the struggle between the government and the opposition press during the later eighteenth century. Most of these cases are concerned with seditious libel (which like blasphemous or obscene libel has nothing to do with personal defamation but uses 'libel' in the sense of *libellus*, a book). Until Fox's Libel Act in 1792, the law gave the government a distinct advantage in trials of this kind, since the jurors, however innocent a publication might seem, were allowed to give a verdict only on questions of fact.

Two questions of fact had to be decided. Firstly, the jury had to say whether the defendant was the publisher of the alleged libel. Second, they had to determine whether the libel meant what the indictment, in its 'innuendoes', said that it meant. For example, when Woodfall was prosecuted in 1770 for publishing Junius's Letter to the * * * *, the indictment alleged that this was a Letter to the King, and that such incomplete words as 'p—t', or 's—n', meant 'parliament' and 'sovereign'. If the jury agreed with this, and agreed that Woodfall was the publisher, they were to find him guilty. The most important issue, whether a publication was seditious or libellous, was a question of law, which the jury was not allowed to decide. Questions of law were decided by judges, often by judges who were regarded as creatures of the prime minister and his administration.

Faced with such a restriction on their power, jurors retaliated increasingly by returning invalid verdicts as in Woodfall's case where they insisted on adding the words 'of printing and publishing only' to their verdict of guilty, or by acquitting the defendant in the face of the evidence. In 1792, at a second attempt, the Libel Act became law, giving the jury power to decide the question of law as well as the questions of fact, though reserving to the judge the right to express his opinion to the jury on the libellousness of a publication, as Sir Charles Abbott did in the trial of John Hatchard in 1817.

The arch-enemies of a free press in the eighteenth century were generally thought to be such men as William Murray, Earl of Mansfield, when acting as judge, and Edward Thurlow,

Attorney-General and later Lord Chancellor, when acting as prosecutor. Mansfield's critics accused him both of incompetence and of blatant pro-government bias. Junius joined in the attack in the *Public Advertiser* of 14 November 1770, addressing himself to Mansfield.

> You will not question my veracity, when I assure you that it has not been owing to any particular respect for your person that I have abstained from you so long. Besides the distress and danger with which the press is threatened, when your Lordship is party, and the party is to be judge, I confess I have been deterred by the difficulty of the task. Our language has no term of reproach, the mind has no idea of detestation, which has not already been happily applied to you, and exhausted.

A quarter of a century later, it was said by Mansfield's enemies that the Libel Act had only been necessary because of the illegal and unconstitutional manner in which he had deprived juries of their traditional rights. By the Act of 1792, 'Juries were restored to their constitutional rights, which fixes upon his memory and character a more indelible stigma than could have been inflicted by an article of impeachment.'[17]

Those trials included in the first volume of the present selection are chosen from proceedings which document 'state prosecutions' between the reigns of Henry VIII and George III. Even the trial of John Hatchard for libel in 1817 was a prosecution sanctioned by the grand jurors of Middlesex and carrying the penalties of criminal law. In Hatchard's case the government libelled was that of Antigua and in Curll's case it was, superficially at least, public morality which had been outraged. All the other trials were direct attempts to suppress treason or seditious publication aimed against the government of Great Britain.

The preservation of law and order in the seventeenth and eighteenth centuries was not so much a matter of making the highways safe for the king's subjects to walk but rather of protecting the monarch and his ministers from subversive criticism and physical danger. It is this hierarchic view of social stability which is reflected in the cases collected here, a view in which the security of ordinary men and women was dependent in the first place upon the security of national leaders, both in body and in reputation.

Press prosecutions of the kind brought against Edmund Curll related obliquely to the preservation of political authority. The most significant aspect of his case is the use of a trial for obscene libel to settle certain personal and political scores. On the other hand, the trials of such men as Richard Baxter for their religious views were certainly defensive political actions by the state. And what applies to Baxter's case must apply more strongly still to those of Prynne, Bastwick, and Burton. In 1676 Sir Matthew Hale enshrined in a legal formula a truth which had long been a political reality.[18]

And Hale saith, that such kind of wicked blasphemous words were not only an offence to God and Religion, but a crime against the Laws, State and Government, and therefore punishable in this Court. For to say, Religion is a Cheat, is to dissolve all those Obligations whereby the Civil societies are preserved, and that Christianity is a parcel of the Laws of England and therefore to reproach the Christian religion is to speak in subversion of the law.

In attempting to preserve its political authority by means of the courts, the Tudor and Stuart state certainly went beyond the limited scope of prosecutions for treason or seditious libel. Yet from the seventeenth century onwards there is a recognizable series of cases in which the state prosecutes less as an arbitrary authority and more as an agent of the public conscience. On occasion, as in the seventeenth-century witchcraft trials, the public conscience could be as barbarous in its effects as any feudal monarchy. If that conscience was transformed into something which we may now look back upon as altogether admirable, the transformation owed much to that type of moral enlightenment which characterized the best minds of the eighteenth century.

'The Public Conscience' is the theme of the second volume in the present series of *State Trials*. The third and fourth volumes, 'Murder' and 'Love and Marriage', mirror the private lives and the more secret conduct of men and women in the domestic world of the seventeenth and eighteenth centuries.

Mr. Salmon's Preface
to the First Edition of the *State Trials*,
in Four Volumes Folio: Printed in the
Year 1719

Since 'tis observable that the best and bravest of mankind are far from being exempted from Criminal Prosecutions, and that potent malice, or prevailing faction, have too often attempted the most consummate merit; that Learning which shews how life, honour, and innocence are to be defended, when they shall happen to be injuriously attack'd, will not, 'tis presum'd, be thought inferior to that, which instructs us how to defend our less important rights. And as the Common Law is nothing else but immemorial Custom, and the custom and methods of Trial, and bringing offenders to Punishment, is no inconsiderable branch of that law; and since these, as other Customs, are only to be collected from former Precedents, 'tis something strange, that amongst the numerous Authors of Reports and Institutes, not one has hitherto thought fit to make any considerable Collection of this kind, or thoroughly to methodize or digest this sort of Learning: nor can any probable reason be assigned for this neglect, unless they have been deterred by the vast trouble and expense it must have been to any private undertaker. As to the Crown Law already extant, 'tis so far from being a complete Direction, even in the most ordinary Trials, that it affords little more than some imperfect Hints of what the Authors intended. And as to the Doctrine of Impeachments, Trials of Peers by Commission, or in Parliament, Bills of Attainder, and the Customs and Usage of Parliaments, in relation to these Matters: this is a Learning that remains entirely untouched, and is only to be collected from Precedents of this nature.

The Undertakers of this Work therefore have spared no pains or expense to procure whatever is valuable of this kind: they have had recourse to every library public and private, where they had intimation there was any thing worth inserting; and they have for some time since offered large encouragement to those who should contribute either Manuscripts or printed Trials, towards rendering the Design complete. And having at length finished their Collection, they have added a Table to the whole, wherein all the various Learning the Work contains is reduced under proper Heads. And that which before lay dispersed in many Volumes, very difficult to be obtained, and several valuable Manuscripts that have been perfectly buried in private hands, are here brought to light; and so disposed, that the studious Reader may make himself master of the subject, with much less labour and expense than has hitherto been requisite.

And as to the Manuscripts, such care has been taken to avoid all mistakes, that the Judges and Counsel, who were concerned in such Trials, and are still living, have been attended with their respective Arguments, and have been pleased so far to encourage the Undertaking, as to correct whatever was amiss.

Nor are the Publishers conscious they have omitted one remarkable Trial that could possibly be obtained, unless that of Mr. Hampden in the Case of Ship-Money, and that of my Lord Strafford; both which being to be found in Mr. Rushworth,[1] are already in the hands of most gentlemen, who are suppos'd to purchase these: and the inserting them could be of no other use than to increase the bulk, and enhance the price of the Book. There is indeed another Account of my Lord Strafford's Trial, which differs in some instances from Mr. Rushworth's and is more concise; and this it has been thought proper to insert.

And as the Union of the two kingdoms of England and Scotland is so near completed, and there remains little else to distinguish us at present but the municipal laws of the respective kingdoms, it has been thought advisable to add some remarkable Scots Trials: in which (to do that nation right) are discovered great learning, eloquence, and strong reasoning. And indeed as the Civil Law prevails very much there, they have at least as large a field to exercise their parts and learning as our more Southern orators, who are so unalterably attach'd to their Common Law; and it must be admitted, that the Party accused has in Scotland all the fair play imaginable: he has what Counsel he thinks fit; he has a Copy of his Charge in his own language; his Counsel are permitted to inspect the very Depositions against him before he is brought to Trial; and they are so little in haste to dispatch a State-Prisoner, that the Trial often lasts some months. This specimen of Scots Trials, as it will at present be acceptable to the curious; so as we have one Senate, and one Legislature, it may hereafter give birth to the introducing such Methods of Trial in each kingdom, as in either shall appear to be founded on the greatest reason and justice.

As to any Partiality in this Undertaking, it seems almost needless to disclaim it; for the Reader has the Evidence and Arguments entire, without any alteration or diminution. It is true, as it falls out in History, so it will do here: the farther we search into Antiquity, and the higher we go, the less perfect will our Accounts be; the same exactness cannot be expected there as in Trials of a more modern date: but thus much may be said for the more ancient Trials, that they are the most perfect and compleat that could possibly be procured. We shall detain the Reader no longer than to observe, that this Collection will not only be useful to the Learned in the Law, and to those whose misfortune it may be to fall under a criminal Prosecution, but in many instances it corrects as well as illustrates our English History: and there is scarce a controverted point in Divinity or Politics, but the Reader will find has been fully debated here by the greatest men our nation has bred. And if Justness of Argument and true Eloquence have any attraction, and these are talents worth improving, here will be found the greatest collection of fine speeches and Arguments, on the most important subjects, that have hitherto been exhibited to the world.

Treason

Chapter One

Sir Thomas More (1535)

Few themes seem more popular in Renaissance literature than that of the fall of princes or great men, while Tudor history from the fate of Cardinal Wolsey to that of the Earl of Essex or the Duke of Norfolk presents the substance of which poetry and drama was the imaginative reflection. It is perhaps only in the case of Sir Thomas More, who became St Thomas More with his canonization in 1935, that a political victim appears with a power of personality beyond almost anything devised by poets or dramatists to illustrate a moral theme. Yet if More seems closer to our own time than other 'traitors' of more recent date, it may be because he is recognizably one of the first martyrs of a modern political system. His crime was to maintain certain beliefs, once shared by his compatriots, at a time when the state regarded those beliefs as no longer politically expedient. He had only to renounce those beliefs (a renunciation which presented little enough difficulty even to some of his finest contemporaries) in order to be assured of his life, wealth, and physical liberty. As a man of formidable political and intellectual reputation, renowned throughout Europe, the Tudor state was reluctant to make him a martyr.

More was probably born in 1478 and was certainly admitted to Lincoln's Inn in 1496. In early life he combined loyalty to the traditions of the medieval Church with an enthusiasm for Renaissance humanism, which induced him to master Greek as well as Latin. In public life, he was a successful lawyer and parliamentarian, as well as an occasional diplomat. He was knighted in 1514 and became Speaker of the House of Commons in 1523. By this time he had written and published his most famous book *Utopia* (1516) and his *Life of John Picus, Earl of Mirandula* (1510). He had written, but not published, his *History of Richard III*, which enshrined the Tudor political view of the Wars of the Roses, with Richard III as the central villain.

Apart from the events of his public life, More holds a place in literary history by virtue of *Utopia* whose picture of an ideal commonwealth was to be ironically copied by Swift in *Gulliver's Travels*, Samuel Butler in the anagrammatic *Erewhon*, and Aldous Huxley in *Brave New World*. More presents a truly utopian state, with universal education for men and women, communal ownership, and freedom of religious belief.

In 1529 More succeeded Wolsey as Lord Chancellor, though without becoming a peer. For two years before this, Henry VIII had considered the possibility of a papal annulment of his own marriage to Catherine of Aragon, his brother's widow whom he had married by papal dispensation in 1509 but who had borne him no children. Wolsey had favoured an annulment and Pope Clement VII, Giulio de' Medici, was requested to grant the king's wish, despite Catherine's protests. As Lord Chancellor, More soon found himself dealing with a Pope who was reluctant to annul the marriage and a king who was determined to be free of Catherine and to marry Anne Boleyn, daughter of a merchant and niece of the Duke of Norfolk. But when he examined the case, More concluded that there could be no justification for an annulment. For the king to protest, after twenty years of ostensible married life, that in God's eyes no marriage had ever existed, was a less than convincing argument. The papal decision was not made until 1534, by which time it was of limited significance to the Tudor government: it was a decision in favour of Catherine of Aragon and against the king.

In 1530 Henry VIII had sent envoys to the Pope and had followed this with a petition signed by lords spiritual and temporal. More and John Fisher, the Bishop of Rochester, had refused to add their signatures. Nonetheless, until May 1532 More continued to hold the office of Lord Chancellor, carrying out its tasks without either publicly condemning the king's actions or doing anything which might seem to indicate approval of them by More as an individual. Yet the king's growing hostility to the Church, as much as the marriage question, divided the Lord Chancellor's loyalties. Papal and ecclesiastical revenues were terminated by Parliament and then, in May 1532, came clear signs of a complete break in allegiance to Rome, and of a demand that Englishmen should swear to be loyal to their king as supreme head of the English Church. On 16 May 1532, More gave up the Great Seal of Lord Chancellor to the king, on the grounds of ill-health. He was succeeded by Sir Thomas Audley, whose conscience was less tender in this matter, as it might well be, since the day before More's resignation the clergy of England had made their submission to the king.

More retired to his house and family at Chelsea, still professing loyalty to his king, as an Englishman, but still refraining, as a Catholic, from giving his approval to the king's actions in the matter of the royal marriage and spiritual authority. With the support of English ecclesiastics, Henry ended his marriage to Catherine and, in January 1533, married Anne Boleyn. As bishops died or were deprived of their sees, they were replaced by men who accepted Henry's views on ecclesiastical and spiritual authority. When Anne Boleyn was to be crowned queen of England, the Bishops of Durham, Bath, and Winchester wrote to More, inviting him to accompany them to the ceremony in June 1533. William Roper, More's son-in-law, describes how More replied to them in the words of a man trapped by the political changes of his time but determined to remain true to his lifelong beliefs. He warned the bishops of the perils of their acquiescence, even in attending the coronation. Their request to him[1]

did put me in remembrance of an emperor who ordained
a law that whosoever had committed a certain heinous
offence (which I now remember not), except it were
a virgin, should suffer the pains of death—such a
reverence had he to virginity. Now so it happened that the
first committer of that offence was indeed a virgin,
whereof the emperor hearing was in no small perplexity,
as he that by some example would fain have had that law
put in execution. Whereupon, when his council had sat
long, solemnly debating this cause, suddenly rose there up
one of his council, a good plain man, amongst them, and
said, 'Why make you so much ado, my lords, about so
small a matter? Let her first be deflowered, and then

after may she be devoured.' And so though your lordships have in the matter of the matrimony hitherto kept yourselves pure virgins, yet take good heed, my lords, that you keep your virginity still. For some there be that by procuring your lordships first at the coronation to be present, and next to preach for the setting forth of it, and finally to write books to all the world in defence thereof are desirous to deflower you, and when they have deflowered you, then will they not fail soon after to devour you. Now, my lords . . . it lieth not in my power but that they may devour me, but God being my good Lord, I will so provide that they shall never deflower me.

Clement VII excommunicated the English king in 1533 and men like More, even in their retirement, could no longer be ignored. More, like John Fisher, was said to be implicated in the affair of Elizabeth Barton, the 'Maid of Kent', who was given to prophetic trances, in which she condemned various acts of iniquity and foretold the punishment of their perpetrators. She even prophesied that if Henry VIII married Anne Boleyn, he would be deposed and killed. A Bill was introduced in the House of Lords in February 1534 condemning Elizabeth Barton as a traitor and naming More and Fisher as having concealed her treason. Elizabeth Barton had already confessed that her prophesies were not divinely inspired, so that her condemnation and execution were inevitable. More had, of course, no connection with her acts and his name was removed from the Bill.

1534 was also the year of the Act of Succession, which recognized Anne Boleyn as the lawful queen and Henry's children by her as heirs to the throne. Although a private citizen, More was one of those required to take an oath of allegiance to the new succession. He refused to take the oath in that form and, in April 1534, was committed to the Tower of London. During the autumn of that year, while More and others remained in prison, Parliament passed the Act of Supremacy, naming the king as supreme head of the English Church and requiring oaths of allegiance to him as such. Thomas Cromwell, as the king's Secretary, and other members of the Privy Council examined More in the Tower to make him affirm or deny the

king's supremacy. More refused to be drawn into either statement but his fate was decided by the Treasons Act of 1534,
which made it a treasonable offence to speak in such a way as to
deprive the king of any of his lawful titles. There followed acts
of attainder against More and Fisher for refusing to take the
oath to the succession. They were condemned to life imprisonment and to the forfeiture of all their possessions.

Though deprived of pen, ink, and books for much of his
imprisonment, More wrote his *Dialogue of Comfort* and some
minor pieces in prison. When without other resources, he used
pieces of coal for writing. His spirit and his wit remained
undimmed by worldly adversity. His family, including his
wife, Alice, visited him and accused him of folly, urging him to
save himself and regain both liberty and royal favour.[2]

'What the good-year, Master More,' quoth she, 'I marvel
that you that have been always hitherto taken for so wise
a man will now so play the fool to lie here in this close
filthy prison, and be content thus to be shut up among
mice and rats, when you might be abroad at your liberty, and
with the favour and good will both of the king and his
council if you would but do as all the bishops and best
learned of this realm have done. And seeing you have at
Chelsea a right fair house, your library, your gallery, your
garden, your orchard, and all other necessaries so handsome
about you, where you might in the company of me your
wife, your children, and household, be merry, I muse what
a God's name you mean here still thus fondly to tarry.'
After he had a while quietly heard her, with a cheerful
countenance he said unto her: 'I pray thee, good
Mistress Alice, tell me one thing!' 'What is that?' quoth
she. 'Is not this house,' quoth he, 'as nigh heaven as mine
own?' To whom she after her accustomed homely
fashion, not liking such talk, answered: 'Tylle valle,
Tylle valle!'

More joked with his gaolers, even with his political enemies,
and for one of those who was an indirect cause of his misfortunes
he showed considerable compassion. When visited by his
daughter Margaret, he asked after the health of Anne Boleyn,

remarking, 'Alas! Meg, alas! it pitieth me to remember into what misery, poor soul, she shall shortly come.'[3]

Spirits like More's, even when imprisoned for life, are too dangerous to a tyrannical régime to be tolerated. A formula was devised for taking his life, as well as that of Fisher. Sir Richard Rich, Solicitor-General, visited them separately and struck up a conversation. In Fisher's case, Rich pretended that there was now some official doubt as to whether the king could be supreme head of the Church. He asked Fisher's opinion. Fisher said that, in his opinion, it was impossible for the king to be head of the Church. This statement was sufficient evidence of Fisher's treason and cost him his life. Rich was more circumspect with More, since he was dealing with a highly successful lawyer and politician. He put to More various hypothetical cases as to whether parliament could decree who should be king or pope. In the end, More was alleged to have said that the king could not be created supreme head of the Church. It was not a complete admission but it was good enough for Rich's purposes and a charge of treason was brought against More.

The consequences of this charge are recorded in his trial and condemnation, where, as throughout almost all accounts of his life, More emerges as a man of worldly ability and spiritual dedication, a martyr without self-importance and a saint with a sharp wit.

The Trial of Sir THOMAS MORE, knight, Lord Chancellor of England, for High Treason, in denying the King's Supremacy: 26 HENRY VIII. A.D. 1535.[4]

A Bill being preferred in Parliament, November 1534, to attaint Elizabeth Barton, and several others, of high treason, Bishop Fisher and Sir Thomas More were also brought into it for misprision [*concealment*] of treason for the refusing of the Oath of Succession—says my Lord Herbert. The same author avows the Bill did so pass;

but Sir Thomas's great-grandson, in his Life, shows the contrary, and that notwithstanding the Archbishop of Canterbury, the Lord Chancellor, Duke of Norfolk, and Secretary Cromwell, by the King's command, went to him and pressed him to a compliance, yet the Chancellor influenced the King so far, that the matter of misprision was dropped. Sir Thomas, was also examined at other times by the Lord Chancellor, Dukes of Norfolk and Suffolk, Mr. Secretary, and others of the Privy Council, who pressed him, with all the arguments they could think of, to own the King's Supremacy in direct and open terms, or plainly to deny it; but he being loath to aggravate the King's displeasure, would say no more than that the statute was like a two-edged sword, for if he spoke against it, he should be the cause of the death of his body; and if he assented to it, he should purchase the death of his soul. Those Examinations being over, Richard Rich, newly made Solicitor-General, and afterwards Lord Rich, with Sir Richard Southwell, and Mr. Palmer, Secretary Cromwell's man, were sent by the King to take away his books. Rich, pretending friendship to him, and protesting he had no commission to talk with him about the former affair of the Supremacy, he put a case to him thus. If it were enacted by Parliament that Richard Rich should be king, and that it should be treason in anybody to deny it, what offence it were to contravene that Act? Sir Thomas More answered, that he should offend if he said so, because he was bound by the Act; but that this was *casus levis* [*a trivial issue*]. Whereupon Sir Thomas said, he would propose a higher case: Suppose it were enacted by parliament, *Quod Deus non sit Deus* [*that God should not be God*] and that it were treason to contravene, whether it were not an offence to say it, according to the said Act? Rich replied, 'Yea;' but said withal, 'I will propose a middle case, because this is too high. The King, you know, is constituted supreme head of the Church upon earth. Why should not you, Master More, accept him for such, as you would me, if I were made king by the aforesaid supposition?' More answered, the case was not the same, because, said he, a parliament can make a king, and depose him, and that every parliament-man may give his consent thereunto, but that a subject cannot be bound so in the case of Supremacy. *Quia consensum ab eo ad Parliamentum præbere non potest* (so, says my Lord Herbert, it is in my copy if it be not mistaken,) *& quanquam Rex sic acceptus sit in Anglia, plurimæ tamen Partes exteræ idem non affirmant* [*that he is unable to offer his consent to Parliament:*

*and though the king may be accepted in England, yet many foreign countries
do not concur in this opinion*].

Sir Thomas, having continued a prisoner in the Tower somewhat
more than a twelvemonth, for he was committed about the middle
of April 1534, and was brought to his trial on the 7th of May, 1535,
he went into the Court leaning on his staff, because he was much
weakened by his imprisonment, but appeared with a cheerful and
composed countenance. The persons constituted to try him, were
Sir Thomas Audley, Lord Chancellor; Thomas, Duke of Norfolk,
Sir John Fitzjames, Lord Chief Justice; Sir John Baldwin, Sir
Richard Leicester, Sir John Port, Sir John Spelman, Sir Walter
Luke, Sir Anthony Fitzherbert.

The indictment was very long, but where to procure a copy of it,
I could never learn; it is said in general, it contained all the crimes
that could be laid to the charge of any notorious malefactor; and
Sir Thomas professed it was so long, that he could scarce remember
the third part of what was objected therein against him. It was read
aloud by the Attorney-General; and Sir Thomas's mortal sin seemed
plainly to be his refusing the Oath of Succession, already mentioned.
To prove this, his double Examination in the Tower was alleged
against him, the first before Secretary Cromwell, Thomas Beade,
John Tregonnel, &c. to whom he professed he had given over all
thoughts of titles either to popes or princes though the whole world
should be given him, he being fully determined only to serve God.
The second time before the Lord Chancellor, the Duke of Suffolk,
Earl of Wiltshire, and others, before whom he compared that oath
to a two-edged sword, as before observed.

Presently after the indictment was read, the Lord Chancellor
and the Duke of Norfolk spoke to him to this effect; 'You see now
how grievously you have offended His Majesty; yet he is so very
merciful, that if you will lay aside your obstinacy, and change your
opinion, we hope you may obtain pardon and favour in his sight.'
But Sir Thomas stoutly replied, 'Most noble lords I have great
reason to return thanks to your honours for this your great civility,
but I beseech Almighty God, that I may continue in the mind I am
in, through His grace, unto death.' Then having intimation given
that he might say what he thought fit in his own defence, he began
thus: 'When I consider the length of my accusation, and what
heinous matters are laid to my charge, I am struck with fear, lest
my memory and understanding, which are both impaired, together

with my bodily health, through a long indisposition contracted by my imprisonment, should now fail me so far, as to make me incapable of making such ready answers in my defence, as otherwise I might have done.'

The Court being sensible of his weakness, ordered a chair to be brought in, wherein he might seat himself, which he did accordingly, and then went on thus: 'This my indictment, if I mistake not, consists of four principal heads, each of which I purpose, God willing, to answer in order. As to the first crime objected against me, that I have been an enemy out of stubbornness of mind to the King's second marriage; I confess I always told His Majesty my opinion, according to the dictates of my conscience, which I neither ever would, nor ought to have concealed: for which I am so far from thinking myself guilty of high treason, that on the contrary, being required to give my opinion by so great a prince in an affair of so much importance, upon which the peace of the Kingdom depended; I should have basely flattered him, and my own conscience, had not I spoke the truth as I thought: then indeed I might justly have been esteemed a most wicked subject, and a perfidious traitor to God. If I have offended the King herein; if it can be an offence to tell one's mind freely when his sovereign puts the question to him; I suppose I have been sufficiently punished already for the fault, by the great afflictions I have endured, by the loss of my estate, and my tedious imprisonment, which has continued already near fifteen months. The second charge against me is, that I have violated the Act made in the last Parliament: that is being a prisoner, and twice examined, I would not, out of a malignant, perfidious, obstinate and traitorous mind, tell them my opinion, whether the King was Supreme Head of the Church or not: but confessed then, that I had nothing to do with that Act, as to the justice or injustice of it, because I had no benefice in the Church: yet then I protested, that I have never said nor done anything against it; neither can any one word or action of mine be alleged, or produced, to make me culpable. Nay, this I own was then my answer to their honours, that I would think of nothing else hereafter, but of the bitter Passion of our Blessed Saviour, and of my exit out of this miserable world. I wish nobody any harm, and if this does not keep me alive, I desire not to live; by all which I know, I would not transgress any law, or become guilty of any treasonable crime. For this statute, nor no other law in the world can punish any man for his silence, seeing they

33

can do no more than punish words or deeds; 'tis God only that is the judge of the secrets of our hearts.'

The Attorney-General (Christopher Hales). Sir Thomas, though we have not one word or deed of yours to object against you, yet we have your silence, which is an evident sign of the malice of your heart: because no dutiful subject, being lawfully asked this question, will refuse to answer it.

Sir Thomas More. Sir, my silence is no sign of any malice in my heart, which the King himself must own by my conduct upon divers occasions; neither doth it convince [*convict*] any man of the breach of the law; for it is a maxim amongst the Civilians and Canonists, *Qui tacet consentire videtur,* he that holds his peace, seems to give his consent. And as to what you say, that no good subject will refuse to give a direct answer; I do really think it to be the duty of every good subject, except he be such a subject as will be a bad Christian, rather to obey God than man; to be more cautious to offend his conscience, than of anything else in the whole world; especially if his conscience be not the occasion of some sedition and great injury to his prince and country: for I do here sincerely protest, that I never revealed it to any man alive. I come now to the third principal article in my indictment, by which I am accused of malicious attempts, traitorous endeavours, and perfidious practices against that statute, as the words therein do allege, because I wrote, while in the Tower, divers packets of letters to Bishop Fisher; whereby I exhorted him to violate the same law, and encouraged him in the like obstinacy. I do insist that these letters be produced and read in court, by which I may be either acquitted or convinced of a lie: but because you say the bishop burnt them all, I will here tell you the whole truth of the matter. Some of my letters related only to our private affairs, as about our old friendship and acquaintance: one of them was in answer to his, wherein he desired me to let him know what answers I made upon my examinations concerning the Oath of Supremacy; and what I wrote to him upon it was this, that I had already settled my conscience, and let him satisfy his according to his own mind. God is my witness, and as I hope He will save my soul, I gave him no other answer; and this I presume is no breach of the laws. As to the principal crime objected against me, that I should say upon my examination in the Tower, that this Law was like a two-edged sword; for in consenting to it, I should endanger my soul, and in rejecting it should lose my life: 'tis evidently concluded, as you say, from this answer, because Fisher made the like, that he was in the same conspiracy. To this I reply, that my answer there was conditional, if there were both danger either in allowing or disallowing that Act; and therefore, like a two-edged sword, it seemed a hard thing it should be put upon me, who had never hitherto contradicted it either in word or deed. These were my words; what the bishop answered, I know not: if his answer was like mine, it did not proceed from any conspiracy of ours, but from the similitude of our learning and understanding. To conclude, I do sincerely avouch, that I never spoke a word against this law to any man living, though perhaps the King's Majesty has been told the contrary.

There was little or no reply made to this full answer, by Mr. Attorney, or anybody else; the word 'Malice' was what was principally insisted on, and in the mouths of the whole Court, though for proof of it nobody could produce either words or actions. Nevertheless, to set the best gloss that could be upon the matter, Mr. Rich was called to give evidence in open court upon oath, which he immediately did, affirming what we have already related concerning a conference between him and Sir Thomas in the Tower. To which Sir Thomas made answer, 'If I were a man, my lords, that had no regard to my oath, I had had no occasion to be here at this time, as is well known to everybody, as a criminal; and if this oath, Mr. Rich, which you have taken, be true, then I pray I may never see God's face, which were it otherwise, is an imprecation I would not be guilty of to gain the whole world.'

More having recited in the face of the Court all the discourse they had together in the Tower, as it truly and sincerely was, he added: 'In good faith, Mr. Rich, I am more concerned for your perjury, than my own danger; and I must tell you, that neither myself, nor anybody else to my knowledge, ever took you to be a man of such reputation, that I or any other would have anything to do with you in a matter of importance. You know that I have been acquainted with your manner of life and conversation a long time, even from your youth to the present juncture, for we lived in the same parish; and you very well know, I am sorry I am forced to speak it, you always lay under the odium of a very lying tongue, of a great gamester, and of no good name and character either there or in the Temple, where you was educated. Can it therefore seem likely to your lordships, that I should in so weighty an affair as this, act so unadvisedly, as to trust Mr. Rich, a man I had always so mean an opinion of, in reference to his truth and honesty, so very much before my sovereign lord the King, to whom I am so deeply indebted for his manifold favours, or any of his noble and grave councillors, that I should only impart to Mr. Rich the secrets of my conscience in respect to the King's supremacy, the particular subject, and only point about which I have been so long pressed to explain myself? Which I never did, nor never would reveal, when the Act was once made, either to the King himself, or any of his Privy Councillors, as is well known to your honours, who have been sent upon no other account at several times by His Majesty to me in the Tower. I refer it to your judgments, my lords, whether this can seem credible to any of your lordships. But supposing what Mr. Rich has swore should be true, seeing the words were spoke in familiar and private conversation, and that there was nothing at all asserted, but only cases put without any offensive circumstances; it cannot in justice be said, that they were spoke maliciously, and where there is no malice, there is no offence. Besides, my lords, I cannot think so many reverend bishops, so many honourable personages, and so many virtuous and learned men, of whom the Parliament consisted in the enacting of that law, ever meant to have any man punished with death, in whom no malice could be found, taking the word *malitia* for *malevolentia*; for if *malitia* be taken in a general signification for any crime, there is no man can be free. Wherefore this word *maliciously* is so far significant in this Statute, as the word *forcible* is in that of *forcible entry*. For in that case if any enter peaceably, and puts his adversary out forcibly, it is no offence; but if he enters forcibly, he shall be punished by that Statute. Besides, all the unspeakable goodness of His Majesty towards me, who has been so many ways my singular good and gracious lord, who has so dearly loved and trusted me, even from my first entrance into his royal service, vouchsafing to honour me with the dignity of being one of his Privy Council, and has most generously promoted me to offices of great reputation and honour, and lastly to that of Lord High-Chancellor, which honour he never did to any layman before, the same being the highest dignity in this famous Kingdom, and next to the King's royal person, so far beyond my merits and qualifications; honouring and exalting me by his incomparable benignity, for these twenty years and upwards, heaping continual favours upon me; and now at last, at my own humble request, giving me liberty to dedicate the remainder of my life to the service of God for the better saving of my soul, has been pleased to discharge and free me from that weighty dignity; before which he had still heaped more and more honours upon me: I say, all this His Majesty's bounty, so long and so plentifully conferred upon me, is enough, in my opinion, to invalidate the scandalous accusation so injuriously surmized and urged by this man against me.'

This touched the reputation of Mr. Rich to the very quick, and was a slur that could not be effaced, without the utmost difficulty; and the only way to do it, was, if possible, to produce substantial and creditable Witnesses to attest the contrary: and therefore he caused Sir Richard Southwell, and Mr. Palmer, who were in the same room with Sir Thomas and Mr. Rich when they conferred together, to be sworn as to the words that passed between them. Whereupon Mr. Palmer deposed, that he was so busy in thrusting Sir Thomas's books into a sack, that he took no notice of their talk. And Sir Richard Southwell likewise swore, that because his business was only to take care of conveying his books away, he gave no ear to their discourse.

Sir Thomas having urged other reasons in his own defence, to the discrediting of Mr. Rich's evidence; the judge proceeded to give the charge to the jury. Whether Sir Thomas had challenged any of the panel, when they were returned to serve, does not appear; but the twelve persons on whose verdict his life now depended, were these: Sir Thomas Palmer, knight, Sir Thomas Peirt, knight, George Lovell, Esq. Thomas Burbage, Esq. Geoffrey Chamber, Edward Stockmore, Jasper Leake, William Browne, Thomas Billington, John Parnel, Richard Bellame, George Stoakes, gents.

Now the jury having withdrawn, scarce were out a quarter of an hour before they returned with their verdict, by which they found the prisoner guilty; upon which the Lord Chancellor, as chief in the commission for this trial, immediately began to proceed to Judgment:

which Sir Thomas observing, he said to him, 'My lord, when I was concerned in the law, the practice in such cases was to ask the prisoner before sentence, whether he had anything to offer why judgment should not be pronounced against him.' The Lord Chancellor hereupon stopping his sentence, wherein he had already proceeded in part, asked Sir Thomas what he was able to say to the contrary. Who presently made answer in these words: 'For as much as, my lords, this indictment is grounded upon an Act of Parliament, directly repugnant to the laws of God and His Holy Church, the supreme government of which, or of any part thereof, no temporal person may by any law presume to take upon him, being what of right belongs to the See of Rome, which by special prerogative was granted by the mouth of our Saviour Christ Himself to St. Peter, and the Bishops of Rome his successors only, whilst He lived, and was personally present here on earth: it is therefore amongst Catholic Christians, insufficient in law, to charge any Christian to obey it.' And in order to the proof of his assertion, he declared among other things, that whereas this Kingdom alone being but one member, and a small part of the Church, was not to make a particular law disagreeing with the general law of Christ's universal Catholic Church, no more than the City of London, being but one member in respect to the whole kingdom, might enact a law against an Act of Parliament, to be binding to the whole realm; so he showed farther, that law was even contrary to the laws and statutes of the kingdom, yet unrepealed, as might evidently be seen by Magna Charta, wherein are these words; *Ecclesia Anglicana libera sit, & habeat omnia jura integra, & libertates suas illæsas* [*the English Church shall be free, with its rights whole and undiminished, and its freedom unimpeded*]: and it is contrary also to that sacred oath which the King's Majesty himself, and every other Christian prince, always take with great solemnity, at their coronations. So great was Sir Thomas's zeal, that he further alleged, that it was worse in the Kingdom of England to refuse obedience to the See of Rome, than for any child to do to his natural parent: for as St. Paul said to the Corinthians, 'I have regenerated you, my children, in Christ:' so might that worthy Pope of Rome, St. Gregory the Great, say of us Englishmen, 'Ye are my children, because I have given you everlasting salvation:' for by St. Augustine and his followers, his immediate messengers, England first received the Christian faith, which is a far higher and better inheritance than any carnal father can leave to his children:

for a son is only by generation, we are by regeneration made the spiritual children of Christ and the Pope.

Here the Lord Chancellor took him up, and said: that seeing all the bishops, universities, and the most learned men in the Kingdom had agreed to that Act, it was much wondered that he alone should so stiffly stickle, and so vehemently argue there against it. His answer was, 'That if the number of bishops and universities were so material as his lordship seemed to make it: then, my lord, I see no reason why that thing should make any change in my conscience: for I doubt not, but of the learned and virtuous men now alive, I do not speak only of this realm, but of all Christendom, there are ten to one of my mind in this matter; but if I should take notice of those learned doctors and virtuous fathers that are already dead, many of whom are saints in heaven, I am sure there are far more, who all the while they lived thought in this case as I do now. And therefore, my lord, I do not think myself bound to conform my conscience to the counsel of one kingdom, against the general consent of all Christendom.'

Here it seems the Lord Chancellor not willing to take the whole load of his condemnation upon himself, asked in open court the advice of Sir John Fitzjames, the Lord Chief Justice of England, whether the indictment was valid or no, who wisely answered thus: 'My lords, all by St. Gillian' [sc. Julian, Juliana] (for that was always his oath) 'I must needs confess that if the Act of Parliament be not unlawful, then the indictment is not in my conscience invalid.' Some have wrote, that the Lord Chancellor should hereupon say, Quid adhuc desideramus testimonium, reus est mortis [We still require evidence: the defendant is on trial for his life], and then presently proceeded to give sentence to this effect: that he should be carried back to the Tower of London, by the help of William Kingston, Sheriff, and, from thence drawn on a hurdle through the City of London to Tyburn, there to be hanged till he should be half dead; that then he should be cut down alive, his privy parts cut off, his belly ripped, his bowels burnt, his four quarters set up over four gates of the city, and his head upon London Bridge.

This was the judgment pronounced upon this great man, who had deserved so well both of the King and Kingdom, and for which Paulus Jovius calls King Henry VIII, another Phalaris. This severe sentence was afterwards, by the King's pardon, changed to beheading, because he had borne the greatest office in the Kingdom;

of which mercy of the King's, word being brought to Sir Thomas, he merrily said, 'God forbid the King should use any more such mercy to any of my friends, and God bless all my posterity from such pardons.' When he had received sentence of death, he spake thus with a resolute and sedate aspect: 'Well, seeing I am condemned, God knows how justly, I will freely speak for the disburdening my conscience, what I think of this law. When I perceived it was the King's pleasure to list out from whence the Pope's authority was derived, I confess I studied seven years together to find out the truth of it, and I could not meet with the works of any one doctor, approved by the Church, that avouch a layman was, or ever could be the Head of the Church.'

Lord Chancellor. Would you be esteemed wiser, or to have
a sincerer conscience than all the bishops, learned doctors,
nobility and commons of this realm?

Sir Thomas More. I am able to produce against one bishop which
you can produce on your side, a hundred Holy and Catholic
bishops for my opinion; and against one realm, the consent
of Christendom for a thousand years.

Duke of Norfolk. Sir Thomas, you show your obstinate and
malicious mind.

Sir Thomas More. Noble sir, it is no malice or obstinacy that
makes me say this, but the just necessity of the cause obliges
me to it for the discharge of my conscience; and I call God
to witness, that nothing but this has excited me to it.

After this the judges kindly offering him their favourable audience if he had anything else to say; he answered most mildly and charitably, 'I have no more to say, but that as the Blessed Apostle St. Paul, as we read in the Acts of the Apostles, was present, and consenting to the protomartyr Stephen, keeping their clothes that stoned him to death, and yet they are both now holy saints in Heaven, and there shall continue friends to eternity; so I verily trust, and shall therefore heartily pray, that albeit your lordships have been on earth my judges to condemnation, yet that we may hereafter meet joyfully together in Heaven to our everlasting salvation: and God preserve you, especially my sovereign lord the King, and grant him faithful counsellors.'

Sir Thomas, after his condemnation, was conducted from the bar to the Tower, an axe being carried before him, with the edge towards him.

Sir Thomas More having remained a prisoner in the Tower about a week after his sentence, on the 6th of July early in the morning, his old friend Sir Thomas Pope came to him with a message from the King and Council, to acquaint him, that his execution was appointed to be before nine that morning. Whereupon Sir Thomas said, he thanked him heartily for his good news. 'I have been,' says he, 'much obliged to His Majesty for the benefits and honours he has most bountifully conferred upon me; yet I am more bound to His Grace I do assure you, for confining me in this place, where I have had convenient place and opportunity to put me in mind of my last end. I am most of all bound to him, that His Majesty is pleased to rid me out of the miseries of this wretched world.' Then Sir Thomas Pope acquainted him, it was the King's pleasure he should not use many words at the place of execution. 'Sir,' said he, 'you do well to acquaint me with the King's pleasure; for I had otherwise designed to have made a speech to the people; but it matters not, and I am ready to conform myself to His Highness's pleasure. And I beseech you, sir, you would become a suitor to His Majesty, that my daughter Margaret may attend my funeral.' To which Pope replied that the King was willing his wife and children, and other friends should be present. Sir Thomas Pope being about to take his leave, could not refrain from tears. Whereupon Sir Thomas More said, 'Let not your spirits be cast down, for I hope we shall see one another in a better place, where we shall be free to live and love in eternal bliss.' And to divert Pope's grief, he took up his urinal and shook it, saying merrily, 'I see no danger but that this man may live longer, if the King pleases.'

About nine he was brought out of the Tower; his beard was long, his face pale and thin, and carrying a red cross in his hand, he often lifted up his eyes to Heaven; a woman meeting with him with a cup of wine, he refused it, saying, 'Christ at His Passion drank no wine, but gall and vinegar.' Another woman came crying, and demanded some papers she said she had left in his hands, when he was Lord Chancellor, to whom he said, 'Good woman, have patience but for an hour, and the King will rid me of the care I have for those papers, and every thing else.' Another woman followed him, crying, he had done her much wrong when he was Lord Chancellor, to whom he said, 'I very well remember the cause, and if I were to decide it now, I should make the same decree.'

When he came to the scaffold, it seemed ready to fall; whereupon he said merrily to the Lieutenant, 'Pray, sir, see me safe up; and as to my coming down, let me shift for myself.' Being about to speak to the people, he was interrupted by the Sheriff, and thereupon he only desired the people to pray for him, and bear witness he died in the faith of the Catholic Church, a faithful servant both to God and the King. Then kneeling, he repeated the *Miserere* Psalm with much devotion; and rising up, the executioner asked him forgiveness. He kissed him, and said, 'Pluck up thy spirits, man, and be not afraid to do thine office; my neck is very short, take heed therefore thou strike not awry for saving thine honesty.' Laying his head upon the block, he bid the executioner stay till he had put his beard aside, for that had committed no treason. Thus he suffered with much cheerfulness; his head was taken off at one blow, and was placed upon London Bridge, where having continued for some months, and being about to be thrown into the Thames to make room for others, his daughter Margaret bought it, enclosed it in a leaden box, and kept it for a relic.

It is said, when the news of his death was brought to the King who was at that time playing at tables, Anne Boleyn looking on, he cast his eye upon her, and said, 'Thou art the cause of this man's death:' and presently leaving his play he betook himself to his chamber, and thereupon, fell into a fit of melancholy. More's great-grandson, in his *Life*, relates that money was miraculously supplied for the purchase of his winding sheet, and that one of his teeth preserved as a relic was miraculously converted into two.

Chapter two

Queen Catherine Howard (1542)

With the fall of Catherine Howard, her reputation changed from that of the hazel-eyed, auburn-haired beauty, twenty years old and the radiant hope for a strong Tudor succession. She was not, it appeared, a beauty after all. She was not as young as some had thought her. Worst of all, her character was disfigured by a life of sexual vice. For a queen, adultery or promiscuity was no ordinary offence. At Anne Boleyn's trial by her peers in 1536 such conduct had been proved an act of treason, since the Act of Succession named her children heirs to the throne and by her conduct she had 'slandered' them and the succession. Such slander was treason under the law.

Catherine Howard's case was not precisely similar but its consequences were much the same. She was probably born just before 1520, daughter of Lord Edmund Howard, an impoverished son of the second Duke of Norfolk. Catherine Howard's mother died and her father, on remarrying, gave up the care of his daughter to her grandmother, the elderly Duchess of Norfolk. It was with the servants and the retainers of this large Tudor household that the girl spent much of her time and it was during this period that the crimes with which she was later charged were alleged to have occurred. The two men involved were Francis Dereham and a musician, Henry Mannock, who had taught her to play the virginals.

On 9 July 1540 the marriage of Henry VIII and his fourth wife, Anne of Cleves, was annulled. Less than three weeks later, Catherine Howard was married to the forty-nine-year-old king. By the autumn of the following year no son had been born to strengthen the Tudor male succession, represented otherwise only by the delicate Prince Edward, born in 1537. The first stories began to circulate of promiscuous conduct by the queen before, and even during, her marriage to the king. As in the case of Sir Thomas More, half-recorded accusations, rumours, reported conversations led to the panoply of judicial homicide. Francis Dereham and Henry Mannock were named as the queen's lovers and if it had occurred to them to deny it, the means used to extract a confession from Mark Smeton in Anne Boleyn's case would have been a strong discouragement.

The story of the queen's infidelity was revealed to the king by the Archbishop of Canterbury, Thomas Cranmer, at Mass on All Souls Day. The charges were investigated and the method of condemnation chosen. A Bill of Attainder, convicting Catherine Howard of treason, was introduced in the House of Lords. Under the circumstances, it was not a piece of legislation likely to be defeated. On 12 February 1542 Catherine Howard was informed that the sentence of beheading was to be carried out on the following day. She calmly arranged a dress-rehearsal of this final event and died as regally as Anne Boleyn had done six years before. Immediately after the beheading followed the execution of Lady Jane Rochford, who was condemned for having facilitated adultery between the queen and Thomas Culpepper, who happened to be Catherine's cousin. Catherine's legacy to the Tudor state was a law, repealed after Henry's death, making it treason in a woman to conceal any previous sexual relationship on marrying the king.

The *State Trials* account comes principally from Lord Herbert's *Life of Henry VIII* (1649).

Proceedings against Queen CATHERINE HOWARD for Incontinency: 33 HENRY VIII. A.D. 1542.

But our King encountered a greater vexation; for the Queen was supposed to offend in incontinency; some particulars whereof being extant in our Records, I have thought fit [says Lord Herbert] to transcribe, rather than to make other narration; the family of which she came being so noble and illustrious, and the honour of her sex, which is tender, being concerned therein. The letter sent from divers of the Council to William Paget, our Ambassador then in France, was this:

'After our hearty commendations, by these our letters, we be commanded to signify unto you a most miserable case, which came lately to revelation, to the intent that if you shall hear the same spoken of, you may declare the truth as followeth. Where the King's Majesty upon the sentence given of the invalidity of the pretended matrimony between His Highness and the Lady Anne of Cleves was earnestly and humbly solicited by his Council and the nobles of this realm to frame his most noble heart to the love and favour of some noble personage to be joined with him in lawful matrimony, by whom His Majesty might have some more store of fruit, and succession to the comfort of this realm; it pleased His Highness upon a notable appearance of honour, cleanness, and maidenly behaviour, to bend his affection towards Mistress Catherine Howard, daughter to the late Lord Edmund Howard, brother to me, the Duke of Norfolk, insomuch as His Highness was finally contented to honour her with his marriage, thinking now in his old days, after sundry troubles of mind which have happened unto him by marriages, to have obtained such a jewel for womanhood, and very perfect love towards him, as should not only have been to his quietness, but also brought forth the desired fruit of marriage, like as the whole realm thought the semblable, and in respect of the virtue and good behaviour which she showed outwardly, did her all honour accordingly. But this joy is turned into extreme sorrow, for when the King's Majesty receiving his Maker on Allhallows day last past, then gave Him most humble and hearty thanks for the good life he led and trusted to lead with her, and also desired the Bishop of Lincoln, his ghostly father, to make like prayer and give like thanks with him; on All Souls day being at Mass, the Archbishop of Canterbury having a little before heard that the same Mistress Catherine Howard was not indeed a woman of that pureness and cleanness that she was esteemed, but a woman who before she was joined with the King's Majesty had lived most corruptly and sensually; for the discharge of his duty opened the same most sorrowfully to His Majesty, and how it was brought to his knowledge, which was in this form following.

'While the King's Majesty was in his Progress, one John Lassells came to the said Archbishop of Canterbury, and declared unto him that he had been with a sister of his married in Sussex, which sometimes had been servant with the old Duchess of Norfolk, who did also bring up the said Mistress Catherine, and being with his said sister chanced to fall in communication with her of the Queen, wherein he advised her, because she was of the Queen's old acquaintance, to sue to be her woman. Whereunto his sister answered that she would not so do, but she was very sorry for the Queen. "Why?" quoth Lassells. "Marry," quoth she, "for she is light both in living and condition." "How so?" quoth Lassells. "Marry," quoth she, "there is one Francis Dereham, who was servant also in my Lady of Norfolk's house, which hath lain in bed with her in his doublet and hose an hundred nights. And there hath been such puffing and blowing between them, that once in the house a maid which lay in the house with her said to me she would lie no longer with her because she knew not what matrimony meant." And further she said unto him that one Mannock, sometime also servant to the said Duchess, knew a privy mark of her body. When the said Lassells had declared this to the said Archbishop of Canterbury, he considering the weight and importance of the matter, being marvellously perplexed therewith, consulted in the same with the Lord Chancellor of England, and the Earl of Hertford, whom the King's Majesty going in his Progress left to reside at London to order his affairs in those parts; who having weighed the matter and deeply pondered the gravity thereof, wherewith they were greatly troubled and unquieted, resolved finally that the said Archbishop should reveal the same to the King's Majesty; which because the matter was such, as he hath sorrowfully lamented, and also could not find in his heart to express the same to the King's Majesty by word of mouth, he declared the information thereof to His Highness in writing. When the King's Majesty had read this information thus delivered unto him, His Grace being much perplexed therewith, yet nevertheless so tenderly loved the woman and had conceived such a constant opinion of her honesty, that he supposed it rather to be a forged matter than of truth. Whereupon it pleased him secretly to call unto him the Lord Privy Seal, the Lord Admiral, Sir Anthony Brown, and Sir Thomas Wriothesley, to whom he opened the case, saying he could not believe it to be true. And yet seeing the information was made, he could not be satisfied till the certainty thereof was known, but he would not in any wise that in the inquisition any spark of scandal should rise towards her. Whereupon it was by His Majesty resolved that the Lord Privy Seal should go straight to London, where the said Lassells that gave the information was secretly kept, and with all dexterity to examine and try whether he would stand to his saying. Who being so examined, answered that his sister so told him, and that he had declared it for the discharge of his duty, and for none other respect; adding that he knew what danger was in it. Nevertheless, he had rather die in declaration of the truth, as it came to him, seeing it touched the King's Majesty so nearly, than live with the concealment of the same. Which asseveration being thus made by the said Lassells, the King's Majesty being informed thereof sent the Lord Privy Seal into Sussex to examine the woman, making a pretence to the woman's husband of hunting, and to her for receiving of hunters: and sent the said Thomas Wriothesley to London at the same instant, both to examine Mannock and also to take the said Dereham upon a pretence of piracy, because he had been before in Ireland and hath been noted before with that offence; making these pretences to the intent no spark of suspicion should rise of these examinations. The said Lord Privy Seal found the woman in her examination constant in her former sayings: and Sir Thomas Wriothesley found by the confession of Mannock that he had commonly used to feel the secrets and other parts of her body, ere ever Dereham was so familiar with her; and Dereham confessed that he had known her carnally many times, both in his doublet and his hose between the sheets, and in naked bed, alleging such witnesses of three sundry women one after another, that had lain in the same bed with them when he did the acts, that the matter seemed most apparent. But what inward sorrow the King's Majesty took when he perceived the information true, as it was the most woeful thing that ever came to our hearts to see it, so it were too tedious to write it unto you. But his heart was so pierced with pensiveness that long it was before His Majesty could speak and utter the sorrow of his heart unto us: and finally with plenty of tears, which was strange in his courage, opened the same. Which done, she was spoken withal in it by the Archbishop of Canterbury, the Lord Chancellor, the Duke of Norfolk, the Lord Great Chamberlain of England, and the Bishop of Winchester; to whom at the first she constantly denied it, but the matter being so declared unto her that she perceived it to be wholly disclosed, the same night she disclosed the whole to the Archbishop of Canterbury, who took the confession of the same in writing subscribed with her hand. Then were the rest of the number, being eight or nine men and women which knew of their doings, examined, who all agreed in one tale.

'Now may you see what was done before the marriage; God knoweth what hath been done since, but she had already gotten this Dereham into her service and trained him upon occasions, as sending of errands and writing of letters when her secretary was out of the way, to come often into her privy chamber. And she had gotten also into her privy chamber to be one of her chamberors, one of the women which had before lain in the bed with her and Dereham. What this pretended is easy to be conjectured. Thus much we know for the beginning, whereof we thought meet to advertise you, to the intent afore specified: and what shall further succeed and follow of this matter we shall not fail to advertise you thereof accordingly.

'You shall also receive herein enclosed a packet of letters, directed unto Sir Henry Knevet, His Grace's Ambassador with the Emperor, which His Highness's pleasure is you shall see conveyed unto him by the next post. Thus fare you right heartily well.

'From the King's Palace at Westminster, the 12th of November. Your loving friends, . . . Thomas Audley, Chancellor; E. Hertford, William Southampton, Robert Sussex, Stephen Winton, Anthony Wingfield.'

[Here were other names, which are now defaced in the original, but 'D. Norfolk' may by the contents of the letter be supposed one.]

Besides the persons specified in this letter, one Thomas Culpepper, being of the same name with the Queen's mother, was indicted for the same fault, as our histories have it, which he and Dereham at their arraignment confessing, Culpepper had his head cut off, and Dereham was hanged and quartered. But it rested not here, for the Lord William Howard, the Queen's uncle newly returned from an ambassage in France, and his wife, and the old Duchess of Norfolk, and divers of the Queen's and the said Duchess's kindred and servants, and a butterwife, were indicted of misprision of treason, as concealing this fact, and condemned to perpetual prison; though yet by the King's favour some of them at length were released. The

King not yet satisfied thus, for more authorising his proceeding, referred the business to the Parliament sitting the 16th of January, 1542. On the 21st of the same month a Bill was brought into the House, and read a first time, for the attainder on the charge of high treason of Catherine Howard, late Queen of England, and Jane, Lady Rochford, with others. And in the same Bill was contained the attainders, on misprision of treason, of Agnes Howard, Duchess of Norfolk, William Howard, &c. On the 28th, the Lord Chancellor declared to the rest of the Peers how much it concerned all their honours not to proceed to give too hasty a judgment on the Bill for the attainder of the Queen and others, which had yet been only once read amongst them. For that they were to remember that a Queen was no mean or private person, but an illustrious and public one. Therefore her cause was to be judged with that sincerity, that there should be neither room for suspicion of some latent quarrel, or that she should not have liberty to clear herself, if perchance, by reason or counsel she was able to do it, from the crime laid to her charge. For this purpose he thought it but reasonable that some principal persons, as well of the lords as commons, should be deputed to go to the Queen, partly to tell her the cause of their coming, and partly in order to help her womanish fears, by advising and admonishing her to have presence of mind enough to say anything to make her cause better. He knew for certain that it was but just that a princess should be judged by equal laws with themselves, and he could assure them that the clearing herself in this manner would be highly acceptable to her most loving husband. But that some answer ought to be had from her, and to report the truth of it to His Majesty, his advice was that they should choose the Archbishop of Canterbury; Charles, Duke of Suffolk, Grand Master of the Household; William, Earl of Southampton, Lord Privy Seal; with the Bishop of Westminster; if the King's Council approved of this, day after day, to repair to the Queen, to treat of this matter, according as their own prudence might think it necessary.

And in the meantime the sentence concerning the Bill against Her Majesty was ordered to be suspended.

On the 30th of January, the Chancellor declared to the Lords openly that the Privy Council, on mature deliberation, disliked the message that was to be sent to the Queen. Nevertheless, in the meantime they had thought of another way, less faulty, to be put to the King, or rather to be altogether demanded of him.

'1st. That His Majesty would condescend, according to his usual wisdom in Council, to weigh by an equal balance the mutability of all human affairs; that nature is weak and corrupt; none made free from accidents; and that no man can be happy in everything. That the whole state of the Kingdom depends on His Majesty's resolution to divert his mind from all trouble and solicitude. Next, that the attainder of Thomas Culpepper and Francis Dereham, with the King's assent, should be confirmed by authority of Parliament. Also the attainder [of] misprision against Lord William Howard. And that the Parliament might have leave to proceed to give judgment, and to finish the Queen's cause, that the event of that business may be no longer in doubt. 3rd. That when all these things are completed in a just parliamentary method, without any loss of time, that then His Majesty would condescend to give his royal assent to them, not by being present and speaking openly, as the custom hath been in other parliaments, but absent, by his letters patents, under the great seal of England, and signed by his own hand. That the remembrance of this late and sorrowful story and wicked facts, if repeated before him, may not renew his grief and endanger His Majesty's health. Lastly, they were to beseech His Majesty that if by chance, by speaking freely on the Queen, they should offend against the statutes then in being, out of his great clemency he would pardon all and every of them for it. And to propound all these matters to His Majesty, the Archbishop of Canterbury; Charles, Duke of Suffolk, with the Earl of Southampton, were deputed for that purpose.'

31st of January, the Lord Chancellor declared to the House that their message and request of yesterday had been delivered to His Majesty by the Lords Commissioners, and that the King had denied no part of their petition but had orderly granted every part of it. That he had returned them thanks for their loving admonition in regard to his health, which he said he took care of, not so much for the sake of his own body, as that of the whole republic. Nay, His Majesty declared further to them than they durst ask of him, as in the case of desiring liberty of speech, &c. For he told them he granted yet more, in giving leave for each man to speak his mind freely, and not incur the penalty which the laws had fixed on those who took the liberty to talk on the incontinency of queens; especially when the said person did not do it out of malice or ill will but out of zeal for his service.

On the 11th of February, the Lord Chancellor produced two statutes, which had passed both Lords and Commons; one concerning the attainder of the Queen, and the other about the method of proceeding against lunatics, who before their insanity had confessed themselves guilty of high treason. Each statute signed with the King's own hand, and together with His Majesty's assent to them, under the broad seal, and signed also, which was annexed to the said statutes. This the Chancellor held forth in both hands, that both Lords and Commons, who were called for that purpose, might apparently see it, and that the statutes might from thence have the full force and authority of a law. Which, when done, the Duke of Suffolk, Grand Master of the King's Household, delivered himself in a very serious discourse to this effect. He told the Houses that he and his fellow deputies, appointed to wait upon the Queen, had been with her, and that she had openly confessed and acknowledged to them the great crime she had been guilty of against the most high God, and a kind Prince, and lastly against the whole English nation. That she begged them all to implore His Majesty not to impute her crime alone to her whole kindred and family. But that His Majesty, howsoever unworthy she might be and undeserving, would yet extend his unbounded mercy and his singular beneficence to all her brothers, that they might not suffer for her faults. Lastly, to beseech His Majesty that it would please him to bestow some of her clothes on those maid-servants who had been with her from the time of her marriage, since she had now nothing else left to recompense them as they deserved.

The Earl of Southampton, Lord Privy Seal, next stood up in the House, and in near the same words confirmed what the Duke had said, adding—

Here the Journal Book again breaks off abruptly, and we are only told that the Chancellor prorogued the Parliament to the Tuesday following. This last *hiatus in manuscripto*, along with the former, makes it seem evident that they were not done by neglect of the clerks, but by design; and that it was a trick of state to prevent posterity from being acquainted with some matters not consistent with the respect they then paid to their grand monarch.

And so the Queen and Lady Jane Rochford, wife to the late Lord Rochford and noted to be a particular instrument in the death of Queen Anne, were brought to the Tower, and after confession of their faults had their heads cut off.

An Act was also passed, declaring that it shall be lawful for any of the King's subjects, if themselves do perfectly know, or by vehement presumption do perceive any will, act, or condition of lightness of body in her which shall be the Queen of this realm, to disclose the same to the King or some of his Council. But they shall not openly blow it abroad or whisper it, until it be divulged by the King or his Council. If the King or any of his successors shall marry a woman which was before incontinent, if she conceal the same it shall be high treason, &c. But this Act was repealed 1 Edward VI. c. 12, and 1 Mary I.

Chapter three

Colonel John Penruddock (1655)

In 1653, with Cromwell's assumption of power as Lord Protector and his dismissal of Parliament, republicans as well as royalists joined the ranks of his enemies. Even though his enemies might ultimately have fought one another, there was sufficient disaffection in the army and elsewhere to make a *coup d'état* seem possible. Moreover, the time appeared to be propitious. Cromwell had assumed power but he had yet to devise a system for imposing his rule effectively on the country as a whole.

Among royalists, there were two opinions. Some, like the secret organization known as the 'Sealed Knot', put little faith in precipitate action. They remained unconvinced that the king's cause was strong enough, either in arms or sentiment, to make the success of an insurrection at all probable. Dedicated though they were to the destruction of Cromwell, they believed this must be accomplished by a royalist invasion from Europe, supported if necessary by foreign arms. The alternative view, held by Colonel John Penruddock and his associates, was that anti-Cromwellian feeling in England had grown so strong that a simultaneous insurrection in various parts of the country might restore the king's government. Penruddock, born in 1619, the son of Sir John Penruddock, royalist High Sheriff of Wiltshire in 1643–4, had been educated at Blandford School and Queen's College, Oxford, having studied law before taking up arms for the king's cause.

Simultaneous risings were planned in areas as far apart as Shrewsbury and Kent, Salisbury and York. Early in 1655, the dismissal of Parliament led certain army officers to denounce Cromwell as a tyrant and there was a mood of disillusionment which inclined men to recall their royalist sympathies. In

March 1655 Colonel Penruddock, Sir Joseph Wagstaffe (formerly a major-general in the army of Charles I), and Colonel Hugh Grove, led their royalist rebels into Salisbury, and took the city in the king's name. But the other insurrections came to nothing. Some were discovered in embryo by John Thurloe, who headed Cromwell's intelligence service, while others failed to occur. Uncertain of what to do, and having been joined by fewer men than they had hoped, Penruddock, Grove, and the others marched towards Exeter. They were intercepted by a government force under Captain Unton Crook, who described the outcome in a latter of 16 March 1655 to Cromwell.[1]

I gave your Highness last night an account how far I had
pursued the Enemy that came out of Wiltshire into
Devon. I sent your Highness the number of them, which
I conceived to be two hundred. It pleased my good God so to
strengthen and direct me, that although I had none but
my own troop, which was not sixty, that about ten
o'clock at night I fell into their quarters at a town called
South Molton, in the County of Devon. I took, after four
hours dispute with them in the town, some sixty prisoners,
near a hundred and forty horse and arms. Wagstaff himself
escaped, and I cannot yet find him, although I am still
sending after him. The party of them was divided into three
troops. Colonel Penruddock commanded one of them and
was to make it a Regiment; Colonel Grove commanded
another, and was to complete it to a Regiment; Colonel
Jones the third, and was to do the like. These three
gentlemen are of Wiltshire and men of estates. One of Sir
Edward Clarke's sons was with them; he was to be Major
to Penruddock, the prisoners tell me that we killed him.
      I have brought all the prisoners to Exon, and have
delivered them over to the High Sheriff, who has put them
into the high Gaol.

Lord Clarendon's account, which appears in *State Trials* as an extended footnote (see pp. 70–6 below), is sympathetic to royalist aspirations but it is not difficult to see how soon disillusionment overtook the rebels. Wagstaff, their leader, made good his escape to Holland; their allies in other parts of England had failed to rise in their support; even those in neighbouring areas showed little sign of coming to their assistance. Predictably, many of them were ready to surrender to Crook's men in exchange for a promise that their lives would be spared.

At Penruddock's trial, the only possible defence to the charge was to argue that Cromwell's government was illegal and that no treason could be committed against it either under common or statute law. Yet since this was a trial held under the authority of political power rather than legal precedent, such a defence was vain. In his final speech to the court, Penruddock came very close to throwing himself on Cromwell's mercy, promising allegiance to the Lord Protector in exchange for his life. His conduct may seem an unedifying contrast to that of Sir Thomas More or, in other circumstances, Wolfe Tone. Yet neither More nor Tone saw their cause so apparently lost and themselves deserted in the way that Penruddock did. If hidden royalist sympathies had not been stimulated by the insurrection, perhaps it was because they did not exist. Among convinced royalists, some might have failed to support him from lack of courage but others, like the 'Sealed Knot', had opposed his action in any case. Whether or not Penruddock appears irresolute at the end of his trial, the psychological motive for resolution had been largely destroyed by the conduct of others.

That Penruddock met his death courageously is a matter of fact recorded by others, and the letters which he exchanged with his wife shortly before his execution are among the most moving documents in all the *State Trials*, since they fail to subordinate grief to a show of patriotic or self-induced high spirits. Penruddock remained an unwilling martyr, though an eager rebel. His unwillingness is even less surprising if one considers that the original sentence, commuted by Cromwell to beheading, was that he should be hanged, drawn, and quartered.

Penruddock, Grove, and five more were convicted of treason, while seven of their other associates were condemned for horse-stealing, since treason could not be proved against them. Three others were acquitted. The executions were carried out in May 1655, and later that year the first plans were introduced for dividing England into administrative areas to be controlled by various major-generals as commanders of militia. Despite the prognostications of certain royalists, the army remained loyal to the Lord Protector, and the opportunity for a successful *coup d'état* was not to re-occur within Cromwell's lifetime.

The Trial of the Hon. Colonel JOHN PENRUDDOCK, at Exon, for High Treason: 7 CHARLES II. A.D. 1655. (Written by Himself)

['When Penruddock's trial was brought on, there was a special messenger sent to Judge Hale, requiring him to assist at it. It was in vacation time, and he was at his country house at Alderley. He plainly refused to go, and said the four terms and two circuits were enough, and the little interval that was between was little enough for their private affairs, and so he excused himself. But if he had been urged, he would not have been afraid of speaking more plainly.' Burnet's *Life and Death of Sir Matthew Hale*.]

Upon Thursday the 19th of April 1655, the Commissioners of Oyer and Terminer being sat in the Castle of Exon, summoned before them myself, Mr. Hugh Grove, Mr. Richard Reeves, Mr. Robert Duke, Mr. George Duke, Mr. Thomas Fitzjames, Mr. Francis Jones, Mr. Edward Davis, Mr. Thomas Poulton, and Mr. Francis Bennet. Being all called to the bar, we were commanded to hold up our hands, and an indictment of high treason was read against us. And being asked whether we would plead guilty or not guilty to the indictment, in the behalf of myself and of the gentlemen therein charged, I spoke as followeth:

Penruddock. My lords, though my education hath been such, as not to give me those advantages which the knowledge of the laws would have assisted me with, for the defending myself; yet upon the hearing this very indictment, my reason tells me that it is illegal; and therefore I do demand counsel, that may dispute the illegality thereof.

Serjeant Glynne.[2] Sir, you desire that which cannot be granted.
Therefore give your answer, whether you are guilty or not
guilty of the treason of which you stand charged.

Penruddock. Sir, by your favour, it is that which hath been granted
to my inferiors, viz. to Mr. Lilburne, and to one Rolf a
shoemaker; and I have as great a right to the laws, as any
person that sits here as my judge: I do therefore challenge it
as my right. Judge Nicholas, whom I there see, will tell you
he himself was counsel for this Rolf. And it is a hard case,
if a free-born gentleman of England cannot have the same
privilege that his inferiors have had before him.

Attorney-General [Sir Edmond Prideaux]. Sir, there is a great
difference between treason acting and acted. The latter is
your case. Therefore, flatter not yourself, and do not think
your being mute shall save your estate in case of treason;[3]
for if you plead not to the indictment, sentence will be
pronounced against you, as if you had been found guilty of
the fact you are charged with.

Penruddock. I observe your distinction. But all the logic you have,
shall not make me nor any rational man acknowledge that
this was either acting or acted, before it be proved. Sir, it is
but a bare suspicion, and I hope you will not condemn me
before I am convicted. I say the indictment is illegal, and I
do demand counsel.

Attorney-General. Sir, the Court must not be dallied withal. I do
peremptorily demand of you, are you guilty or not guilty?
If you plead, you may have favour. Otherwise we shall proceed
to sentence.

Penruddock. Sir, put case I do plead, shall I then have counsel
allowed me?

Attorney-General. Sir, the Court makes no bargains. Refer yourself
to us.

(Hereupon, my fellow prisoners persuaded me to plead not guilty.
Which being done, I demanded counsel, as being partly promised it.
Mr. Attorney told me I could have none. Then I replied.)

Penruddock. Sir, *durus est hic sermo* [*this is a harsh declaration*], it is no
more than I expected from you. But rather than I will be
taken off unheard, I will make my own defence as well as
I can.

(The jurors being then called, I challenged about twenty-four
of the thirty-five I might have challenged. The rest of the gentlemen
were sent from the bar, I was left alone upon my trial: and the
jurors were so packed, that had I known them the issue had been
the same that it was. The jurors being sworn, and the indictment
again read, Mr. Attorney demanded what exception I could make
to it.)

Penruddock. Sir, I except against every part thereof, for I take it
to be illegal *in toto composito* [*in its whole composition*].

Recorder Steele.[4] Sir, it is not usual for any court to admit of
general exceptions, therefore we expect that you should make
it to some particular.

Penruddock. Sir, I desire a copy of my indictment, and time until
tomorrow to make my defence.

Attorney-General. Sir, you cannot have it. The Court expects you
should do it now.

Penruddock. Then if I cannot have time, if my general exception
might have been admitted, it would have told you that there
can be no high treason in this nation, but it must be grounded
either upon the common or statute law. But this is neither
grounded upon the common law, or the statute; *ergo,* no
treason—against a Protector, who hath no power according to
law. Neither is there any such thing in law as a Protector,
for all treasons and such pleas are *propria causa regis* [*the King's
own cause*].

Serjeant Glynne. Sir, you are peremptory, you strike at the
government. You will fare never a whit the better for this
speech. Speak as to any particular exception you have to the
indictment.

Penruddock. Sir, if I speak anything which grates upon the present
government, I may confidently expect your pardon. My life
is as dear to me as this government can be to any of you.
The holy prophet David, when he was in danger of his life,
feigned himself mad, and the spittle hung upon his beard.
You may easily therefore excuse my imperfections. And since
I am now forced to give you my particular exception, more
plainly, to the indictment, I am bold to tell you, I observe
in the latter part of the indictment you say I am guilty
of high treason, by virtue of a statute in that case made and

provided. If there be any such statute, pray let it be read.
I know none such. My actions were for the King, and I well
remember what Bracton saith.

[*Penruddock then cited passages from Henry de Bracton's
thirteenth-century* De Legibus et Consuetudinis Angliae *to
show that the King was the supreme temporal power and that only
God might overrule regal authority.* 'Omnes sub rege, et ipse
nullo nisi tantum Deo; non est inferior sibi subjectis;
non parem habet in regno suo,' *was, in Penruddock's view,
the justification for his actions and the unanswerable defence to the
charges which had been brought against him.*]

Penruddock. This shows us where the true power is. You shall find
also that whoever shall refuse to aid the King when war is
levied against him, or against any that keep the King from his
just rights, offends the law and is thereby guilty of treason.
Again, all men that adhere to the King in personal service are
freed from treason by law. And yet you tell me of a statute
which makes my adhering to my King according to law to be
high treason. Pray let it be read.
Attorney-General. Sir, you have not behaved yourself so as to have
such a favour from the Court.
Penruddock. I require it not as a favour but as my right.
Attorney-General. Sir, you cannot have it.
Penruddock. If I cannot have it, these gentlemen that are the
jurors have not offended you, their verdict reaches to
their souls, as to my life. Pray let not them go blindfold, but
let that statute be their guide.
Attorney-General. Sir, the jury ought to be satisfied with what
hath been already said, and so might you too.
Penruddock. Sir, I thank you. You now tell me what I must trust
to.

Mr. Attorney then made a large speech in the face of the Court,
wherein he aggravated the offence with divers circumstances; as
saying I had been four years in France and held a correspondency
with the King my master, of whom I had learned the Popish religion.
That I endeavoured to bring in a debauched, lewd young man, and
to engage this nation in another bloody war. And that if I had not

been timely prevented, I had destroyed them—meaning the jurors—
and their whole families. I interrupted him and said:

Penruddock. Mr. Attorney, you have been heretofore of counsel for
me. You then made my case better than indeed it was. I see
you have the faculty to make men believe falsehoods to be
truth too.

Attorney-General. Sir, you interrupt me. You said but now you
were a gentleman.

Penruddock. I have been thought worthy heretofore to sit on the
bench, though now I am at the bar.

Mr. Attorney then proceeded in his speech, and called the witnesses.

Then I said, 'Sir, you have put me in a bear's skin, and now you
will bait me with a witness. But I see the face of a gentleman here
in Court (I mean Captain Crook) whose conscience can tell him,
that I had articles from him which ought to have kept me from
hence.' Captain Crook hereupon stood up, and his guilty conscience,
I suppose, advised him to sit down again, after he had made this
speech, that is to say, he opened his lips and spake nothing. The
several witnesses now came in. Mr. Dove the Sheriff of Wilts and
others; my charity forbids me to tell you what many of them swore.
I shall therefore omit that, and only tell you that one of our own
party, and indeed I think an honest man, being forced to give his
evidence, I said, 'My lords, it is a hard case that when you find
you cannot otherwise cleave me in pieces, that you must look after
wedges made of my own timber.' The virtuous crier of Blandford
being asked what were the words I used in the proclaiming King
Charles at the market, he said, I declared for Charles the Second,
and settling the true Protestant religion: for the liberty of the subject,
and privilege of parliaments.

Then I said to the Attorney-General and the whole Court, 'You
said even now, that I had learned of the King my master the Popish
religion, and endeavoured to bring him in. Your own witness tells
you what and whom I would bring in; and that it was the true
Protestant and not the Popish religion His Majesty is of, and intends
to settle.' I urged divers cases to make the business but a riot, as
my lord of Northumberland's, pretending that it was for the taking
of taxes; and that the power was not declared to be where they say
it is. I required the judges to be of counsel for me, and told them it

was their duty. Commissioner Lisle told me, I should have no wrong, (but he meant right); but Judge Rolle and Nicholas confessed themselves parties, therefore would say nothing. Then I told the Court, 'If I had seen a crown upon the head of any person, I had known what had been treason. The law of England would have taken hold of me, out of the respect it has to monarchy. There were no such landmarks before me, therefore I conceive I cannot be guilty of what I am charged with. And my lord, and Mr. Attorney, you here indict me for a treason committed at South Molton in Devonshire; and gentlemen, ye swear witnesses against me for facts done in other countries [*counties*]; Sarum, Blandford, and South Molton, are not in a parish. You puzzle the jurors with these circumstances, pray go to the kernel. And you, gentlemen of the jury, save your labour by taking those notes.' Mr. Attorney then addressed himself to the jury; and, to be short, after the space of half-an-hour long, gave them directions to bring me in guilty. This being done, I craved the favour from the Court, that I might speak to the jury: which being allowed, I said to them as followeth, or to the same effect:

'Gentlemen; you are called a jury of life and death; and happy will it be for your souls, if you prove to be a jury of life. You have heard what hath been said to make my actions treason; and with what vigour many untruths have been urged to you. I have made appear to you, that there can be no treason but against the King; that the law knows no such person as a Protector. Mr. Attorney pretends a statute for it, but refuseth the reading thereof either to me or you; vilifies me at pleasure, and tells you that I am a Papist, and would bring in the Popish religion; and that if I had not been timely prevented I had destroyed you. I hope you are also satisfied of the contrary, from the mouth of one of the bitterest witnesses. You are now judges between me and these judges. Let not the majesty of their looks, or the glory of their habits, betray you to a sin which is of a deeper dye than their scarlet; I mean that sin, blood: which calls to heaven for vengeance. Gentlemen, you do not see a hair on my head but is numbered neither can you make any one of them, much less can you put breath into my nostrils, when it is taken out. A sparrow doth not fall to the ground without the providence of God, much less shall man, to whom he hath given dominion and rule over all the creatures of the earth. Gentlemen look upon me, I am the image of my Creator, and that stamp of

His which is in my visage, is not to be defaced, without an account given wherefore it was. I have here challenged, as I am a gentleman, and free-born man of England, the right which the law allows me. I demanded a copy of my indictment and counsel, but it is denied me. The law which I would have been tried by is the known law of the land, which was drawn by the wise consultation of our princes, and by the ready pens of our progenitors. The law which I am now tried by, is no law, but what is cut out by the point of a rebellious sword; and the sheets in which they are recorded, being varnished with the moisture of an eloquent tongue, if you look not well to it, may chance to serve for some of your shrouds. If the fear of displeasing others, shall betray you to find me guilty of anything, you can at the most but make a riot of this. Pray, by the way, take notice, that the last Parliament would not allow the legislative power to be out of themselves; seventeen of twenty in this very county were of that opinion, and deserted the House; they were your representative; if you should find me guilty, you bring them in danger, and in them yourselves. Have a care of being drawn into a snare. Gentlemen, your blood may run in the same channel with mine. If what I have said do not satisfy you, so as to acquit me; if you bring a special verdict, you do in some measure acquit yourselves, and throw the blood that will be spilt upon the judges. Consider of it, and the Lord direct you for the best!'

The jury, after a quarter of an hour's retirement, brought me in guilty. The Lord forgive them, for they knew not what they did.

Upon Monday the 23rd of April, we were again called to the bar, being then in number twenty-six. Serjeant Glynne asked of me first, what I could say for myself, that I should not have sentence according to law? Then I said,

'My Lords and gentlemen, you ask what I can say for myself, that I should not have sentence passed upon me. The jury found me guilty. If I should go about to make a defence now, it would signify no more than as if my friends should petition for my pardon after I am executed. I could have offered you articles here, but I thought them inconsistent with this Court. When I look upon my offence, as to the Protector, I conclude myself a dead man; but when I reflect upon the favour he hath showed to others of my condition, and the hopes I have of your intercession, methinks I feel my spirits renewed again. My lords, death is a debt due from me to nature; the Protector has now the keeping the bond, and has put in suit by his Attorney; if he please to forbear the serving me with an execution, and let me keep it a little longer, I will pay him the interest of thanks for it as long as I live, and engage my posterity and a numerous alliance to be bound for me. So the Lord direct you all for the best. If I have found favour, I shall thank you; if not I shall forgive you!'

This being done, Serjeant Glynne, after a most bitter and non-sensical speech, gave sentence against us; viz. to be drawn, hanged and quartered. A pretty exchange for unworthy Crook's Articles for life, liberty, and estate; which I can prove, and will die upon. My trial held at least five hours. This is as much as at present I can remember of it; excuse the errors.

One of the jury being asked by a gentleman, why he found me guilty, answered, he was resolved to hang me, before he did see me.

I observe treason in this age to be an *individuum vagum* [*an unknown quantity*], like the wind in the Gospel, which bloweth where it listeth; for that shall be treason in me to-day, which shall be none in another to-morrow, as it pleaseth Mr. Attorney. The judges are sworn to do justice according to the law of the land, and therefore have miserably perjured themselves in condemning me contrary to law. And (not so contented) must cause the jury (so wise they were) through their false and unjust directions, to destroy their own rights and properties, and set up a new, arbitrary and tyrannical government.

The judges would not give me their advice in point of law (as was their duty,) because they said they were parties; yet could sit still on the bench in their robes, to countenance and approve of my sentence. No man can be a judge where he is a party in the same cause; therefore my trial was contrary to law. The judges being parties, ought not to sit upon the bench, but stand by; therefore my trial was illegal. The rest being no judges, but the Protector's immediate servants, so could not be my judges in case of high treason; for none but the sworn judges of the land are capable of it by law.

One thing of Colonel Dove, the reverend Sheriff of Wilts, who, that the jury might be sufficiently incensed, complaining of the many incivilities he pretended were offered him by our party, being upon his oath, said, that one of our men did run him through the side with a carbine. Surely it was a very small one, for the wound is not discernible.

A great deal of pains every man in his place took for the carrying on his master's work.

Be merciful unto me, O Lord, be merciful unto me: Under the shadow of Thy wings will I hide myself till this tyranny be overpast.

Glory to God on high, on earth peace, goodwill towards men; and so have mercy on me, O Lord!

The Sentence was ordered to be executed the 16th of May following.

As he was ascending the scaffold, he said, 'This, I hope, will prove to be like Jacob's ladder; though the feet of it rest on earth, yet I doubt not but the top of it reacheth to heaven.'

When he came upon the scaffold, he spoke to the people as follows:

'Gentlemen; it hath ever been the custom of all persons whatsoever, when they come to die, to give some satisfaction to the world, whether they be guilty of the fact of which they stand charged. The crime for which I am now to die, is loyalty, but, in this age called high treason. I cannot deny but I was at South Molton, in this County; but whether my being there, or my actions there, amount to so high a crime as high treason, I leave to the world and to the law to judge: truly, if I were conscious to myself of any base ends that I had in this undertaking, I would not be so injurious to my own soul, or disingenuous to you, as not to make a public acknowledgment thereof. I suppose that divers persons, according as they are biased in their several interests and relations, give their opinions to the world concerning us. I conceive it impossible, therefore, so to express myself in this particular, as not to expose both my judgment and reputation to the censure of many whom I shall leave behind me; because I will not put others, therefore, upon a breach of charity concerning me, or my actions, I have thought fit to decline all discourses which may give them a capacity either to injure themselves or me. My trial was public, and my several examinations, I believe, will be produced when I am in my grave. I will refer you therefore to the first, which I am sure some of you heard; and to the latter, which many of you, in good time, may see. Had Captain Crook done himself and us that right which a gentleman and a soldier ought to have done, I had not now been here. The man I forgive with all my heart: but truly, gentlemen, his protesting against those articles he himself with so many protestations and importunities put upon us, hath drawn so much dishonour and blood upon his head, that I fear some heavy judgment will pursue him; though he hath been false to us, I pray God I do not prove a true prophet to him; nay, I must say more, that coming on the road to Exon, he, the said Captain Crook, told me, Sir Joseph Wagstaff was a gallant gentleman, and that he was sorry he was not taken with us; that then he might have had the benefit of our articles. "But now," said he, "I have beset all the country for him, so that he cannot escape, but must be hanged." He also questioned me, as I passed through Salisbury from London, whether he had given me conditions; which I endeavouring to make appear to Major Butler, he interrupted me, and unwillingly confessed it, saying I proffered him four hundred pounds to perform his articles; which had been a strange proffer of mine, had I not really conditioned with him; and I told him then, having found him unworthy, I would have given him five hundred pounds, believing him to be mercenary. To make it yet farther appear I injure him not, by styling him unworthy; after these articles were given, he proffered to pistol me, if I did not persuade another house to yield, which then were boldly resisting. To which my servant John Biby, now a prisoner, replied, "I hope you will not be so unworthy as to break the law of arms." Thus much I am obliged to say to the honour of the soldiery, that they have been so far from breaking any articles given to others, that they have rather bettered them than otherwise. It is now our misfortune to be made precedents and examples together: but I will not do the Protector so much injury, as to load him with dishonour, since I have been informed, that he would have made our conditions good, if Crook, that gave them, had not abjured them. This is not a time for me to enlarge upon any subject, since I am now become the subject of death; but since the articles were drawn by my hand, I thought myself obliged to a particular justification of them. I could tell you of some soldiers which were turned out of his troop for defending those conditions of ours; but let that pass, and henceforward, instead of life, liberty and estate, which were the articles agreed upon, let drawing, hanging and quartering bear the denomination of "Captain Crook's Articles". However I thank the Protector for granting me this honourable death. I should now give you an account of my faith; but, truly, gentlemen, this poor nation is rent into so many several opinions, that it is impossible for me to give you mine, without displeasing some of you. However, if any man be so critical as to enquire of what faith I die, I shall refer him to the Apostles, Athanasius, and the Nicene creed, and to the testimony of this reverend gentleman, Dr. Short, to whom I have unbosomed myself: and if this do not satisfy, look in the thirty-nine Articles of the Catholic Church of England, to them I have subscribed, and do own them as authentic. Having now given you an account concerning myself, I hold myself obliged in duty to some of my friends, to take off a suspicion which lies upon them. I mean, as to some persons of honour; which upon my examination I was charged to have held correspondency with; the Marquis of Hertford, the Marquis of Winchester, and my Lord of Pembroke, were the persons nominated to me. I did then acquaint them, and do now second it with this protestation, that I never held any correspondency with either, or any of them, in relation to this particular business, or indeed to anything which concerned the Protector or his government. As for the Marquis of Winchester, I saw him some twelve years since, and not later; and if I should see him here present I believe I should not know him; and for the Earl of Pembroke, he was not a man likely to whom I should discover my thoughts, because he is a man of contrary judgment. I was examined likewise concerning my brother Freke, my cousin Hastings, Mr. Dorrington, and others: it is probable their estates may make them liable to this my condition; but I do here so far acquit them, as to give the world this further protestation, that I am confident they are as innocent in this business as the youngest child here. I have no more to say to you now, but to let you know that I am in charity with all men, I thank God; I both can and do forgive my greatest persecutors, and all that ever had any hand in my death. I have offered the Protector as good security for my future demeanour, as I suppose he could have expected; if he had thought fit to have given me my life, certainly I should not have been so ungrateful as to have employed it against him. I do humbly submit to God's pleasure, knowing that the issues of life and death are in His hand; my blood is but a small sacrifice; if it had been saved, I am so much a gentleman as to have given thanks to him that preserved it, and so much a Christian as to forgive them which take it; but seeing God by His providence hath called me to lay it down, I willingly submit to it, though terrible to nature; but blessed be my Saviour, who hath taken out the sting; so that I look upon it without terror. Death is a debt, and a due debt; and it hath pleased God to make me so good a husband that I am come to pay it before it is due. I am not ashamed of the cause for which I die, but rather rejoice that I am thought worthy to suffer in the defence and cause of God's true Church, my lawful King, the liberty of the subject, and privilege of parliaments; therefore I hope none of my alliance and friends will be ashamed of it; it is so far from pulling down my family, that I look upon it as the raising of it one storey higher; neither was I so prodigal of nature, as to throw away my life, but have used, though none but honourable and honest, means to preserve it. These unhappy times indeed have been very fatal to my family, two of my brothers already slain, and myself going to the slaughter; it is God's will, and I humbly submit to that providence. I must render an acknowledgment of the great civilities that I have received from the City of Exon, and some persons of quality, and for their plentiful provision made for the prisoners. I thank Mr. Sheriff for his favour towards us, in particular to myself, and I desire him to present my due respects to the Protector, and though he had no mercy for myself, yet that he would have respect to my family. I am now a-stripping off my clothes to fight a duel with death, I conceive no other duel lawful; but my Saviour hath pulled out the sting of this mine enemy, by making Himself a sacrifice for me, and truly I do not think that man deserving one drop of His blood that will not spend all for Him in so good a cause. The truth is, gentlemen, in this age treason is an *individuum vagum*; like the wind in the gospel, it bloweth where it listeth. So now treason is what they please, and lighteth upon whom they will. Indeed no man, except he will be a traitor, can avoid this censure of treason. I know not to what end it may come, but I pray God my own and my brother's blood, that is now to die with me, may be the last upon this score. Now, gentlemen, you may see what a condition you are in without a King; you have no law to protect you, no rule to walk by: when you perform your duty to God, your King and country, you displease the arbitrary power now set up, (I cannot call it government). I shall leave you to peruse my trial, and there you shall see what a condition this poor nation is brought into; and (no question) will be utterly destroyed, if not restored, by loyal subjects, to its old and glorious government. I pray God He lay not His judgments upon England for their sluggishness in doing their duty, and readiness to put their hands in their bosoms, or rather taking part with the enemy of truth. The Lord open their eyes that they may be no longer led or drawn into such snares, else the child that is unborn will curse the day of their parents' birth. God Almighty preserve my lawful King, Charles II from the hands of his enemies, and break down that wall of pride and rebellion, which so long hath kept him from his just rights! God preserve his royal mother, and all His Majesty's royal brethren: and incline their hearts to seek after Him! God incline the hearts of all true Englishmen to stand up as one man to bring in the King, and redeem themselves and this poor Kingdom out of its more than Egyptian slavery. As I have now put off these garments of cloth, so I hope I have put off my garments of sin, and have put on the robes of Christ's righteousness here, which will bring me to the enjoyment of His glorious robes anon.'—Then he kneeled down and kissed the block and said thus: 'I commit my soul to God my Creator and Redeemer. Look upon me, O Lord, at my last gasping, hear my prayer, and the prayers of all good people. I thank Thee, O God, for all their dispensations towards me.'—Then kneeling down, he prayed most devoutly as follows:

'O Eternal, Almighty, and most merciful God, the righteous Judge of all the world, look down in mercy on me a miserable sinner. O blessed Jesus, Redeemer of mankind, which takest away the sins of the world, let Thy perfect manner of obedience be presented to Thy heavenly Father for me. Let Thy precious death and blood be the ransom and satisfaction of my many and heinous transgressions. Thou that sittest at the right hand of God make intercession for me. O holy and blessed Spirit which art the Comforter, fill my heart with Thy consolations. O holy, blessed, and glorious Trinity, be merciful to me, confirm my faith in the promises of the Gospel, revive and quicken my hope and expectation of joys prepared for true and faithful servants. Let the infinite love of God my Saviour, make my love to Him steadfast, sincere, and constant.

'O Lord, consider my condition, accept my tears, assuage my grief, give me comfort and confidence in Thee: impute not unto me my former sins, but most merciful Father receive me into Thy favour, for the merits of Christ Jesus. Many and grievous are my sins, for I have sinned many times against the light of knowledge, against remorse of conscience, against the motions and opportunities of grace. But accept, I beseech Thee, the sacrifice of a broken and contrite heart, in and for the perfect sacrifice, oblation, and satisfaction of Thy Son Jesus Christ. O Lord receive my soul after it is delivered from the burden of the flesh, into perfect joy in the sight and fruition of Thee. And at the general resurrection, grant that my body may be endowed with immortality, and received with my soul into glory.

'I praise Thee O God, I acknowledge Thee to be the Lord; O Lamb of God, that takest away the sins of the world, have mercy on me. Thou that sittest at the right hand of God, hear my prayer. O Lord Jesus Christ, God and man, Mediator betwixt God and man, I have sinned as a man, be thou merciful to me as a God. O holy and blessed Spirit, help my infirmities with those sighs and groans which I cannot express.'

Then he desired to see the axe, and kissed it, saying, 'I am like to have a sharp passage of it, but my Saviour hath sweetened it unto me.' Then he said, 'If I would have been so unworthy as others have been, I suppose I might by a lie have saved my life, which I scorn to purchase at such a rate. I defy such temptations and them that gave them me. Glory be to God on high, on earth peace, good-will towards men, and the Lord have mercy upon my poor soul! *Amen.*'

So laying his neck upon the block, after some private ejaculations, he gave the headsman a sign with his hand, who at one blow severed his head from his body.

The night before his Execution he received the following Letter from his Lady:

'My dear Heart:

'My sad parting was so far from making me forget you, that I scarce thought upon myself since, but wholly upon you. Those dear embraces which I yet feel, and shall never lose, being the faithful testimonies of an indulgent husband, have charmed my soul to such a reverence of your remembrance, that were it possible, I would, with my own blood, cement your dead limbs to life again; and (with reverence) think it no sin to rob heaven a little while longer of a martyr. O my dear! you must now pardon my passion, this being my last (oh fatal) word that ever you will receive from me; and know, that until the last minute that I can imagine you shall live, I will sacrifice the prayers of a Christian, and the groans of an afflicted wife. And when you are not (which sure by sympathy I shall know) I shall wish my own dissolution with you, that so we may go hand in hand to heaven. It is too late to tell you what I have, or rather what I have not done for you; how turned out of doors because I came to beg mercy; the Lord lay not your blood to their charge. I would fain discourse longer with you, but dare not; passion begins to drown my reason, and will rob me of my *devoir*, which is all I have left to serve you. Adieu therefore ten thousand times my dearest dear! and since I must never see you more, take this prayer; may your faith be so strengthened, that your constancy may continue, and then I know heaven will receive you; whither grief and love will in a short time, I hope, translate, my dear, your sad, but constant wife, even to love your ashes when dead.

ARUNDEL PENRUDDOCK.'

'May the 15th, 1655, eleven o'clock at night. Your children beg your blessing, and present their duties to you.'

To which he wrote this Answer.

'Dearest, best of Creatures!

'I had taken leave of the world when I received yours. It did at once recall my fondness for life, and enable me to resign it. As I am sure I shall leave none behind me like you, which weakens my resolution to part from you; so when I reflect I am going to a place where there are none but such as you, I recover my courage. But fondness breaks in upon me; and as I would not have my tears flow tomorrow, when your husband and the father of our dear babes is a public spectacle; do not think meanly of me, that I give way to grief now in private, when I see my sand run so fast, and I within few hours am to leave you helpless, and exposed to the merciless and insolent, that have wrongfully put me to a shameless death, and will object that shame to my poor children. I thank you for all your goodness to me, and will endeavour so to die, as do nothing unworthy that virtue in which we have mutually supported each other, and for which I desire you not repine that I am first to be rewarded; since you ever preferred me to yourself in all other things, afford me, with cheerfulness, the precedence in this.

'I desire your prayers in the article of death, for my own will then be offered for you and yours.

J. PENRUDDOCK.'

[Clarendon, after speaking of the various insurrections of Charles II's friends, which had been projected and proposed to the King a little before this time, says: 'There cannot be

a greater manifestation of the universal prejudice and aversion
in the whole kingdom towards Cromwell, and his
government, than that there could be so many designs and
conspiracies against him, which were communicated to so
many men, and that such signal and notorious persons
could resort to London, and remain there, without any such
information or discovery, as might enable him to cause them
to be apprehended; there being nobody intent and zealous
to make any such discoveries, but such whose trade it was
for great wages to give him those informations, and they
seldom care whether what they inform be true or no.
The Earl of Rochester consulted with great freedom in
London with the King's friends; and found that the persons
imprisoned were only taken upon general suspicion, and
as being known to be of that party, not upon any particular
discovery of what they designed or intended to do; and
that the same spirit still possessed those who were at liberty.
The design in Kent appeared not reasonable, at least not
to begin upon; but he was persuaded, and he was very
credulous, that in the north there was a foundation of
strong hope, and a party ready to appear powerful enough
to possess themselves of York; nor had the army many
troops in those parts. In the West likewise there seemed
to be a strong combination, in which many gentlemen were
engaged, and their agents were then in London, and were
exceedingly importunate to have a day assigned, and
desired no more than that Sir Joseph Wagstaff might be
authorised to be in the head of them; who had been well
known to them; and he was as ready to engage with them.
The Earl of Rochester liked the countenance of the North
better; and sent Marmaduke Darcy, a gallant gentleman,
and nobly allied in those parts to prepare the party there;
appointed a day and place for the rendezvous; and promised
to be himself there; and was contented that Sir Joseph
Wagstaff should go into the West; who upon conference
with those of that country, likewise appointed their
rendezvous upon a fixed day, to be within two miles of
Salisbury. And it was an argument that they had no mean
opinion of their strength, that they appointed to appear
that very day when the judges were to keep their assizes in

that city, and where the Sheriff, and principal gentlemen of the county were obliged to give their attendance. And of both these resolutions the Earl of Rochester, who knew where the King was, took care to advertise His Majesty; who, from hence, had his former faint hopes renewed; and in a short time after they were so improved, that he thought of nothing more, than how he might with the greatest secrecy transport himself into England; for which he did expect a sudden occasion.

'Sir Joseph Wagstaff had been formerly major-general of the foot in the King's Western army, a man generally beloved; and though he was rather for execution than counsel, a stout man, who looked not far before him; yet he had a great companionableness in his nature, which exceedingly prevailed with those, who, in the intermission of fighting, loved to spend their time in jollity and mirth. He, as soon as the day was appointed, left London, and went to some of his friends' houses in the country, near the place, that he might assist the preparations as much as was possible. Those of Hampshire were not so punctual at their own rendezvous, as to be present at that near Salisbury at the hour; however, Wagstaff, and they of Wiltshire, appeared to expectation. Penruddock, a gentle-man of a fair fortune, and great zeal and forwardness in the service, Hugh Grove, and other persons of condition, were there with a body of near two hundred horse well armed; which, they presumed, would every day be improved upon the access of those who had engaged themselves in the Western association, especially if the fame of their being up, and effecting anything, should come to their ears. They accounted that they were already strong enough to visit Salisbury in all its present lustre, knowing that they had many friends there, and reckoning that all who were not against them, were for them; and that they should there increase their numbers both in foot, and horse; with which the town then abounded; nor did their computation and conjecture fail them. They entered the city about five of the clock in the morning: they appointed some officers, of which they had plenty, to cause all the stables to be locked up, that all the horses might be at their devotion; others, to break open the gaols, that all there might attend their benefactors. They kept a good body of horse upon the market-place, to encounter all opposition; and gave order to apprehend the judges and the Sheriff, who were yet in their beds, and to bring them into the market-place with their several commissions, resolving or not caring to seize upon the persons of any others.

'All this was done with so little noise or disorder, as if the town had been all of one mind. And they who were within doors, except they were commanded to come out, stayed still there, being more desirous to hear than to see what was done; very many being well pleased, and not willing that others should discern it in their countenance. When the judges were brought out in their own robes, and humbly produced their commissions, and the Sheriff likewise, Wagstaff resolved, after he had caused the King to be proclaimed, to cause them all three to be hanged, who were half dead already, having well considered, with the policy which men in such actions are naturally possessed with, how he himself should be used if he were under their hands, and therefore choosing to be beforehand with them. But having not thought fit to deliberate this beforehand with his friends, whereby their scrupulous consciences might have been confirmed, many of the country gentlemen were so startled with this proposition, that they protested against it; and poor Penruddock was so passionate to preserve their lives, as if works of this nature could be done by halves, that the Major-General durst not persist in it; but was prevailed with to dismiss the judges, and, having taken their commissions from them, to oblige them upon another occasion to remember to whom they owed their lives, resolving still to hang the Sheriff; who positively, though humbly, and with many tears, refused to proclaim the King; which being otherwise done, they likewise prevailed with him rather to keep the Sheriff alive, and to carry him with them to redeem an honester man out of the hands of their enemies. This was an ill-omen to their future agreement, and submission to the commands of their General, nor was the tender-heartedness so general but that very many of the gentlemen were much scandalised at it,

both as it was a contradiction to their commander-in-chief;
and as it would have been a seasonable act of severity to
have cemented those to perseverance who were engaged in
it, and kept them from entertaining any hopes but in
the sharpness of their swords.

'The noise of this action was very great both in and out of
the Kingdom, whither it was quickly sent. And without doubt
it was a bold enterprise, and might have produced wonderful
effects, if it had been prosecuted with the same resolution,
or the same rashness, it was entered into. All that was
reasonable in the general contrivance of insurrection
and commotion over the whole Kingdom, was founded
upon a supposition of the division and faction in the army;
which was known to be so great, that Cromwell durst not
draw the whole army to a general rendezvous, out of
apprehension that, when they should once meet together,
he should no longer be master of them. And thence it was
concluded, that, if there were in any one place such a body
brought together as might oblige Cromwell to make the
army, or a considerable part of it to march, there would at
least be no disposition in them to fight to strengthen that
authority, which they abhorred. And many did at that time
believe, that if they had remained with that party at
Salisbury for some days, which they might well have done
without any disturbance, that their numbers would have
much increased, and their friends farther West must have
been prepared to receive them, when their retreat had been
necessary by a stronger part of the army's marching against
them. Cromwell himself was amazed; he knew well the
distemper of the Kingdom, and in his army, and now when
he saw such a body gathered together without any noise,
that durst, in the middle of the Kingdom, enter into the
chief city of it, when his judges and all the power of that
county was in it, and take them prisoners, and proclaim the
King in a time of full peace, and when no man durst so
much as name him but with a reproach, he could not
imagine that such an enterprise could be undertaken
without a universal conspiracy; in which his own army
could not be innocent; and therefore knew not how to trust
them together. But all this apprehension vanished, when it

was known that within four or five hours after they had performed this exploit, they left the town with very small increase or addition to their numbers.

'The truth is, they did nothing resolutely after their first action; and were in such disorder, and discontent between themselves, that without staying for their friends out of Hampshire (who were, to the number of two or three hundred horse upon their way, and would have been at Salisbury that night) upon pretence that they were expected in Dorsetshire, they left the town, and took the Sheriff with them, about two of the clock in the afternoon: but were so weary of their day's labour, and their watching the night before, that they grew less in love with what they were about, and differed again amongst themselves about the Sheriff; whom many desired should be presently released; and that party carried it in hope of receiving good offices afterwards from him. And in this manner they continued on their march westward. They from Hampshire and other places, who were behind them, being angry for their leaving Salisbury, would not follow, but scattered themselves; and they who were before them, and heard in what disorder they had left Wiltshire, likewise dispersed: so that after they had continued their journey into Devonshire, without meeting any who would join with them, horse and man were so tired for want of meat and sleep, that one single troop of horse, inferior in number, and commanded by an officer of no credit in the war, being in those parts by chance, followed them at a distance, till they were so spent that he rather entreated than compelled them to deliver themselves; some, and amongst those Wagstaff, quitted their horses, and found shelter in some honest houses; where they were concealed till opportunity served to transport them into the parts beyond the seas, where they arrived safely. But Mr. Penruddock, Mr. Grove, and most of the rest, were taken prisoners, upon promise given by the officer that their lives should be saved: which they quickly found he had no authority to make good. For Cromwell no sooner heard of his cheap victory, than he sent judges away with a new commission of oyer and terminer, and order to proceed with the utmost severity against the offenders. But Rolle, his Chief Justice, who had so luckily escaped at Salisbury, had not recovered the fright; and would no more look those men in the face who had dealt so kindly with him; but expressly refused to be employed in the service, raising some scruples in point of law, whether the men could be legally condemned; upon which Cromwell, shortly after, turned him out of his office, having found others, who executed his commands. Penruddock, and Grove, lost their heads at Exeter; and others were hanged there; who having recovered the faintness they were in when they rendered, died with great courage and resolution, professing their duty and loyalty to the King. Many were sent to Salisbury, and tried and executed there, in the place where they had so lately triumphed; and some who were condemned, where there were fathers, and sons, and brothers, that the butchery might appear with some remorse, were reprieved, and sold, and sent slaves to the Barbados; where their treatment was such, that few of them ever returned into their own country. And thus this little fire, which probably might have kindled and enflamed all the Kingdom, was for the present extinguished in the West; and Cromwell secured without the help of his army: which he saw, by the countenance it then showed when they thought he would have use of them, it was high time to reform; and in that he resolved to use no longer delay.'5

In the third volume of Thurloe's *State Papers* are several letters and other documents relative to this and the contemporaneous insurrections.]

Chapter four

Theobald Wolfe Tone (1798)

At the end of the eighteenth century, England faced the hostility of two groups in Ireland: Catholic nationalists and Protestant republicans. The second group derived some of its inspiration from the revolution in France and was often hostile to Catholic Ireland as well as to monarchist England. To this second group Theobald Wolfe Tone belonged, though he was also sympathetic to the Catholics as victims of political oppression. Born in 1763, Tone was a reluctant student at Trinity College, Dublin, and was called to the Bar before he started his first political club in the city during the winter of 1790–1. His aim was threefold: to destroy the existing form of government in Ireland; 'to break the connection with England, the never-failing source of all our political evils'; and to unite Catholics and Protestants as Irish patriots.

Until the Union with England in 1800, there was a separate Parliament for Ireland, though owing allegiance to the British Crown. To Wolfe Tone and his supporters this represented no true independence at all, while the proposed Union with England, which was aimed at removing economic grievances, could only be abhorrent. In September 1791 Tone published *An Argument on behalf of the Catholics of Ireland*, a pamphlet written to persuade Irish Protestants to support their Catholic compatriots. A month later he and James Napper Tandy were two of the founders of the Society of United Irishmen, trying to unite Catholic and Protestant enemies of England. Pressure upon Parliament produced a Catholic Relief Bill in 1793, granting some civil rights to Catholics, though not the right to sit in Parliament.

By 1795 Irish Protestants and Catholics were fighting among themselves, while Tone and Lord Edward Fitzgerald were in contact with the revolutionary régime in France to see what French support they might count on in driving the English from Ireland. In that year Tone left Ireland for America and then, in turn, left America for France, where he arrived in February 1796. For some months he tried to persuade the French government to send an army to Ireland, which would be the signal for Irishmen to take up arms against English oppression. In June 1796 Tone was given the rank of *chef de brigade* in the French army, while General Hoche was put in command of a force to invade Ireland. The invasion fleet of forty-three ships carrying 15,000 soldiers set sail in December 1796. The ships were scattered by a storm but Tone with the *Indomptable* and other ships, as well as some 7,000 troops, arrived in Bantry Bay. Continuing storms made a landing impossible and there was no alternative but to sail back to France.

A further expedition in July 1797 was also defeated by the weather and soon afterwards General Hoche died, depriving the Irish exiles of the most influential of their supporters in the counsels of the French government. In Ireland itself, the Society of United Irishmen had been encouraged by French attempts to assist them and had laid plans for an insurrection. Some of the leaders were arrested before this could take place, though Lord Edward Fitzgerald remained at large as the co-ordinator of the rebellion. The general rising in Ireland was planned for 23 May 1798. Two days earlier an attempt was made to arrest Lord Edward Fitzgerald, but in the struggle he killed one officer, injured a second, and was himself mortally wounded. On 23 May the insurrection broke out and for a month the rebels were virtually in control of Wexford. Tone, in France, urged the French government to send troops to Ireland at once, but nothing was done. The rebels were defeated and, despite an amnesty offered to those who laid down their arms, many were hanged or shot.

Eventually, the French decided on a number of smaller landings to be made in August and September 1798. On 22 August, General Humbert and about 800 men landed at Kilala in Mayo. They advanced on the positions held by General Lake and his 3,000 militia at Castlebar. The retreat of the defenders was so rapid that the battle became known as 'The Castlebar Races'. Yet within a short time Humbert was defeated and surrendered to Lord Cornwallis, who had succeeded Lord Camden as Lord-Lieutenant of Ireland.

In September 1798 Tone sailed with a force which was to reinforce Humbert and consisted of the *Hoche*, eight small frigates, the fast schooner *La Biche*, and 3,000 troops. Off Lough Swilly these ships encountered an English fleet and it was suggested to Wolfe Tone and Napper Tandy that they should transfer to *La Biche*, which could easily outdistance any English pursuers and would carry the Irish leaders safely back to France. Tandy agreed to this but Tone insisted on remaining aboard the *Hoche* and commanding one of her batteries in the fight which followed. It was hardly an equal battle. After resisting for four hours the *Hoche* was compelled to surrender and Tone was among those taken prisoner. Two days later the men who had been captured were landed in Ireland, where Tone was recognized, despite his French uniform. He was put in irons and brought to face trial in Dublin by court martial.

Tone did not live to see the complete constitutional subjugation of Ireland, when the Irish Parliament, the subject of financial inducement and political coercion, voted itself out of existence in 1800 so that the Union with England might be formed. This, in turn, helped to provoke the rebellion of 1803, led by Robert Emmet. For some hours Dublin was in the grip of an uncontrolled insurrection and Lord Justice Kilwarden was murdered by the crowd. The rebels had a supply of arms and uniforms but they were no match for the troops who soon re-established order in the city. The hope of success in 1803, without positive military intervention by France, was even more unrealistic than it had been in 1798. Emmet suffered the sentence which Tone, by his own determination and the quirks of civil law, contrived to escape. Ironically, Kilwarden who was to be lynched in 1803 was the judge who prevented the authorities from executing Wolfe Tone in 1798, while the girl whom Emmet risked and lost his life to see again, was the daughter of John Philpot Curran, who argued Tone's case before Kilwarden.

The Trial of THEOBALD WOLFE TONE for High Treason, before a Court Martial holden at Dublin on Saturday, November 10th, together with Proceedings in the Court of King's Bench on Monday, November 12th: 39 GEORGE III. A.D. 1798.

'Mr. Tone was one of the most active promoters of the designs of the United Irishmen; and according to the concurring testimony of all his co-temporaries, was the ablest man who had given his support to that cause. He was originally a member of the Irish bar, where his talents could not have failed to have raised him to distinction; but the principles of the French revolution, and the hope of successfully applying them to change the condition of his own country, soon diverted his ardent mind from legal pursuits, and involved him in that political career which subsequently occupied his life. In this new field he, at a very early period, became conspicuous for his zeal in supporting the claims of the Roman Catholics, who appointed him a secretary to their committee, and voted him a sum of money as the reward of his exertions. He was also one of the original projectors of the plan of combining the popular strength and sentiment, which was afterwards matured into the Irish Union. That association existed some years before its object was to effect a revolution; but it has already been shown that, as early as 1791, Mr. Tone recommended precisely the same views which the future leaders vainly attempted to accomplish.

['By the test of the more early of these societies,' (of United Irishmen), 'the members pledged themselves 'to persevere in endeavouring to form a brotherhood of affection among Irishmen of every religious persuasion, and to obtain an equal, full, and adequate representation of all the people of Ireland *in the Commons House of Parliament.*' In the year 1795 the latter words were struck out, in order to accommodate the test to the revolutionary designs that began to be generally entertained.—Report of the Secret Committee 1798.

'It is a received opinion, that the celebrated Theobald Wolfe Tone was the author of the constitution of the later United Irishmen; but the writer of this work is informed by a gentleman now in Ireland, who was intimately connected with Mr. Tone, that he himself denied this to be the fact. "He assured me," adds the gentleman alluded to, "that Captain Thomas Russell, to whom he was for many years so warmly attached, was the person who drew up that remarkable paper, and that he (Tone) was not a member of the *close* society of United Irishmen till the eve of his embarking at Belfast for America, in the summer of 1795." It is, however, certain that Mr. Tone, as far back as 1791, strongly recommended to the societies of United Irishmen, then in their infancy, to attempt a revolution, as appears from his letter written in that year to the society at Belfast. —Report of the Secret Committee (Appendix).' W. H. Curran, *Life of the Rt. Hon. John Philpot Curran* (London, 1819), vol. 2, pp. 11–12 n.]

In 1794, when Jackson arrived in Ireland upon his secret mission from the French government, he soon discovered that Mr. Tone was one of the persons the most likely to approve and assist his designs. He accordingly communicated them to him, and was not disappointed in his expectation. Mr. Tone so cordially embraced the proposal of an invasion of Ireland by the French, that had not the urgency of his private affairs prevented, he would have passed over to France, in order to confer in person with the French authorities upon the subject. Some of the discussions upon this topic took place in the prison of Newgate, in the presence of Cockayne and Mr. Hamilton Rowan, the latter of whom was at that time under sentence of confinement for the publication of a libel. Jackson being shortly after arrested upon the information of Cockayne, Mr. Rowan, who was aware that the evidence of that witness would equally involve himself, effected his escape, and fled to France.[1] Mr. Tone remained. Whatever his more private communications might have been with Jackson, upon whose fidelity he relied, he conceived that the amount of Cockayne's testimony could convict him of no higher an offence than misprision of treason. Considerable exertions were also used by his private friends to dissuade the government from a prosecution; and, in consequence, he was not arrested. The evidence upon Jackson's trial, however, having publicly shown that some degree of treasonable connection had subsisted between him and Mr. Tone, the latter was advised, if he consulted his safety, to withdraw from Ireland. He accordingly, in the summer of 1795, transported himself and his family to America.

> ['The vessel in which he was a passenger, no sooner arrived in sight of an American port, than she was boarded by a boat from a British man-of-war. Mr. Tone was (among others) impressed to serve as a sailor in His Majesty's navy; but, after considerable difficulties, his own remonstrances, and the solicitations of Mrs. Tone, obtained his release.'
> *Life of John Philpot Curran*, vol. 2, p. 157 n.]

Here he did not remain many months. He tendered his services to the French Directory, and having met with all the encouragement he could desire, he procured a passage to France, where he arrived in the beginning of the year 1796. He was most favourably received, and appointed to a commission in the French army. His efforts to persuade the Directory to send an armament to Ireland have been previously mentioned.

> ['The United Irishmen despatched an agent to France for this purpose,' (to obtain military aid in order to effect a separation from England) 'about the middle of 1796.
> Mr. Tone was then at Paris, and exerting all his influence to the same effect. In the first memorial which Mr. Tone presented to the French Directory, in order to induce them to send an expedition to Ireland, he stated that at that period more than two-thirds of the sailors in the British navy were Irish; that he was present when the Catholic delegates urged this to Lord Melville as one reason for granting emancipation, and that his lordship had not denied the fact. This statement was understood to have had great weight with the Directory, who immediately committed the whole of the subject to the consideration of Carnot (then one of the Directory) and Generals Clarke and Hoche.
> 'The gentleman who has communicated the preceding circumstance has added the following anecdote:
> 'Soon after the question of an expedition to Ireland had been left to the decision of Carnot, Clarke, and Hoche, they named an evening to meet Tone at the palace of the Luxembourg. Tone arrived at the appointed hour, eight

o'clock. He was ushered into a splendid apartment. Shortly after, the director and the generals made their appearance: they bowed coldly, but civilly, to Tone, and almost immediately retired, without apology or explanation, through a door opposite to that by which they had entered. Tone was a good deal struck by so unexpected a reception; but his surprise increased when ten o'clock arrived, without the appearance of, or message of any kind from, those on whom all his hopes seemed to depend. The clock struck eleven, twelve, one—all was still in the palace; the steps of the sentinels, on their posts without, alone interrupted the dead silence that prevailed within. Tone paced the room in considerable anxiety; not even a servant had entered of whom to inquire his way out, or if the director and the generals had retired. About two o'clock the folding doors were suddenly thrown open; Carnot, Clarke and Hoche entered; their countenances brightened, and the coldness and reserve so observable at eight o'clock had vanished. Clarke advanced quickly to Tone, and taking him cordially by the hand, said, "Citizen! I congratulate you. We go to Ireland." The others did the same; and having fixed the time to meet again, the persons engaged in this remarkable transaction separated.' *Life of John Philpot Curran*, vol. 2, pp. 19–21 n. See also p. 36 of the same volume.]

The first expedition having failed, a second attempt was made in the autumn of 1798. This was equally unsuccessful; and Mr. Tone, who was on board the *Hoche* French line-of-battle ship, one of the vessels captured by Sir John Borlase Warren's squadron off the Irish coast, fell into the hands of the English government, and was brought to trial by court martial in Dublin, on the 10th of November 1798.' *Life of John Philpot Curran*, vol. 2, pp. 154–58.

DUBLIN BARRACK

Saturday 10 *November* 1798

The Court was composed of the following members:

Major-General Loftus, *President*
Colonel Vandeleur
Colonel Wolfe
Colonel Tytler

Lieutenant-Colonel Daly
Major Armstrong
Captain Corry

Mr. Tone was brought into court under a corporal's guard, from the Provost Marshalsea, where he had been confined. He was dressed in the French uniform—a large and fiercely cocked hat, with broad gold lace, and the tricoloured cockade, a blue uniform coat, with gold and embroidered collar, and two large gold epaulets, blue pantaloons with gold laced garters at the knees, and short boots bound at the tops with gold lace.

At first he seemed a good deal agitated, and called for a glass of water, having drank which, he seemed much composed and collected.

The charges were read by the Judge Advocate against Mr. Tone, implicating him as a natural-born subject of our Lord the King, having traitorously entered into the service of the French republic, at open war with His Majesty, and being taken in the fact, bearing arms against his King and country, and assuming a command in an enemy's army approaching the shore of his native land for the purpose of invasion, and acting in open resistance to His Majesty's forces, with several other charges of a treasonable nature.

On the conclusion of the charges read against him, he was called upon to plead, whether guilty or not guilty.

['When asked what he would plead, he exclaimed, "Guilty! for I have never, during my life, stooped to a prevarication." ' *Life of John Philpot Curran*, vol. 2, p. 158 n.]

Mr. Tone, bowing to the Court, said, he presumed this was the time in which he might read to the Court the statements of a few points, which he had committed to paper, for the occasion of his trial.

He was asked, in the first instance, if he would plead to the charge against him guilty, or not guilty.

He answered, that it was not his wish to avail himself of any subterfuge, or to give the Court any unnecessary trouble; he was ready to admit the whole of the charge exhibited against him.

He was then asked what was his object in reading the papers in his hand; was it anything which his own sense must tell him might be improper for the Court to hear?

Mr. Tone answered, the paper was certainly drawn up with a view to vindication, though possibly it could not be considered as a defence against the accusation on which he was now called to trial. He could not say whether it was a kind of defence which the Court might choose to hear. He had endeavoured in the formation to be as collected and moderate as his feelings could possibly admit, and if the Court would do him the honour of permitting him to read the paper, its contents would best suggest how far it was admissible as to the reading.

Court. Sir; before you read that paper, you will do well to consider whether it contains anything irrelevant to the question now at issue, or anything which your own good sense may suggest the Court ought not to hear.

Prisoner. In what I am about to read, I trust there is nothing irrelevant to my situation, nor anything but what I should hope the Court will not think improper to hear. I have endeavoured to be as collected and moderate as possible; and I should not wish to offer any language offensive to the Court.

Judge Advocate. Is there anything in the paper which you wish should go before his excellency the Lord Lieutenant?

Prisoner. I have no objection.

A Member. You have already pleaded guilty to the charge of having acted traitorously.—Do you mean by anything contained in that paper to retract that plea?

Prisoner. Certainly I have admitted the charge, and consequently the appellation by which I am technically described.

President. It is not the wish of the Court, sir, to deny you any indulgence which, consistently with their duty, they can grant; but they must reserve to themselves the power of stopping you, if you shall utter anything irrelevant to the case before them, or unfitting for them to listen to.

Prisoner. The Court, no doubt, will reserve to itself that discretionary power, but I repeat that I have endeavoured to be as moderate as possible, and if any of my expressions should happen to appear objectionable, I shall be willing to substitute others less so.

Here the President having given permission, the prisoner read the paper which was as follows:

Mr President and Gentlemen of the Court; it is not my

intention to give this Court any trouble respecting the purport of what has been alleged against me: my admission of the charge prevents a prolongation of those forms which could not be more irksome to you than they would be to me. What I have done has been purely from principle and the fullest conviction of its rectitude. I wish not for mercy—I hope I am not an object of pity. I anticipate the consequence of my caption, and am prepared for the event. The favourite object of my life has been the independence of my country, and to that object I have made every sacrifice.

Placed in honourable poverty, the love of liberty was implanted by nature and confirmed by education in my heart. —No seduction, no terror, could banish it from thence; and seduction and terror have not been spared against me. To impart the inestimable blessings of liberty to the land of my birth, I have braved difficulties, bondage, and death.

After an honourable combat, in which I strove to emulate the bravery of my gallant comrades, I was forced to submit, and was dragged in irons through the country, not so much to my disgrace, as that of the person by whom such ungenerous and unmanly orders were issued.

[*Copy of a Letter from T. W. Tone to Major-General the Earl of Cavan*

Derry Prison, 12 Brumaire, an. 6.
(3 *November*, 1798.)

My Lord;

On my arrival here, Major Chester informed me, that his orders from your lordship, in consequence, as I presume, of the directions of government, were that I should be put in irons. I take it for granted, those orders were issued in ignorance of the rank I have the honour to hold in the armies of the French Republic. I am, in consequence, to apprize your lordship, that I am breveted as *Chef de Brigade* in the infantry since the 1st Messidor, an. 4; that I have been promoted to the rank of adjutant-general the 2nd Nivose, an. 6; and finally, that I have served as such, attached to General Hardy since the 3rd Thermidor, an. 6, by virtue of the orders of the Minister-at-War:—Major Chester, to whom I have showed my commission, can satisfy your lordship as to the fact, and General Hardy will ascertain the authenticity of the documents.

Under these circumstances, I address myself to your lordship as a man of honour and a soldier; and I do protest, in the most precise and strongest manner, against the indignity intended against the honour of the French army in my person; and I claim the rights and privileges of a prisoner of war, agreeably to my rank and situation in an army, not less to be respected, in all points, than any other which exists in Europe.

From the situation your lordship holds under your government, I must presume you to have discretionary power to act according to circumstances; and I cannot, for a moment, doubt, but what I have now explained to your lordship, will induce you to give immediate orders, that the honour of the French nation and the French army be respected in my person, and of course that I shall suffer no coercion, other than in common with the rest of my brave comrades, whom the fortune of war has for the moment deprived of their liberty.

I am, my lord,
With great respect,
Your lordship's most
obedient servant,
T. W. TONE,
dit SMITH, Adjutant General.

Answer from Major-General the Earl of Cavan to T. W. Tone.

Buncranna, 3 November, 1798.

Sir;

I have received your letter of this date from Derry gaol, in which you inform me, that you consider your being ordered into irons as an insult and degradation to the rank you hold in the army of the French Republic, and that you protest, in the most precise and strongest manner, against such indignity.—Had you been a native of France, or of any other country not belonging to the British empire, indisputably it would be so; but the motive that directed me to give the order that I did this morning for your being put in irons, was, that I looked upon you (and you have proved yourself) a traitor and rebel to your Sovereign and native country, and as such you shall be treated by me.

I shall enforce the order I gave this morning, and I lament, as a man, the fate that awaits you. Every indulgence shall be granted you by me, individually, that is not inconsistent with my public duty.

I am, Sir, your humble servant,
CAVAN, Major-General.

Whatever I have written and said on the fate of Ireland, I here reiterate.

The connexion of England I have ever considered as the bane of Ireland, and have done everything in my power to break it, and to raise three millions of my countrymen to the rank of citizens.

Here he was stopped by the Court.

Mr. President. Mr. Tone, it is impossible we can listen to this.

A Member. It appears to me, that this paper has been produced here, with a design of making injurious impressions on the minds of persons who may be in this room.

President. I cannot think there are any persons of that description here.

Prisoner. I do not think either that there are any such persons here, nor have I read the paper with the intention imputed to me. What follows will be found less exceptionable.

Judge Advocate. If what follows be of such a nature as you described to me yesterday, I really am of opinion, Mr. Tone, it must operate to your prejudice; you will therefore do well to consider before you read it.

On the farther advice which the Court and the Judge Advocate humanely urged, the prisoner consented to cancel part of the most exceptionable of what he read, and also some subsequent matter, which he said was only the expression of his thanks to the Roman Catholics, a body which he had once, he said, the honour of serving. He then desired to know if he might proceed?

President. It is a principle by which we shall be scrupulously ruled, to avoid most carefully everything not immediately relative to your case and the ends of justice; and it is but fitting that we expect you to confine yourself simply to the charge made against you; a reverse conduct can tend to no good purpose.

Prisoner. I have said nothing, nor do I mean to say anything, that has not been already uttered, with respect to me, in both Houses of Parliament, where my name has been so often quoted.

He was then suffered to proceed.

Having considered the resources of the country, and being convinced they were too weak to effect her independence without assistance, I sought that assistance in France: and without any intrigue, but asking, in the open honesty of my principles, and that love of freedom which has ever distinguished me, I have been adopted by the French Republic; and in the active discharge of my duty of a soldier, acquired what is to me invaluable, and what I will never relinquish but with my existence—the friendship of some of the best characters in France, and the attachment and esteem of my brave companions in arms.

It is not the sentence of any court that can weaken the force, or alter the nature, of those principles on which I have acted, and the truth of which will outlive those ephemeral prejudices that may rule for the day. To her I leave the vindication of my fame, and, I trust, posterity will not listen to her advocation without being instructed.

It is now more than four years since persecution drove me from this country, and I need hardly say that personally I cannot be involved in anything that has happened during my absence. In my efforts to accomplish the freedom of my country, I never have had recourse to any other than open and manly war. There have been atrocities committed on both sides, which I lament; and if the generous spirit which I had assisted to raise in the breasts of Irishmen, has degenerated into a system of assassination, I believe all who had any knowledge of me from my infancy will be ready to admit, that no man in existence could more heartily regret, that the tyranny of any circumstances or policy should so pervert the natural disposition of my countrymen.

I have little more to say.—*Success* is all in this life; and, unfavoured of her, virtue becomes vicious in the ephemeral estimation of those who attach every merit to prosperity.—In the glorious race of patriotism, I have pursued the path chalked out by Washington in America, and Kosciuszko in Poland.[2] Like the latter, I have failed to emancipate my country; and, unlike both, I have forfeited my life.—I have done my duty, and I have no doubt the Court will do theirs. —I have only to add, that a man who has thought and acted as I have done, should be armed against the fear of death.

A Member. This paper, then, which you have read, contains nothing in denial of the charge against you.

Prisoner. What I have once done, I should be ashamed to deny.

Here the prisoner having been asked by the Judge Advocate if there was anything else which he wished to address to the Court, he replied, that if he was not to be brought up again before the decision of the Court, he would wish to say a few words more; which being permitted, the prisoner proceeded.

I conceive, that I stand here in the same light with our *emigrés*; and, if the indulgence lie within the power of the Court, I would only request what French magnanimity allowed to Charette and to the Count de Sombreuil[3]—the death of a soldier, and to be shot by a file of grenadiers. This is the only favour I have to ask; and I trust that men, susceptible of the nice feelings of a soldier's honour, will not refuse the request. It is not from any personal feeling that I make this request, but from a respect to the uniform which I wear and to the brave army in which I have fought. From papers which I yesterday delivered into the hands of the brigade major, it will be seen, that I am as regularly breveted an officer in the French service, as any here is in the British army, and it will be seen that I have not my commission as a protection.

Judge Advocate. I wish you to be aware, that your acceptance of a commission in the French service amounts to positive proof of the charge advanced against you; but, from your admissions already, I suppose, that by the production of those papers, you merely want to show, that you were an officer in the French army.

Prisoner. Nothing more.

The papers were then produced, and were a brevet for the rank of Chef de Brigade, and a letter of service, both bearing the signatures of the President of the French Directory and the Minister of War. By one of those it appeared, that his last appointment was to proceed to Brest, to join the

Army of England; and to some questions asked of him, he answered, that he had been appointed to three several armies, destined on three several expeditions under BUONAPARTE, HOCHE, *and* KILMAINE, *an Irishman. Having been asked, why he was designated, in the brevet and letter of service, by the name of* SMITH, *together with that of* TONE, *he explained by saying, that in proceeding from America to France, it was necessary that he should have a passport, and accordingly took the first that fell in his way, which happened to be made out in the name of* SMITH. *On entering France, he was accordingly registered by that and his real name, which he had added thereto:—* 'Indeed,' *said he,* 'amost every soldier in France has, what they call* Un Nom de Guerre.'—*He repeated his desire to be indulged with death in the most honourable manner; and as he had no doubt of the decision of the Court, he expressed a wish, that the confirmation of it by the Lord Lieutenant might be had as soon as possible, and execution of the sentence immediately follow— within an hour, if it were practicable.*

The President replied, that the Court would proceed forthwith to a consideration and judgment of his case, after which no delay would take place in transmitting the proceedings to His Excellency, and that it was probable, whoever went with them, would bring back the Lord Lieutenant's determination on the subject.

The prisoner then thanked the Court for the indulgence which had been extended to him.—He was brought back to the Provost Marshalsea.

Mr. Tone retired from his trial, surrounded by the guard which escorted him there, leaning on the arm of Brigade Major Sandys. There was a considerable number of yeomanry officers, and other loyal citizens, assembled, to witness this termination of the career in the political race of a man, viewed as uniting in his own person the *Alpha* and *Omega* of the Irish Union. He walked with an air of unconcern, and seemed to feel his situation as one who had fully made up his mind to the worst.

The whole of Saturday and Sunday, however, he expressed much anxiety to learn the decision of His Excellency the Lord-Lieutenant, concerning the request he had made as to the mode of his execution, having no doubt at all as to the sentence of the Court, and its confirmation by His Excellency.

On Sunday evening he was informed, that his conviction and sentence of death had been confirmed by His Excellency, but that his request as to the mode of execution could not be complied with; that he must suffer the same fate with the other traitors who were taken in war against their king and country; and that the peculiar circumstances of his case rendered it necessary, that his execution should be in the most public manner, for the sake of a striking example; that he must be executed in front of the New Prison, where his former accomplices had forfeited their lives to the justice of their country.

This, however, was an arrangement for which all his fortitude and philosophy could not string the nerves of Mr. Tone. Such a torrent of public ignominy was too much for reflection, and he took the resolution of anticipating the execution by his own hand, and relieving his mind from the intolerable load of horror which the manner of his approaching fate impressed; for, when the sentinel who watched in his room went to rouse him on Monday morning, he found him exhausted, weltering in his blood, with his throat cut across, and apparently expiring. The sentinel immediately alarmed the Provost Marshal; a military surgeon of the 5th regiment of Dragoons immediately attended, and on examining the wound, pronounced it not mortal, though extremely dangerous; to which Mr. Tone faintly answered—'I find, then, I am but a bad anatomist.'

['It was directed by the government that he should be executed in the ordinary form, and in the most public manner; but this the prisoner took the resolution of preventing, by an act, which, in his case, shows the uncertain security of any speculative determinations respecting suicide, against the pressure of the actual calamity, or of the many other motives which impel a man to raise his hand against himself.

'Upon the evening before the *Hoche* sailed from Brest, the subject of suicide was fully discussed among the Irish, who formed a part of the expedition. They felt confident of success, should the French troops debark in safety upon the coast of Ireland; but they were equally certain that, if captured at sea, they would all be condemned and executed. Upon this a question arose whether, in the latter event, they should suffer themselves to be put to death according to the sentence and forms of law. Mr Tone maintained that they ought, and, with his usual eloquence and animation, delivered his decided opinion that, in no point of view in which he had ever considered suicide, could he hold it to be justifiable. It is supposed that, in his own particular instance, he did not at this time anticipate an ignominious mode of death; but that he expected, in case of capture and condemnation, to be allowed the military privilege, which, he afterwards so earnestly claimed.'* Disappointed in this hope, he now committed the act which he had so lately reprobated. He was induced to do so either by a natural impulse of personal pride, of which he had not previously contemplated the powerful influence, or (as is conjectured by those who best knew him) out of consideration for the army of which he was a member, and for whose honour, in his estimation, no sacrifice could be too great.' *Life of John Philpot Curran*, vol. 2, pp. 160–2.]

The wound, which was inflicted with a penknife, intersected the windpipe between two of the cartilaginous rings which form that organ, and amounted to what surgeons style the operation of bronchotomy;—it was dressed, but only with a view to prolong life till the fatal hour of one o'clock appointed for execution; to which end the cart was prepared, and an escort of cavalry and infantry under orders to attend.

In the interval a motion was made in the Court of King's Bench by Mr. Curran, on an affidavit of Mr. Tone's father, stating that his son had been brought before a bench of officers, calling itself a court martial, and by them sentenced to death.

'I do not pretend to say,' observed Mr. Curran, 'that Mr. Tone is not guilty of the charges of which he was accused;—I presume the officers were honourable men;—but it is stated in the affidavit, as a solemn fact, that Mr. Tone had no commission under His Majesty, and therefore no court martial could have cognizance of any crime imputed to him, while the Court of King's Bench sat in the capacity of the great criminal court of the land. In times when

* 'The gentleman who has communicated the above circumstances was present at the conversation. Independent of the moral arguments adduced against suicide, it was suggested by one of the company that, from political considerations, it would be better not to relieve, by any act of self-murder, the Irish government from the discredit in which numerous executions would involve it—an idea which, he says, Mr. Tone warmly approved. He adds that when it appeared that the *Hoche* was likely to be captured, a boat was despatched to her from the *Biche* (a small fast sailing vessel, which afterwards escaped into Brest) in order to bring off all the Irish on board; but that Mr. Tone could not be persuaded to avail himself of the opportunity.' *Life of John Philpot Curran*, vol. 2, pp. 161–2 n.

war was raging, when man was opposed to man in the field, courts martial might be endured; but every law authority is with me, while I stand upon this sacred and immutable principle of the constitution—*that martial law and civil law are incompatible*; and that the former must cease with the existence of the latter. This is not the time for arguing this momentous question. My client must appear in this court. *He is cast for death this day.* He may be ordered for execution while I address you. I call on the Court to support the law. I move for a *habeas corpus* to be directed to the Provost Marshal of the barracks of Dublin, and Major Sandys to bring up the body of Mr. Tone.

Lord Chief Justice (Kilwarden). Have a writ instantly prepared.

Mr. Curran. My client may die while this writ is preparing.

Lord Chief Justice. Mr. Sheriff, proceed to the barracks, and acquaint the Provost Marshal that a writ is preparing to suspend Mr. Tone's execution; and *see that he be not executed.*

The Court awaited, in a state of the utmost agitation, the return of the Sheriff.

Mr. Sheriff. My lords, I have been at the barracks, in pursuance of your order. The Provost Marshal says he must obey Major Sandys. Major Sandys says he must obey Lord Cornwallis.

Mr. Curran. Mr. Tone's father, my lords, returns, after serving the *habeas corpus.* He says General Craig will not obey it.

Lord Chief Justice. Mr. Sheriff, take the body of Tone into your custody. Take the Provost Marshal and Major Sandys into custody, and show the order of this Court to General Craig.

Mr. Sheriff, who was understood to have been refused admittance at the barracks, returns.

Mr. Sheriff. I have been at the barracks. Mr. Tone, having cut his throat last night, is not in a condition to be removed. As to the second part of your order, I could not meet the parties.

A French Emigrant Surgeon, whom General Craig had sent along with the Sheriff, was sworn.

Surgeon. I was sent to attend Mr. Tone this morning at four o' clock, his windpipe was divided. I took instant measures to secure his life, by closing the wound. There is no knowing, for four days, whether it will be mortal. His head is now kept in one position. A sentinel is over him, to prevent his speaking. His removal would kill him.

Mr. Curran applied for farther surgical aid, and for the admission of Mr. Tone's friends to him. (Refused.)

Lord Chief Justice. Let a rule be made for suspending the execution of Theobald Wolfe Tone; and let it be served on the proper persons.

The prisoner lingered until the 19th day of November, when he expired, after having endured in the interval the most excruciating pain.

It was generally understood that Mr. Tone was to have been paraded through the streets previous to his execution, and some assign this to be the cause of his attempt on his life. He seemed on his trial unmoved and unterrified.

['Mr. Tone had reached only his thirty-fourth year. His father was an eminent coachmaker in Dublin. He had sixteen children (thirteen sons and three daughters), of whom only five attained the age of maturity, and whose fates afford a singular instance of the wanderings and calamities of a single family. Theobald died as above related. Matthew was executed the same year, in Dublin barracks, for high treason; it is said that no more than five persons were present at the execution. William was killed in India, a major in Holkar's service. Arthur accompanied his brother Theobald to America, and was subsequently, at the early age of eighteen, appointed to the command of a frigate in the service of the Dutch republic. He is supposed to have perished at sea, as no account was ever after received of him. Mary was married to a foreign merchant, and died at St. Domingo. Their aged mother survives, and now [1819] resides in Dublin.

'After the death of Mr. Wolfe Tone, his widow and infant children were protected by the French republic, and, on the motion of Lucien Buonaparte, a pension granted for their support.' *Life of John Philpot Curran,* vol. 2, p. 166 n.]

Libel

Chapter five

John Bastwick, Henry Burton, and William Prynne (1637)

In all the cases reported in *State Trials* there are no more willing martyrs than the three Puritan propagandists William Prynne (1600–69), Dr John Bastwick (1593–1654), and Henry Burton (1578–1648). Victims of the most barbaric punishments, they showed a faith in their own righteousness which would unnerve any enemy, and which certainly heartened their own supporters and won them thousands of sympathizers. Only Burton was a clergyman, Rector of St Matthews, Friday Street. Bastwick was a doctor of medicine and Prynne, the best known of the trio, a barrister.

Their trial in 1637 was not the first time that any of them had been prosecuted for libels against the political or ecclesiastical establishment. Early in the reign of Charles I, Bastwick published his *Flagellum Pontificis*, attacking the bishops and defending the Presbyterians, for which he was fined £1,000 and imprisoned by the Court of High Commission. In 1626 Henry Burton was cited before the same court for having denounced the alleged Catholic sympathies of Archbishop Laud. He was imprisoned in 1629 for another attack on the bishops in *Babel no Bethel*. William Prynne's literary career attracted fewer penalties at first, since he was more specifically concerned than the others with what he regarded as the vices of social behaviour. In 1628 he published a pamphlet condemning 'the unloveliness of love-locks', in which he attacked the custom of long hair for men as 'unseemly' and 'unlawful' in a Christian. On the other hand, women who wore their hair short were 'mannish, un-natural, impudent, and unchristian'. More decisive was his attack on theatres and the morality of actors or actresses in *Histriomastix* (1633), though the book dealt with other 'still-increasing evils' as well. His references to the unpleasant fates which Providence had decreed for those who indulged in such unwholesome pleasures were taken by his enemies as inciting the people against their monarch, since Charles I happened to enjoy dancing, stage plays, and other evils condemned by Prynne. Moreover, the motto in *Histriomastix*, 'Women Actors Notorious Whores', was unfortunate at a time when the queen took part in amateur theatricals. Proceedings were taken against Prynne early in 1633, and he was sentenced by Star Chamber to be imprisoned for life, to be fined £5,000, and to have his ears cut off in the pillory. Later it was discovered that part of his ears still remained because, according to one account, Prynne had offered the executioner five shillings not to cut them off at the base.

From his prison, Prynne smuggled out a new attack on his enemies in *News from Ipswich: Discovering the Practices of Domineering Lordly Prelates*, as well as his *Divine Tragedy*. Bastwick and Burton were both implicated in the publication of *News from Ipswich* but they had also issued tracts of their own: *The Litany of John Bastwick* and his πράξεις τῶν επισκόπων, a Latin defence of his views. Burton's *Apology of an Appeal* included two sermons in which he had libellously but picturesquely attacked the bishops as 'caterpillars' rather than as pillars of the state, and derided them as 'antichristian mushrumps'. The case in Star Chamber and its immediate consequences are the subject of the account reprinted here. No lawyer seemed willing to defend the three men and when an attorney eventually read Burton's rebuttal of the charges, he deleted sixty-four pages, leaving only the first six and the last twenty-four lines, for fear the rest might involve Burton in further danger.

The public mutilation of the three defendants on 30 June 1637 did more to promote their cause among the common people than any amount of pamphleteering. Representing as they did the professions of law, medicine, and the Church, there was an added sense of revulsion among contemporary observers at the manner of their treatment and disfigurement. Well might Burton proclaim from the pillory, 'Little do you know what fruit God is able to produce from this dry tree.' When Burton was taken away to life imprisonment, five hundred sympathizers rode with him on the first stage of the journey, while 100,000 people are said to have lined the route, making it seem a triumphal procession. Naturally, the faith of the martyrs themselves was the more strengthened by their sufferings. When Bastwick was warned that he would remain in his prison cell, if necessary for the rest of his life, unless he recanted, he promised that his gaolers should wait until Doomsday and that even on Doomsday he would not recant until the afternoon.

Neither Bastwick nor his two associates had to wait until Doomsday for their release. In 1641 they were freed by order of the Long Parliament and returned from their remote prisons in the Channel Islands and the Isles of Scilly to an enthusiastic reception by those crowds, to whom they were a popular emblem of suffering endured under Star Chamber. Bastwick became captain of a Leicester trained band (having served as a soldier in the Low Countries many years before) and though captured by the royalists during the Civil War, he was soon released again. His compensation for the sufferings he had endured amounted to some £9,000, paid to him from confiscated royalist estates. Burton, after his release, received £6,000 and returned to the life of a Puritan clergyman. If the compensation in both cases seems generous, it appears less so when seen as compensation for the money spent (and owed) by the three men in defending themselves in 1637.

William Prynne was only forty years old at the time of his release and still had a busy life ahead of him. With the change in political fortunes he became an eminent prosecuting counsel on the parliamentary side, taking part in the case of Archbishop Laud who was condemned for treason in 1644 but who had been one of Prynne's accusers in Star Chamber seven years earlier. Yet Prynne was rarely free of controversy. Though he defended Parliament, he attacked the army and was consequently imprisoned during Pride's Purge in 1648. He was released the following year, only to become involved in a quarrel against the Commonwealth over the imposition of taxes. He went back to prison in 1650 and was kept there until 1653. Released once more, he produced numerous, if ephemeral, pamphlets on a scale to make him a bibliographer's despair. Surprisingly, after the death of Cromwell he joined those who favoured the restoration of Charles II. Yet Prynne had never opposed monarchy in principle, he had attacked only evil monarchs or those, like Charles I, whom he regarded as under the sway of evil men.

Prynne was on good terms with the restored king, even dedicating one of his publications to him. In 1662 Charles made him Keeper of the Records in the Tower of London with an annual salary of £500. As the last survivor of the trio who had provided so gruesome a spectacle in 1637, and as the author of some two hundred books and pamphlets, Prynne in his final years became something of a curiosity to diarists like Anthony à Wood. Pepys met him at dinner at Trinity House in 1662 and records an incident which makes a very human contrast to the image of the spiritually self-confident Puritan, as well as showing that Puritanism is not necessarily synonymous with prudery.

> I seated myself close by Mr. Prin, who, in discourse with me, fell upon what records he hath of the lust and wicked lives of the nuns heretofore in England, and showed me out of his pocket one wherein thirty nuns for their lust were ejected out of their house, being not fit to live there, and by the Pope's command to be put, however, into other nunnerys.[1]

Proceedings in the Star Chamber against Dr. JOHN BASTWICK, Mr. HENRY BURTON, and WILLIAM PRYNNE, Esq. for several Libels: 13 CHARLES I. A.D. 1637. Written by their Friends.

[Clarendon, *History of the Rebellion* (1704), vol. 1, pp. 73 and 158–60; Rushworth, *Historical Collections* (1721), vol. 2, pp. 380–5.

Kennet, after mentioning the opinion which the judges had given on the legality of Ship-Money, proceeds: 'It was a less invidious opinion which the same judges had delivered in the case of Burton and Bastwick, who had been so fierce in their Libels against the Government, that it was considered by the King's counsel how to draw them into an arraignment of high treason. For which purpose there was a meeting of the judges at Serjeant's Inn, before whom the King's counsel laboured to prove that divers passages in the books of the said authors did amount to high treason. But when the counsel withdrew, the judges in debate among themselves, came to these resolutions. 1. That if there were anything in the books that amounted to treason, no indictment could be found good for treason, unless it was grounded upon the statute of 25 Edward III, either for compassing the King's death, or imagining the same, or else for levying of war. 2. That if any man seditiously, maliciously and of purpose to raise rebellion, and to incite rebellion, did take arms to reduce the course of government of the state, either ecclesiastical or civil, and thereby to compass the King's destruction, this was treason. 3. That such indictment was to be framed upon the said statute of 25 Edward III. This resolution being delivered by the Lord Chief Justice to the King and council, had this regular effect, that the said offenders were not indicted of high treason, but prosecuted in a softer manner, though afterwards thought severe and arbitrary.' White Kennet, *History of England* (1706), vol. 3, p. 79.]

An information was exhibited in the Star Chamber by the Attorney-General, against John Bastwick, doctor in physic, Henry Burton, bachelor of divinity, and William Prynne, barrister-at-law, defendants, for writing and publishing seditious, schismatical and libellous books against the hierarchy. They prepared their answers, but the counsel being backward for fear of offending the Court, they petitioned they might sign their answers themselves, which was denied; and the 28th of April the Court ordered them to put in their answers by Monday seven-night under their counsels' hands, or else the matters of the information to be taken *pro confesso* [*as if admitted*]. Mr. Prynne, 5 May, again petitioned them, that having been for above a week debarred access to his counsel, and his servant who should solicit for him being detained close prisoner in a messenger's hands, and it being difficult to get his counsel to repair to him during the term; he having been a barrister-at-law, prayed he might (according to former precedents in that court) have liberty to put in his answer by the day prefixed, under his own hand, and not under his counsel's, who refused it out of fear and cowardice.

*　　*　　*

Upon reading this and a petition from Dr. Bastwick to the same purpose, alleging his counsel refused to sign his answer, the Court adhered to their former order, that they should by Monday put in their answers under counsel's hands, or else to be taken *pro confesso*. Prynne and Bastwick thereupon left their answers under their own hands at the office, and tendered another draught thereof to the Court.

Before this petition of Mr. Prynne, he and the two other defendants put in a cross-bill under all their hands, against the Archbishop of Canterbury and others of the prelates, wherein they charged them with usurping upon His Majesty's prerogative royal, with innovations, licensing popish and Arminian Books, &c. and set forth the substance of their answers. The bill being engrossed and signed by them, Mr. Prynne tendered it to my Lord Keeper, praying it might be accepted without counsels' hands, who durst not sign it. The Lord Keeper upon reading the cross-bill refused to admit it, but delivered it to the King's Attorney. The Archbishop nettled thereat, demanded the opinion of the judges, whether they could not be punished as libellers; who all but one answered negatively: for it was tendered in a legal way, and the King's courts are open to all men. The Archbishop then applied to the Court of Star Chamber, and informed them, that in some books and pamphlets lately published, His Grace and the other bishops are said to have usurped upon the King's prerogative, and proceeded in their courts contrary to law.

*　　*　　*

Mr. Burton in his answer, set forth the substance of his sermon which he preached the 5th of November in his parish church in Friday Street, touching the innovations brought into the Church.

Dr. Bastwick in his answer termed the prelates invaders of the King's prerogative, condemners of the scriptures, advancers of Popery, superstition, idolatry, profaneness, oppression of the King's subjects, in the impious performance whereof they showed neither wit nor honesty; enemies of God and the King, and servants of the Devil.

Mr. Prynne's answer was much against the hierarchy, but in more moderate and cautious expressions.

14 June. The Lords being set in their places in the Star Chamber, and the three defendants brought to the bar, to receive their sentences, the Lord Chief Justice Finch looking earnestly on Mr. Prynne, said, 'I had thought Mr. Prynne had no ears, but methinks he hath ears'; which caused many of the Lords to take the stricter view of him, and for their better satisfaction, the usher of the court was commanded to turn up his hair, and show his ears: upon the sight whereof the Lords were displeased they had been formerly no more cut off, and cast out some disgraceful words of him. To which Mr. Prynne replied, 'My lords, there is never a one of your honours, but would be sorry to have your ears as mine are.'

Lord Keeper. In good faith he is somewhat saucy.
Mr. Prynne. I hope your honours will not be offended, pray God give you ears to hear.
Lord Keeper. The business of the day is to proceed on the prisoners at the bar.

Mr. Prynne then humbly desired of the Court to give him leave to make a motion or two, which being granted, he moved, first, that their honours would be pleased to accept of a cross-bill against the prelates, signed with their own hands, being that which stands with the justice of the Court, which he humbly craves; and so tendered it.

Lord Keeper. As for your cross-bill, it is not the business of the day; hereafter if the Court shall see just cause, and that it savours not of libelling, we may accept of it: for my part I have not seen it, but have heard somewhat of it.
Mr. Prynne. I hope your honours will not refuse it, being it is on His Majesty's behalf. We are His Majesty's subjects, and therefore require the justice of the Court.
Lord Keeper. But this is not the business of the day.
Mr. Prynne. Why then, my lords, I have a second motion, which I humbly pray your honours to grant; which is, that your lordships will be pleased to dismiss the prelates here now sitting, from having any voice in the censure of this cause, being generally known to be adversaries, as being no way

agreeable with equity or reason, that they who are our adversaries, should be our judges. Therefore we humbly crave they may be expunged out of the court.

Lord Keeper. In good faith, it is a sweet motion, is it not? Herein you are become libellous. And if you should thus libel all the lords and reverend judges, as you do the most reverend prelates, by this your plea, you would have none to pass sentence upon you for your libelling, because they are parties.

Mr. Prynne. Under correction, my lord, this doth not hold, the case is not alike, for here are only one or two members of the Court, who are said to be libelled against, and your lordship yourself in your case against Norton absented yourself from the hearing, because a party, which is usually done by the lords in like cases.—(*But this prevailed nothing.*)

Mr. Prynne. Then I have a third motion, which is, that your lordships will receive my answer to the information signed with one counsel's hand, which as soon as I could get signed, I tendered at the office, but it was refused.

Lord Keeper. Your answer comes now too late, proceed to the business of the day. Read the information. (*Which was read being very large, and having these five books thereto annexed, Dr. Bastwick's Latin* Apology, *his* Litany, *Mr. Burton's book entitled,* An Apology of an Appeal to the King's most excellent Majesty, *with two Sermons for God and the King, preached on the 5th of November last:* The News from Ipswich, *and the* Divine Tragedy, *recording God's fearful Judgments against Sabbath-Breakers.*—The King's counsel being five, took each of them a several book.*)

Mr. Attorney began with Dr. Bastwick's Latin *Apology*; next unto the Attorney, Serjeant Whitfield falls upon Mr. Burton's book, saying, 'In good faith, my lords, there is never a page in this book, but deserves a heavier and deeper censure than this Court can put upon him.'

Next followed the Archbishop, who in like manner descanted on *The News from Ipswich*, charging it to be full of pernicious lies; and especially vindicating the honour of Matthew Wren, Bishop of Norwich, as being a learned, pious, and reverend father of the Church.

Next followed the King's Solicitor, (Mr. Littleton) who descanted upon the *Divine Tragedy*; to which part of it concerning God's judgments on sabbath-breakers, he said, that they sat in the seat of God, who judged these accidents which fell out upon persons suddenly struck, to be the judgments of God for sabbath-breaking. He enlarged himself upon that passage which reflected upon his Majesty's late Attorney-General, Mr. William Noy, who, (he said) was most shamefully abused by a slander laid upon him, as if God's judgment fell upon him, for so eagerly prosecuting Mr. Prynne for his *Histriomastix*, which judgment was this; that he laughing at Mr. Prynne, while he was suffering upon the pillory, was struck with an issue of blood in his privy parts, which could never be stopped till the day of his death, which followed soon after. 'But the truth of this, my lords, you shall find to be as probable as the rest, for we have here three or four gentlemen of good credit and rank, to testify upon oath that he had that issue long before.' And the Solicitor called out for room to be made for the gentlemen to come in, but none such appeared.

Lastly followed Mr. Herbert, who descanting upon Dr. Bastwick's *Litany*, concluded jointly with the rest, that it deserved a heavy censure.

Lord Keeper. You hear, gentlemen, wherewith you are charged, and now lest you should say you cannot have liberty to speak for yourselves, the Court gives you leave to speak what you can, with these conditions: 1. That you speak within the bounds of modesty. 2. That your speeches be not libellous.

They all three answered, they hoped so to order their speech, as to be free from any immodest or libellous speaking.

Lord Keeper. Then speak in God's name, and show cause why the Court should not proceed in censure (*as taking the cause* pro confesso.)

Mr. Prynne. I expected some particular charge to be proved against me. Dr. Bastwick and Mr. Burton are charged with particular books to the information annexed, but none of the books are laid to me; my sole offence, for which the information must be taken *pro confesso*, is my not putting in my answer under counsel's hand by a day pre-fixed; whereas I entered my appearance, and took out a copy of the information, which being taken out, I endeavoured to draw up my answer; but being shut up close prisoner, I was deserted of all means by which I should have done it; for I was no sooner

served with the subpoena, but I was shortly after shut up close
prisoner, prohibited of pen, ink, and paper, and so disabled
to draw up my answer, or instructions for counsel; my
servant who should solicit for me was in prison, without
being admitted to bail, my friends denied access, and my
chamber twice searched; and after I had drawn some
instructions, and part of my answer, having then obtained
liberty of pen and ink, they were taken away by Mr.
Nicolas, Clerk of the Council; your lordships refused to let
me put in my answer under my own hand, though a
counsellor at law, contrary to former precedents; your
lordships did at last assign me counsel, but they neglected to
come to me, and when, by order of the Court, Mr. Holt came to
me in the Tower, I gave him my fee and instructions, and
afterwards Mr. Holt and my other counsel agreed upon my
answer, caused it to be engrossed, and promised to sign it,
but Mr. Holt refused to do it then; afterwards Mr. Tomlins
signed it, and it was carried to the office, but they refused it.
Here it is, I tender it upon my oath, which your lordships
cannot deny with the justice of the Court.

Lord Keeper. We can give you a precedent, that this Court hath
proceeded and taken a cause *pro confesso*, for not putting in an
answer in six days; you have had a great deal of favour
showed you, in affording you longer time, and therefore the
Court is free from all calumny or aspersion for rejecting your
answer, not signed with counsels' hands.

Mr. Prynne. But one word or two, my lords, I desire your honours
to hear me. I put a case in law. If an award be made that A
shall together with B and C enter into a bond of 100*l.* to S,
the award is void, because A hath no power to compel B and
C to enter into such a bond. My case is the same. The Court
ordered me to put in my answer under counsels' hands;
I endeavoured it, they refused to sign it, I had no power to
compel them, and desired the Court to order them to sign it;
but the Court replied they had no power to force them. How
then could I, a close prisoner, compel them, if the Court
could not? By this means the most innocent person in the
world may be made guilty of what crimes you please. I appeal
to Mr. Holt, if I have not used all my endeavours to get him
to sign my answer.

Mr. Holt. There was so long time spent ere I could do anything after I was assigned his counsel, that it was impossible his answer could be drawn up in so short a time as was allotted. For after long expectation, seeing he came not to me, I went to him, where I found him shut up close prisoner, so that I could not have access to him. Whereupon I motioned to the Lieutenant of the Tower to have free liberty of speech with him concerning his answer, which being granted me, I found him very willing and desirous to have it drawn up. Whereupon I did move in this Court for pen and paper, which was granted, the which he no sooner had gotten but he set himself to draw up instructions, and in a short time sent me forty sheets, and soon after I received forty more; but I found the answer so long, and of such a nature, that I durst not set my hand to it, for fear of giving your honours distaste.

Mr. Prynne. My lords, I did nothing but according to the directions of my counsel, only I spake my own words: my answer was drawn up by his consent, it was his own act, and he did approve of it; and if he will be so base a coward, to do that in private which he dares not acknowledge in public, I will not have such a sin lie on my conscience, let it rest with him. Here is my answer, which though it be not signed with their hands, yet here I tender it upon my oath, which you cannot in justice deny.

Lord Keeper. Your case is good law, but ill applied; the Court desires no such long answer, but whether you are guilty or not guilty.

Mr. Prynne. By the statutes of Philip and Mary and of Elizabeth in the case of libelling the King or Queen,[2] the party's confession, or two witnesses face to face are required, else no conviction, and here is neither; nor is there in all the information one clause that doth particularly fall on me, but only in general. There is no book laid to my charge, and shall I be condemned for a particular act, when no accusation of any particular act can be brought against me? This were most unjust and wicked. Here I tender my answer to the information upon my oath. My lord, you do impose impossibilities upon me, I could do no more than I did.

Lord Keeper. Well, hold your peace, your answer comes too late. What say you Dr. Bastwick?

Dr. Bastwick. My honourable lords, methinks you look like an
assembly of gods, and sit in the place of God. Ye are called
the Sons of God; and since I have compared you to gods,
give me leave a little to parallel the one with the other, to
see whether the comparison between God and you doth hold
in this noble and righteous cause. This was the carriage of
Almighty God in the cause of Sodom, before he would
pronounce sentence, or execute judgment, he would first
come down, and see whether the crime was altogether
according to the cry that was come up. And with whom
doth the Lord consult, when he came down? With his servant
Abraham, and he gives the reason; 'for I know,' saith he,
'that Abraham will command his children and household
after him, that they shall keep the way of the Lord to do
justice and judgment.' My good lords, thus stands the case
between your honours and us this day. There is a great cry
come up into your ears against us from the King's
Attorney; why now be you pleased to descend and see if the
crime be according to the cry, and consult with God, not the
prelates, being in the adversary part; who, as it is
apparent to all the world, do proudly set themselves against
the ways of God, and from whom none can expect justice or
judgment, but with righteous men, that will be impartial on
either side, before you proceed to censure, which censure you
cannot pass on us without great injustice before you hear our
answers read. Here is my answer, which I here tender upon
my oath. My good lords, give us leave to speak in our own
defence. We are not conscious to ourselves, of anything we
have done that deserves a censure this day in this honourable
Court, but that we have ever laboured to maintain the
honour, dignity, and prerogative royal of our Sovereign Lord
the King; let my lord the King live for ever. Had I a thousand
lives, I should think them all too little to spend for the
maintenance of His Majesty's royal prerogative. My good
lords, can you proceed to censure before you know my cause?
I dare undertake, that scarce any one of your lordships have
read my books. And can you then censure me for what you
know not, and before I have made my defence? O my noble
lords! Is this righteous judgment? This were against the law
of God and man, to condemn a man before you know his

crime. The Governor before whom St. Paul was carried, who was a very heathen, would first hear his cause before he would pass any censure upon him; and doth it beseem so noble and Christian assembly to condemn me before my answer be perused, and my cause known? Men, brethren, and fathers, into what an age are we fallen? I desire your honours to lay aside your censure for this day, to inquire into my cause, and hear my answer read; which if you refuse to do, I here profess, I will clothe it in Roman buff, and send it abroad unto the view of all the world, to clear mine innocency, and show your great injustice in this cause.

Lord Keeper. But this is not the business of the day. Why brought you not in your answer in due time?

Dr. Bastwick. My lord, a long time since I tendered it to your honour, I failed not in any one particular. And if my counsel be so base and cowardly, that they dare not sign it for fear of the prelates, as I can make it appear, therefore have I no answer? My lord, here is my answer, which though my counsel out of a base spirit dare not set their hands unto, yet I tender it upon my oath.

Lord Keeper. But, Mr. Doctor, you should have been brief; you tendered it in too large an answer, which, as I heard, is as libellous as your books.

Dr. Bastwick. No, my lord, it is not libellous though large; I have none to answer for me but myself, and being left to myself, I must plead my conscience in answer to every circumstance of the information.

Lord Keeper. What say you, Mr. Doctor, are you guilty, or not guilty? Answer yea, or no: you needed not to have troubled yourself so much about so large an answer.

Dr. Bastwick. I know none of your honours have read my books; and can you with the justice of the Court, condemn me before you know what is written in my books?

Lord Keeper. What say you to that was read to you even now?

Dr. Bastwick. My lord, he that read it did so murder the sense of it, that had I not known what I had written, I could not tell what to have made of it.

Lord Keeper. What say you to the other sentence read to you?

Dr. Bastwick. That was none of mine, I will not father that which was none of my own.

Lord Dorset. Did not you send that book, as now it is, to a nobleman's house, together with a letter directed to him?

Dr. Bastwick. Yea, my lord, I did so, but withal you may see in my Epistle set before the book, I did at first disclaim what was not mine. I sent my book over by a Dutch merchant, who it was that wrote the addition I do not know, but my Epistle set to my book made manifest what was mine, and what was not; and I cannot justly suffer for what was none of mine.

Lord Arundel. My lord, you hear by his own speech the cause is taken *pro confesso.*

Lord Keeper. Yea, you say true, my lord.

Dr. Bastwick. My noble Lord of Arundel, I know you are a noble prince in Israel, and a great peer of this realm; there are some honourable lords in this court, that have been forced out as combatants in a single duel; it is between the prelates and us, at this time, as between two that have appointed the field. The one being a coward goes to the magistrate, and by virtue of his authority disarms the other of his weapons, and gives him a bullrush, and then challenges him to fight. If this be not base cowardice, I know not what belongs to a soldier. This is the case between the prelates and us, they take away our weapons, our answers, by virtue of your authority, by which we should defend ourselves, and yet they bid us fight. My lord, doth not this savour of a base cowardly spirit? I know, my lord, there is a decree gone forth, for my sentence was passed long since, to cut off our ears.

Lord Keeper. Who shall know our censure, before the Court pass it? Do you prophesy of yourselves?

Dr. Bastwick. My lord, I am able to prove it, and that from the mouth of the prelates' own servants, that in August last it was decreed, that Dr. Bastwick should lose his ears. O my noble lords! Is this righteous judgment? I may say, as the Apostle once said, 'What, whip a Roman!' I have been a soldier able to lead an army into the field, to fight valiantly for the honour of their prince. Now I am a physician, able to cure nobles, kings, princes, and emperors; and to curtalize a Roman's ears like a cur, O my honourable lords! Is it not too base an act for so noble an assembly, and for so righteous and honourable a cause? The cause, my lords, is great, it concerns the glory of God, the honour of our King, whose prerogative we labour to maintain and to set up in a high manner, in which your honours' liberties are engaged. And doth not such a cause deserve your lordships' consideration, before you proceed to censure? Your honours may be pleased to consider, that in the last cause heard and censured in this court, between Sir James Bagg and the Lord Mohun, wherein your lordships took a great deal of pains, with a great deal of patience, to hear the bills on both sides, with all the answers and depositions largely laid open before you; which cause when you had fully heard, some of your honours now sitting in court, said, you could not in conscience proceed to censure, till you had taken some time to recollect yourselves. If in a cause of that nature, you could spend so much time, and afterwards recollect yourselves before you would pass censure; how much more should it move your honours to take some time in a cause wherein the glory of God, the prerogative of His Majesty, your honours' dignity, and the subject's liberty is so largely engaged? My good lords, it may fall out to be any of your lordships' cases to stand as delinquents at this bar, as we now do. It is not unknown to your honours, the next cause that is to succeed ours, is touching a person that sometimes hath been in greatest power in this court.[3] And if the mutations and revolutions of persons and times be such, then I do most humbly beseech your honours to look on us, as it may befall yourselves. But if all this will not prevail with your honours to peruse my books, and hear my answer read, which here I tender upon the word and oath of a soldier, a gentleman, a scholar, and a physician, I will clothe them, as I said before, in Roman buff, and disperse them throughout the Christian world, that future generations may see the innocency of this cause, and your honours' unjust proceedings in it; all which I will do, though it cost me my life.

Lord Keeper. Mr. Doctor, I thought you would be angry.

Dr. Bastwick. No, my lord, you are mistaken, I am not angry or passionate; all that I do press, is, that you would be pleased to peruse my answer.

Lord Keeper. Well, hold your peace. Mr. Burton, what say you?

Mr. Burton. My good lords, your honours, it should seem, do determine to censure us, and take our cause *pro confesso,* although we have laboured to give your honours satisfaction in all things. My lords, what you have to say against my book, I confess I did write it, yet did I not anything out of intent of commotion, or sedition. I delivered nothing but what my text led me to, being chosen to suit with the day, namely the 5th of November; the words were these, &c.

Lord Keeper. Mr. Burton, I pray stand not naming texts of scripture now; we do not send for you to preach, but to answer to those things that are objected against you.

Mr. Burton. My lord, I have drawn up my answer to my great pains and charges, which answer was signed with my counsel's hands, and received into the Court, according to the rule and order thereof. And I did not think to have been called this day to a censure, but have had a legal proceeding by way of bill and answer.

Lord Keeper. Your answer was impertinent.

Mr. Burton. My answer, after it was entered into the court, was referred to the judges, but by what means I do not know. Whether it be impertinent, and what cause your lordships had to cast it out, I know not; but after it was approved of, and received, it was cast out as an impertinent answer.

Lord Finch. The judges did you a good turn to make it impertinent, for it was as libellous as your book, so that your answer deserved a censure alone.

Lord Keeper. What say you, Mr. Burton, are you guilty or not?

Mr. Burton. My lord, I desire you not only to peruse my book here and there, but every passage of it.

Lord Keeper. Mr. Burton, time is short, are you guilty or not guilty! What say you to that which was read? Doth it become a minister to deliver himself in such a railing and scandalous way?

Mr. Burton. In my judgment, and as I can prove it, it was neither railing nor scandalous; I conceive that a minister hath a larger liberty than always to go in a mild strain. I being the pastor of my people, whom I had in charge, and was to instruct, I supposed it was my duty to inform them of these innovations that are crept into the Church, as likewise of the danger and ill consequence of them; as for my answer, ye blotted out what ye would, and then the rest which made best for your own ends, you would have to stand; and now for me to tender

THE FIRST ACT.

Enter the Bishop of Canterbury, and with him a Doctor of Physicke, a Lawyer, and a Divine : who being set downe, they bring him variety of Dishes to his Table,

C *Anterbury,* is here all the dishes, that are provided?
  Doct. My Lord, there is all : and 'tis enough, wert for a Princes table,
Ther's 24. severall dainty dishes, and all rare.
  B, Cant. Are these rare : no, no, they please me not,
Give me a Carbinadoed cheek, or a tippet of a Cocks combe :
None of all this, here is meate for my Pallet.
  Lawyer. My Lord, here is both Cocke and Phesant,
Quaile and Partridge, and the best varieties the shambles yeeld.

A 2

Cant.

---

1   *A New Play Called Canterbury His Change of Diet* (1641). Archbishop Laud dining on the ears of William Prynne, John Bastwick, and Henry Burton.

2   Edward, 1st Baron Thurlow, by Thomas Phillips (1806).

only what will serve for your own turns, and renounce the rest, were to desert my cause, which before I will do, or desert my conscience, I will rather desert my body, and deliver it up to your lordships to do with it what you will.

Lord Keeper. This is a place where you should crave mercy and favour, Mr. Burton, and not stand upon such terms as you do.

Mr. Burton. There wherein I have offended through human frailty, I crave of God and man pardon: and I pray God, that in your Sentence you may so censure us, that you may not sin against the Lord.

Thus the Prisoners desiring to speak a little more for themselves, were commanded to silence. And so the lords proceeded to censure.

[*The proceedings ended with a long speech by Archbishop Laud, attacking the arguments of the condemned publications. Laud did not censure the defendants, since 'the business hath some reflection upon myself'.*]

On the 30th of June following, the sentence was executed, when Dr. Bastwick, Mr. Prynne and Mr. Burton, were conveyed to the pillory in the Palace Yard, Westminster.

Dr. Bastwick and Mr. Burton first meeting, they did close one in the other's arms three times, with as much expressions of love as might be, rejoicing that they met at such a place, upon such an occasion, and that God had so highly honoured them, as to call them forth to suffer for His glorious truth.

Then immediately after, Mr. Prynne came, the doctor and he saluting each other, as Mr. Burton and he did before. The doctor then went up first on the scaffold, and his wife immediately following came up to him, and saluted each ear with a kiss, and then his mouth. Her husband desired her not to be in the least manner dismayed at his sufferings: and so for a while they parted, she using these words 'Farewell my dearest, be of good comfort, I am nothing dismayed.' And then the doctor began to speak these words:

Dr. Bastwick. There are many that are this day spectators of our standing here, as delinquents, though not delinquents, we bless God for it. I am not conscious to myself wherein I have committed the least trespass, (to take this outward shame) either against my God, or my King. And I do the rather speak it, that you that are now beholders may take notice how far innocency will preserve you in such a day as this is; for we come here in the strength of our God, who hath mightily supported us, and filled our hearts with greater comfort than our shame or contempt can be. The first occasion of my trouble was by the prelates, for writing a book against the Pope, and the Pope of Canterbury said I wrote against him, and therefore questioned me: but if the presses were as open to us as formerly they have been, we would shatter his Kingdom about his ears. But be ye not deterred by their power, neither be affrighted at our sufferings; let none determine to turn from the ways of the Lord, but go on, fight courageously against Gog and Magog. I know there be many here who have set many days apart for our behalf, (let the prelates take notice of it) and they have sent up strong prayers to Heaven for us, we feel the strength and benefit of them at this time; I would have you to take notice of it, we have felt the strength and benefit of your prayers all along this cause. In a word, so far I am from base fear, or caring for anything that they can do, or cast upon me, that had I as much blood as would swell the Thames, I would shed it every drop in this cause; therefore be not any of you discouraged, be not daunted at their power; ever labouring to preserve innocency, and keep peace within, go on in the strength of your God, and He will never fail you in such a day as this. As I said before, so I say again, had I as many lives as I have hairs on my head, or drops of blood in my veins, I would give them all up for this cause. This plot of sending us to those remote places, was first consulted and agitated by the Jesuits, as I can make it plainly appear. O see what times we are fallen into, that the lords must sit to act the Jesuits' plots! For our own parts, we own no malice to the persons of any of the prelates, but would lay our necks under their feet to do them good as they are men, but against the usurpation of their power, as they are bishops, we do profess ourselves enemies till Doomsday.

Mr. Prynne shaking the doctor by the hand, desired him that he might speak a word or two. 'With all my heart,' said the doctor.

*   *   *

Mr. Prynne.[4] You all at this present see there be no degrees of men exempted from suffering: Here is a reverend divine for the soul, a physician for the body, and a lawyer for the estate.

I had thought they would have let alone their own society, and not have meddled with any of them. And the next, for aught I know, may be a bishop. You see they spare none of what society or calling soever, none are exempted that cross their own ends. Gentlemen, look to yourselves; if all the martyrs that suffered in Queen Mary's days are accounted and called schismatical heretics and factious fellows; what shall we look for!

[The Archbishop of Canterbury being informed by his spies what Mr. Prynne said, moved the lords then sitting in the Star Chamber, that he might be gagged, and have some further censure presently executed upon him; but that motion did not succeed.]

Yet so they are called in a book lately come forth under authority. And such factious fellows are we, for discovering a Plot of Popery. Alas, poor England, what will become of thee, if thou look not the sooner into thine own privileges, and maintainest not thine own lawful liberty? Christian people, I beseech you all, stand firm, and be zealous for the cause of God, and His true religion, to the shedding of your dearest blood, otherwise you will bring yourselves, and all your posterities, into perpetual bondage and slavery.

Now the executioner being come to sear him, and cut off his ears, Mr. Prynne spake these words to him. 'Come, friend, come, burn me, cut me, I fear not. I have learned to fear the fire of hell, and not what man can do unto me. Come sear me, sear me, I shall bear in my body the marks of the Lord Jesus.' Which the executioner performed with extraordinary cruelty, heating his iron twice to burn one cheek: and cut one of his ears so close, that he cut off a piece of his cheek. He said, 'The more I am beaten down, the more am I lift up.'

Upon the day for execution, Mr. Burton being brought into the Palace Yard, unto a chamber that looked into the yard, where he viewed three pillories there set up: 'Methinks,' said he, 'I see Mount Calvary, where the three crosses, one for Christ, and the other two for the two thieves were pitched. And if Christ were numbered among thieves, shall a Christian, for Christ's cause, think much to be numbered among rogues, such as we are condemned to be? Surely, if I be a rogue, I am Christ's rogue, and no man's.' And a little after, looking out at the casement towards the pillory, he said, 'I see no difference between looking out of this square window and yonder round hole.' Pointing towards the pillory, he said, 'It is no matter of difference to an honest man' And a little after that, looking somewhat wishfully upon his wife, to see how she did take it, she seemed to him to be something sad; to whom he thus spake. 'Wife, why art thou so sad?' To whom she made answer, 'Sweetheart, I am not sad.' 'No?' said he, 'See thou be not, for I would not have thee to dishonour the day, by shedding one tear, or fetching one sigh; for behold there, for thy comfort, my triumphant chariot, on which I must ride for the honour of my Lord and Master: and never was wedding day so welcome and joyful a day as this day is; and so much the more, because I have such a noble Captain and Leader, who hath gone before me with such undauntedness of spirit, that He saith of Himself, "I gave my back to the smiters, my cheeks to the nippers, they plucked off the hair, I hid not my face from shame and spitting, for the Lord God will help me, therefore shall I not be confounded. Therefore have I set my face like a flint, and I know I shall not be ashamed." ' At length being carried toward the pillory, he met Dr. Bastwick at the foot of the pillory, where they lovingly saluted and embraced each other; and parting a little from him, he returned and most affectionately embraced him the second time, being heartily sorry he missed Mr. Prynne, who was not yet come, before he was gone up to his pillory, which stood alone next the Star Chamber, and about half a stone's cast from the other double pillory, wherein the other two stood; so as all their faces looked southward, the bright sun all the while, for the space of two hours, shining upon them. Being ready to be put into the pillory, standing upon the scaffold, he spied Mr. Prynne new come to the pillory, and Dr. Bastwick in the pillory, who then hasted off his band, and called for a handkerchief, saying, 'What! shall I be last, or shall I be ashamed of a pillory for Christ, who was not ashamed of a cross for me?' Then being put into the pillory, he said, 'Good people, I am brought hither to be a spectacle to the world, to angels and men; and howsoever I stand here to undergo the punishment of a rogue, yet except to be a faithful servant to Christ, and a loyal subject to the King, be the property of a rogue, I am no rogue. But yet if to be Christ's faithful servant, and the King's loyal subject, deserve the punishment of a rogue, I glory in it, and I bless my God, my conscience is clear, and is not stained with the guilt of any such crime as I have been charged with, though otherwise I confess myself to be a man subject to many frailties and human infirmities. Indeed that book entitled, *An Apology of an Appeal, with sundry Epistles and two Sermons, for God and the King*, charged against me in the information, I have and do acknowledge, the misprinting excepted, to be mine, and will by God's grace never disclaim it whilst I have breath within me.' After a while, he having a nosegay in his hand, a bee came and pitched on the nosegay, and began to suck the flowers, which he beholding, and well observing, said, 'Do ye not see this poor bee? she hath found out this very place to suck sweetness from these flowers; and cannot I suck sweetness in this very place from Christ?' The bee sucking all this while, and so took her flight. By and by, he took occasion from the shining of the sun, to say, 'You see how the sun shines upon us, but that shines as well upon the evil as the good, upon the just and unjust, but that the Sun of Righteousness, Jesus Christ, who hath healing under His wings, shines upon the souls and consciences of every true believer only, and no cloud can hide Him from us, to make Him ashamed of us, no not of our most shameful sufferings for His sake. And why should we be ashamed to suffer for His sake who hath suffered for us? All our sufferings be but fleabitings to that He endured. He endured the cross and despised the shame, and is set on the right hand of God. He is a most excellent pattern for us to look upon, that treading His steps, and suffering with Him, we may be glorified with Him. And what can we suffer, wherein He hath not gone before us even in the same kind? Was He not degraded, when they scornfully put on Him a purple robe, a reed into His hand, a thorny crown upon His head, saluting Him with, "Hail King of the Jews!" and so disrobed Him again? Was not He deprived when they smote the shepherd, and the sheep was scattered? Was not violence offered to His sacred person, when He was buffeted and scourged, His hands and His feet pierced, His head pricked with thorns, His side gored with a spear, &c.? Was not the cross more shameful, yea and more painful than a pillory? Was not He stripped of all He had, when He was left stark naked upon the cross, the soldiers dividing His garments, and casting lots upon His vesture? And was He not confined to perpetual close imprisonment in man's imagination, when His body was laid in a tomb, and the tomb sealed, lest He should break prison, or His disciples steal Him away? And yet did He not rise again, and thereby brought deliverance and victory to us all, so as we are more than conquerors through Him that loved us? Here then we have an excellent pattern indeed.'

One said unto Mr. Burton, 'Christ will not be ashamed of you at the last day.' He replied, he knew whom he had believed, and that Christ was able to keep that he had committed to Him against that day. One asked him how he did? He said, 'Never better, I bless God, who hath accounted me worthy thus to suffer.' The keeper keeping off the people from pressing near the pillory; he said, 'Let them come and spare not, that they may learn to suffer.' The same keeper being weary, and sitting down, asked Mr. Burton if he were well, and bad him be of good comfort. To whom he replied, 'Are you well? If you be well, I am much more, and full of comfort, I bless God.' Some asked him if the pillory were not uneasy for his neck and shoulders? He answered, 'How can Christ's yoke be uneasy? This is Christ's yoke, and He bears the heavier end of it, and I the lighter; and if mine were too heavy, He would bear that too. O good people, Christ is a good and sweet master, and worth the suffering for! And if the world did but know His goodness and had tasted of His sweetness, all would come and be His servants; and did they but know what a blessed thing it were to bear His yoke, O who would not bear it?' The keeper going about to ease the pillory by putting a stone or a brickbat between, Mr. Burton said, 'Trouble not yourself, I am at very good ease, and feel no weariness at all.' And espying a young man at the foot of the pillory, and perceiving him to look pale on him, he said, 'Son, son, what is the matter you look so pale? I have as much comfort as my heart can hold, and if I had need of more, I should have it.' One asked him a while after if he would drink some *aqua vitae*. To whom he replied, that he needed it not; 'For I have,' said he, (laying his hand upon his breast,) 'the true Water of Life, which like a well doth spring up to eternal life.' Pausing a while he said with a most cheerful and grave countenance, 'I was never in such a pulpit before, but little do ye know,' (speaking to them that stood about him) 'what fruits God is able to produce from this dry tree.' They looking steadfastly upon him, he said, 'Mark my words, and remember them well. I say, little do you know what fruits God is able to produce from this dry tree; I say, remember it well, for this day will never be forgotten; and through these holes,' (pointing to the pillory) 'God can bring light to His Church.' The keeper going about again to mend the pillory, he said, 'Do not trouble yourself so much. But indeed we are the troublers of the world.' By and by, some of them offering him a cup of wine; he thanked them, telling them he had the wine of consolation within him, and the joys of Christ in possession, which the world could not take away from him, neither could it give them unto him. Then he looked towards the other pillory, and making a sign with his hand, cheerfully called to Dr. Bastwick, and Mr. Prynne, asking them how they did? Who answered, 'Very well.' A woman said unto him, 'Sir, every Christian is not worthy of this honour, which the Lord hath cast upon you this day.' 'Alas,' said he, 'Who is worthy of the least mercy, but it is His gracious favour and free gift, to account us worthy in the behalf of Christ to suffer anything for His sake?' Another woman said, 'There are many hundreds which by God's assistance would willingly suffer for the cause you suffer for this day.' To whom he said, 'Christ exalts all of us that are ready to suffer afflictions for His name with meekness and patience; but Christ's military discipline in the use of His spiritual warfare, in point of suffering, is quite forgotten, and we have in a manner lost the power of religion, in not denying ourselves, and following Christ as well in suffering as in doing.' After a while Mr. Burton calling to one of his friends for a handkerchief, returned it again, saying, 'It is hot, but Christ bore the burden in the heat of the day; let us always labour to approve ourselves to God in all things, and unto Christ, for therein stands our happiness, come of it what will in this world.'

One said to Mr. Burton, 'The Lord strengthen you.' To whom he replied, 'I thank you, and I bless His name He strengthens me. For though I am a poor sinful wretch, yet I bless God for my innocent conscience in any such crime as is laid against me; and were not my cause good, and my conscience sound, I could not enjoy so much unspeakable comfort in this my suffering, as I do, I bless my God.' Mrs. Burton sending commendation to him by a friend: he returned the like to her, saying, 'Commend my love to my wife, and tell her I am heartily cheerful, and bid her remember what I said to her in the morning; namely, that she should not blemish the glory of this day with one tear, or so much as one sigh.' She returned answer, that she was glad to hear him so cheerful, and that she was more cheerful of this day than of her wedding day. This answer exceedingly rejoiced his heart, who thereupon blessed God for her, and said of her, 'She is but a young soldier of Christ's, but she hath already endured many a sharp brunt, but the Lord will strengthen her unto the end.' And he having on a pair of new gloves, showed them to his friends thereabout him, saying, 'My wife yesterday of her own accord bought me these wedding gloves, for this is my wedding day.'

One said to him, 'Sir, by this sermon, your suffering, God may convert many unto Him.' He answered, 'God is able to do it indeed.' And then he called again to Dr. Bastwick and Mr. Prynne, asking them how they did; who answered as before. Some speaking to him concerning that suffering of shedding his blood, he answered, 'What is my blood to Christ's blood? Christ's blood is a purging blood, but mine is corrupted and polluted with sin.' One friend asked another standing near Mr. Burton, if there should be anything more done unto him? Mr. Burton overhearing him answered, 'Why should there be no more done? For what God will have done must be accomplished.' One desired Mr. Burton to be of good cheer. He thus replied, 'If you knew my cheer, you would be glad to be partaker with me; for I am not alone, neither hath God left me alone in all my sufferings and close imprisonment since first I was apprehended.' The halberd-men standing round about, one of them had an old rusty halberd, the iron whereof was tacked to the staff with an old crooked nail; which one observing, and saying, 'What an old rusty halberd is that!' Mr. Burton said, 'This seems to me to be one of those halberds which accompanied Judas when he went to betray and apprehend his Master.' Mr. Burton said again, 'I am persuaded that Christ my Advocate is now pleading my cause at the Father's right hand, and will judge my cause, though none be found here to plead it, and will bring forth my righteousness as the light at noonday, and clear my innocency in due time.' A friend asked Mr. Burton, if he would have been without this particular suffering? To whom he said, 'No, not for a world.' Moreover, he said that his conscience in the discharge of his ministerial duty and function, in admonishing his people to beware of the creeping in of Popery and superstition, exhorting them to stick close unto God and the King in duties of obedience, was that which first occasioned his sufferings; and he said, 'As for this truth I have preached, I am ready to seal it with my blood, for this is my crown both here and hereafter. I am jealous of God's honour, and the Lord keep us that we may do nothing that may dishonour Him, either in doing or suffering; God can bring light out of darkness, and glory out of shame. And what shall I say more? I am like a bottle which is so full of liquor, that it cannot run out freely; so I am so full of joy, that I am not able to express it.'

In conclusion, some told him of the approach of the executioner, and prayed God to strengthen him. He said, 'I trust He will. Why should I fear to follow my Master, Christ, who said, "I gave my back to the smiters, and my cheek to the nippers that plucked off my hair; I hid not my face from shame and spitting, for the Lord God will help me, therefore shall I not be confounded; therefore have I set my face like a flint, and I know that I shall not be ashamed." '

When the executioner had cut off one ear, which he had cut deep and close to the head in an extraordinary cruel manner; yet he never once moved and stirred for it, though he had cut an artery, so as the blood ran streaming down upon the scaffold, which divers persons standing about the pillory seeing, dipped their handkerchiefs in, as a thing most precious, the people giving a mournful shout, and crying for the surgeon, whom the crowd and other impediments for a time kept off, so that he could not come to stop the blood; he all the while held up his hands, said, 'Be content, it is well, blessed be God.' The other ear being cut no less deep, he then was freed from the pillory, and came down, where the surgeon waiting for him, presently applied remedy for stopping the blood after a large effusion thereof, yet for all this he fainted not in the least manner, though through expense of much blood he waxed pale. And one offering him a little wormwood-water, he said, 'It needs not;' yet through importunity he only tasted of it, and no more, saying, his Master, Christ, was not so well used, 'For they gave Him gall and vinegar, but you give me good strong water to refresh me, blessed be God.' His head being bound up, two friends led him away to an house provided him in King Street, where being set down, and bid to speak little, yet he said after a pause, 'This is too hot to hold long.' Now lest they in the room, or his wife should mistake, and think he spake of himself concerning his pain, he said, 'I speak not this of myself; for that which I have suffered is nothing to that my Saviour suffered for me, who had His hands and feet nailed to the cross.' And lying still awhile, he took Mr. Prynne's sufferings much to heart, and asked the people how he did, 'For,' said he, 'his sufferings have been great.' He asked also how Dr. Bastwick did, with much compassion and grief, that himself, being the first that was executed, could not stay to see how they two fared after him.

Soon after the execution of the sentence, they were severally sent prisoners to the respective castles of Caernarvon, Launceston in Cornwall, and Lancaster, and afterwards on the 27th of August following, it was ordered by the King and Council, that Dr. Bastwick should be removed to the castle or fort of the Isles of Scilly, Mr. Burton to the Isle of Guernsey, and Mr. Prynne to which of the two castles of the Isle of Jersey the Governor should think fit; and that none be admitted to have conference with them, or to have access to them, but whom the captains of the said castles or their deputies should appoint; they not to be allowed pen, paper, or ink, nor any books, but the Bible and Common-Prayer book, and other books of devotion, consonant to the doctrine and discipline of the Church of England; no letters or writings to be brought them, but what shall be opened, nor any to be sent from them: that the wives of Bastwick and Burton should not land or abide in any of the said islands, and if they did, they should be detained in prison till further order from the board; and the conductors of the said three prisoners, either by sea or land, to suffer none but themselves to speak to them in their passage. Accordingly they were sent to the said three islands, where they remained till the beginning of the Long Parliament 1641, when upon their respective petitions they were sent for up, discharged and restored.

Chapter six

Richard Baxter (1685)

Not all reporting of trials is impartial and this account of Richard Baxter's trial for seditious libel in 1685 is drawn principally from the versions of those who looked forward with enthusiasm to the downfall of the presiding judge, Lord Chief Justice Jeffreys.

Richard Baxter (1615–91), though ordained a clergyman of the Church of England, emerged in the years following the Restoration as one of the most eminent and respected leaders of English Nonconformity. The Act of Ejectment in 1662 had made it impossible that Baxter and his followers should remain within the Church of England. For the next twenty-five years he was both persecuted and prosecuted for his activities as a preacher and writer. The book which brought him before Jeffreys was his *Paraphrase on the New Testament,* in which he attacked the character and conduct of bishops, according to the indictment which included, among others, the following passages from the book.[1]

> Are not these Preachers and Prelates then the least and basest that preach and tread down Christian love of all that dissent from any of their presumptions, and so preach down not the least but the great command?
>
> Let not those proud hypocrites deceive you who by their long liturgies, and ceremonies, and claim of superiority, do but cloak their worldliness, pride and oppression, and are religious to their greater damnation.
>
> To be dissenters and disputants against errors and tyrannical impositions upon conscience is no fault but a great duty.

According to the Crown, such passages amounted to an

attack upon the bishops of the Church of England. In John Taylor's case, in 1676, Chief Justice Hale had ruled that blasphemy and attacks on established religion were a political crime, since they threatened the security of the state. Hence, Baxter was charged with seditious libel, and offered as his defence that the only bishops attacked were bishops of the Church of Rome. He protested that the indictment strained the meaning of his words to make innocent statements appear seditious.

The account of the trial is less remarkable for the persecution of Baxter than for the performance of Jeffreys. The coarse, bullying repartee, remembered by his enemies after such cases as Baxter's and the treason trials of the Duke of Monmouth's rebellion, earned him the reputation of a bloodthirsty clown. He was said to have been a heavy drinker and, if the present account of Baxter's trial is correct, drink or mental unbalance might explain his conduct.

Yet Jeffreys has traditionally been at the mercy of the most partisan Whig historians. John Tutchin was one of the first to attack him after the Monmouth rebellion, while Bishop Burnet laid twice the number of deaths to Jeffreys's charge as actually occurred, according to the official figures. He was no better served by Victorian Whigs like Macaulay. It is only in our own time that the balance has been corrected by such books as P. J. Helm, *Judge Jeffreys* (1966), and G. W. Keeton, *Lord Chancellor Jeffreys and the Stuart Cause* (1965). There is certainly a case for thinking that Jeffreys was less of an ogre or buffoon, and a better Lord Chancellor than his legend allows. The legend true or false, is the creation of such documents as the present account of Richard Baxter's trial.

Proceedings against RICHARD BAXTER, Clerk, for a seditious Libel, at Guildhall, before Lord Chief Justice Jeffreys: 1 JAMES II. A.D. 1685.

On the 28th of February, 1685, Mr. Baxter was committed to the King's Bench Prison by the Lord Chief Justice Jeffreys's warrant, for his *Paraphrase on the New Testament*, printed a little before, which was called a scandalous and seditious book against the government. On the 6th of May, which was the first day of term, he appeared in Westminster Hall, and an information was ordered to be drawn up against him. May 14th he pleaded not guilty to the information. May 15th, he, being much indisposed, moved by his counsel that he might have farther time given him for his trial. But it was denied him, and Jeffreys cries out in a passion, 'I will not give him a minute's time more to save his life. We have had,' says he, 'to do with other sort of persons, but now we have a saint to deal with; and I know how to deal with saints as well as sinners. Yonder,' says he, 'stands Oates in the pillory,' as he actually did at that very time in the New Palace Yard, 'and he says he suffers for the truth, and so says Baxter. But if Baxter did but stand on the other side of the pillory with him, I would say two of the greatest rogues and rascals in the Kingdom stood there.' On May 30th, in the afternoon, he was brought to his trial before the Lord Chief Justice Jeffreys at Guildhall. Sir Henry Ashurst, who could not forsake his own and his father's friends, stood by him all the while. Mr. Baxter came first into court, and with all the marks of serenity and composure, waited for the coming of the Lord Chief Justice, who appeared quickly after with great indignation in his face. He no sooner sat down than a short cause was called and tried; after which the Clerk began to read the title of another cause. 'You blockhead you,' says Jeffreys, 'The next cause is between Richard Baxter and the King.' Upon which, Mr. Baxter's cause was called. The passages mentioned in the information were his paraphrase on Matthew v, 19; Mark ix, 39; Mark xi, 31; Mark xii, 38, 39, 40; Luke x, 2; John xi, 57, and Acts xv, 2. These passages were picked out by Sir Roger L'Estrange[2] and some of his companions: and a certain noted clergyman, who shall be nameless, put into the hands of his enemies some accusations out of Romans xiii, &c. as against the King, to touch his life, but no use was made of them. The great charge was, 'That in these several passages he reflected on the prelates of the Church of England, and so was guilty of sedition &c.' The King's counsel opened the information at large with its aggravations. Mr. Wallop, Mr. Williams, Mr. Rotheram, Mr. Atwood, and Mr. Phipps, were Mr. Baxter's counsel, and had been feed by Sir Henry Ashurst.

Mr. Wallop said that he conceived, the matter depending being a point of doctrine, it ought to be referred to the bishop his ordinary; but if not, he humbly conceived the doctrine was innocent and justifiable, setting aside the *Innuendoes*, for which there was no colour, there being no antecedent to refer them to, that is, no bishop or clergy of the Church of England named. He said the book accused, *i.e.* the comment on the New Testament, contained many eternal truths, but they who drew the information were the libellers, in applying to the prelates of the Church of England those severe things which were written concerning some prelates, who deserved the character he gave. 'My lord,' says he, 'I humbly conceive the bishops Mr. Baxter speaks of, as your lordship if you have read church history must confess, were the plagues of the Church and the world.' 'Mr. Wallop,' says the Lord Chief Justice, 'I observe you are in all these dirty causes; and were it not for you, gentlemen of the long robe, who should have more wit and honesty than to support and hold up these factious knaves by the chin, we should not be at the pass we are at.'—'My lord,' says Mr. Wallop, 'I humbly conceive that the passages accused are natural deductions from the text.'—'You humbly conceive,' says Jeffreys, 'and I humbly conceive. Swear him, swear him.'—'My lord,' saith he, 'under favour, I am counsel for the defendant, and if I understand either Latin or English, the information now brought against Mr. Baxter upon so slight a ground is a greater reflection upon the Church of England than anything contained in the book he is accused for.' Says Jeffreys to him, 'Sometimes you humbly conceive, and sometimes you are very positive. You talk of your skill in church history, and of your understanding Latin and English. I think I understand something of them as well as you but, in short, must tell you that if you do not understand your duty better, I shall teach it you.' Upon which Mr. Wallop sat down.

Mr. Rotheram urged that if Mr. Baxter's book had sharp reflections upon the Church of Rome by name, but spake well of the prelates of the Church of England, it was to be presumed that the sharp reflections were intended only against the prelates of the Church of Rome. The Lord Chief Justice said Baxter was an enemy to the name and thing, the office and persons of bishops.—Rotheram added that Mr. Baxter frequently attended Divine Service, went to the Sacrament, and persuaded others to do so too, as was certainly and publicly known, and had, in the very book so charged, spoken very moderately and honourably of the bishops of the Church of England.—Mr. Baxter added, 'My lord, I have been so moderate with respect to the Church of England, that I have incurred the censure of many of the dissenters upon that account.'—'Baxter for bishops!' saith Jeffreys, 'That is a merry conceit indeed! Turn to it, turn to it.'—Upon this Rotheram turned to a place, where it is said that great respect is due to those truly called to be bishops among us; or to that purpose.—'Ay,' says Jeffreys, 'This is your Presbyterian cant, "Truly called to be bishops." That is himself, and such rascals called to be bishops of Kidderminster, and other such like places; bishops set apart by such factious, snivelling Presbyterians as himself.

[After the Restoration, Baxter had been offered by Lord Chancellor Clarendon the Bishopric of Hereford, which he refused, alleging in a letter his reasons of conscience, and he only requested permission to continue his ministry at Kidderminster, which was not granted.]

'A Kidderminster bishop he means, according to the saying of a late learned author, and every parish shall maintain a Tithe-pig Metropolitan.' Mr. Baxter beginning to speak again, saith Jeffreys to him, 'Richard, Richard, dost thou think we will hear thee poison the court? Richard, thou art an old fellow, an old knave. Thou hast written books enough to load a cart. Every one is as full of sedition —I might say treason—as an egg is full of meat. Hadst thou been whipped out of thy writing trade forty years ago, it had been happy. Thou pretendest to be a preacher of the gospel of peace, and thou hast one foot in the grave. It is time for thee to begin to think what account thou intendest to give. But leave thee to thyself, and I see thou wilt go on as thou hast begun, but by the grace of God I'll look after thee. I know thou hast a mighty party, and I see a great many of the brotherhood in corners, waiting to see what will become

of their mighty Don, and a doctor of the party,' looking to Doctor
Bates, 'at your elbow. But by the grace of Almighty God, I will
crush you all.'

Mr. Rotheram sitting down, Mr. Atwood began to show that not
one of the passages mentioned in the information ought to be
strained to that sense, which was put upon them by the innuendoes,
they being more natural when taken in a milder sense. Nor could
any one of them be applied to the prelates of the Church of England,
without a very forced construction. To evidence this, he would have
read some of the text, but Jeffreys cried out, 'You shan't draw me
into a conventicle with your annotations, nor your snivelling
parson either.'

'My lord,' says Mr. Atwood, 'I conceive this to be expressly within
Rosewall's case, lately before your lordship.'—'You conceive,'
saith Jeffreys, 'You conceive amiss: it is not.'—'My lord,' saith
Atwood, 'that I may use the best authority, permit me to repeat
your lordship's own words in that case.'—'No, you shan't,' says he,
'You need not speak, for you are an author already, though you
speak and write impertinently.'—Says Atwood, 'I cannot help that,
my lord, if my talent be no better, but it is my duty to do my best
for my client.'—Jeffreys thereupon went on, inveighing against
what Atwood had published, and Atwood justified it to be in defence of the English constitution, declaring that he never disowned
anything he had written. Jeffreys several times ordered him to sit
down, but he still went on. 'My lord,' says he, 'I have matters of law
to offer for my client,' and he proceeded to cite several cases,
wherein it had been adjudged that words ought to be taken in the
milder sense, and not in the strained, by innuendoes. 'Well,' says
Jeffreys when he had done, 'you have had your say.'

Mr. Williams and Mr. Phipps said nothing, for they saw it was
to no purpose. At length says Mr. Baxter himself, 'My lord, I think
I can clearly answer all that is laid to my charge, and I shall do it
briefly. The sum is contained in these few papers, to which I shall
add a little by testimony.'—But he would not hear a word.—At
length the Chief Justice summed up the matter in a long and ful-
some harangue.

' 'Tis notoriously known,' says he, 'there has been a design to
ruin the King and nation. The old game has been renewed, and
this has been the main incendiary. He is as modest now as can be,
but time was when no man was so ready at, "Bind your kings in

3 *Strike but Hear* (1774). John Horne defending himself at the Bar of the House of Commons, as he defended himself against Thurlow three years later.

4 *The State Cotillon* (1773). Lord Chief Justice Mansfield is shown in the centre of the dance, trampling on Magna Carta.

chains and your nobles in fetters of iron," and, "To your tents, O Israel!" Gentlemen, for God's sake, don't let us be gulled twice in an age, &c.'—And when he concluded, he told the jury that if they in their conscience believed he meant the bishops and clergy of the Church of England, in the passages which the information referred to, they must find him guilty—and he could mean no men else—if not, they must find him not guilty.

When he had done, says Mr. Baxter to him, 'Does your lordship think any jury will pretend to pass a verdict upon me upon such a trial?'—'I'll warrant you, Mr. Baxter,' says he, 'Don't you trouble yourself about that.'

The jury immediately laid their heads together at the bar, and found him guilty.

As Mr. Baxter was going from the bar, he told the Lord Chief Justice, who had so loaded him with reproaches and yet continued them, that a predecessor of his—meaning Sir Matthew Hale—had other thoughts of him. Upon which the judge replied that there was not an honest man in England but what took him for a great knave.

He had subpoenaed several clergymen, who had appeared in court, but were of no use to him, through the violence of the Chief Justice.

The trial being over, Sir Henry Ashurst led Mr. Baxter through the crowd, 'I mention it to his honour,' says Bishop Kennet, and conveyed him away in his coach. On June 29th following, he had judgment given against him. He was fined five hundred marks, to lie in prison till he paid it and be bound to his good behaviour for seven years.

Mr. Baxter afterwards obtained the King's pardon, by the mediation of the Lord Powis. His fine was remitted, and on Wednesday, November 24th, Sir Samuel Astry sent his warrant to the Keeper of the King's Bench Prison to discharge him. But he gave sureties for his good behaviour, His Majesty declaring, for his satisfaction, that it should not in him be interpreted a breach of the good behaviour for him to reside in London, which was not allowable according to the Oxford Act. And this was entered upon his bail-bond. Notwithstanding this, he continued some time after in the rules, and on February 28th following, removed to a house he took in Charterhouse Yard, where he preached to a separate congregation without interruption as long as he lived, his death happening after the Revolution, viz. December 8th, 1691.

Chapter seven

Edmund Curll (1727)

The case of the publisher Edmund Curll marks a new stage in the history of English morals. Curll, who was born in 1675 and died in 1747, is denounced by Pope in the second book of the *Dunciad*, while his purveying of 'rubbish' is referred to by Swift in the verses 'On the Death of Dr. Swift'. As a pirate, Curll was the unauthorized publisher of some of Pope's letters and, in general, of any material which he felt would stimulate public curiosity. In one of its forms, Pope's revenge was to oblige Curll to drink half a pint of wine laced with an emetic, which provoked Curll to publish a pamphlet complaining of an attempt to poison him. Curll combined pornography with piracy, hence Pope's ironic reference in the *Duciad*, I, 40, to 'Curll's chaste Press'. Much of Curll's output was, in fact, extremely feeble and only the unremitting gullibility of his customers can have brought them back to buy yet more of his works on hermaphrodites or flagellation, let alone his *School of Venus*, which had no more than its title in common with the seventeenth-century best-seller.

However, Curll's case is interesting as the first successful major prosecution for obscenity, though not, as is sometimes said, the first successful case at any level. At Guildhall Sessions, for instance, as far back as 1683, John Wickens was fined forty shillings for publishing *The Whore's Rhetorick*. At the Sessions for April and May 1688, Benjamin Crayle, *alias* Carle, was fined twenty shillings for selling the *School of Venus* (a translation of Michel Millot's *L'Escole des Filles*, 1655), while Joseph Streater was fined forty shillings for printing this book and *A Dialogue between a Married Lady and a Maid* (a translation of Nicolas Chorier's *L'Académie des Dames*, 1680). Both men were prosecuted again in 1689 for issuing *Sodom: or, The Quintessence of Debauchery*, attributed to the Earl of Rochester. The charge against Streater was apparently not proceeded with but Crayle was fined £20 at the Guildhall Quarter Sessions of January 1690 and committed to prison until the fine was paid. In July 1693, Elizabeth Latham was fined five marks and committed to prison at Guildhall Quarter Sessions for publishing another work attributed to Rochester, *Poems on Several Occasions by the E. of R.*

These may have been minor cases but they were an indication of the official attitude towards such literature. Indeed, though the first Society for the Reformation of Manners did not specifically concern itself with literature at its foundation in 1692, it is clear that hostility to obscene or indecent literature spread quickly with the advent of a new and literate middle class.

In 1698 the first major prosecution relating to an obscene publication was brought against Hill, a printer, in the Court of King's Bench for publishing *Poems on Several Occasions by the E of R*. This was, potentially, a case in which the legal question of obscene literature could be decided by the King's judges. But Hill absconded from justice and his case went by default. Then, as the report of Curll's case indicates, the prosecutions of James Read, Angell Carter, and John Marshall, in 1707, reached the Court of Queen's Bench. All three were charged with publishing obscene libels, in Marshall's case *Sodom* and *The School of Love* (another translation of Chorier); in the cases of Read and Carter a collection of fifteen poems, *The Fifteen Plagues of a Maidenhead*. The Court decided that they had committed no crime with which it could deal and, indeed, that the only body competent to deal with the defendants would be an ecclesiastical court. Moreover, the judges insisted that the word 'libel' must imply defamation of a person. It was to be pointed out in Curll's case that it was simply a translation of *libellus*, a book.

Whether or not Read and his co-defendants had committed an offence against the law, there was no doubt that such publications as theirs offended the moral susceptibilities of a growing number of people. Even in the light of what had happened at Guildhall Sessions in the 1680s and 1690s they were lucky to be acquitted. The legal definition of obscene literature as tending to deprave or corrupt its readers was not pronounced until the Hicklin case of 1868 but the deleterious influence of such literature was a well-established maxim of literary criticism even before the eighteenth century.

Curll was prosecuted for the publication of two books, neither of them particularly new. His own edition of Meibomius, *De Usu Flagrorum* had been published in 1718, seven years before the charges were brought. *Venus in the Cloister: or, The Nun in her Smock* (1724) was a translation of Jean Barrin's *Vénus dans le Cloître, ou la Religieuse en Chemise* (1683). The anomaly in this case is that the book had first been published in English in 1683 and was listed in the *Term Catalogue* for Easter that year. No action was taken against it until Curll's edition of 1724.

Curll was, of course, the most obvious target in his time for this type of prosecution, but just as his literary rivals had scores to settle with him over his pirating of their works, so the government had a political grudge to work off. During the course of his trial, Curll published the *Memoirs of John Ker*, a government spy in the reign of Queen Anne, whose political revelations were apparently unwelcome to those in power in the 1720s. Curll was fined fifty marks for publishing his pornography but the more dangerous sentence of the pillory was for publishing Ker's *Memoirs*.

Curll was a rogue, and not a particularly lovable one. He was prosecuted at a time when immorality in literature was inevitably about to come within the scope of the law. The Attorney-General's argument that the case was analogous to that of Sir Charles Sedley and his friends who had removed their breeches and insulted the crowd, in the reign of Charles II, may seem far-fetched, but it was persuasive enough in an age of new middle-class and female readership. Indeed, despite its popular image as a rumbustious age, the eighteenth century, in its literature, was to be much more the century of Samuel Richardson than even of Laurence Sterne or Henry Fielding. As Richardson wrote in 1741, the time had come when it was a moral duty to 'decry such Novels and Romances, as have a Tendency to inflame and corrupt.'[1] Given this atmosphere, it would have taken more than legal precedents, or the lack of them, to save Edmund Curll.

The Case of EDMUND CURLL, Bookseller, in the King's Bench, for publishing a Libel: 1 GEORGE II. A.D. 1727.

[Probably the notorious bookseller. As to whom see the *Dunciad*, II, 58 ff.]

Michaelmas Term. 1 George II.

DOMINUS REX *v.* EDMUND CURLL

Information exhibited by the Attorney-General against the Defendant, Edmund Curll, for that he 'existens homo iniquus et sceleratus, ac nequiter machinans et intendens bonos mores subditorum hujus regni corrumpere et eos ad nequitiam inducere, quendam turpem iniquum et obscoenum libellum, intitulat Venus in the Cloister, or, The Nun in her Smock, impie et nequiter impressit et publicavit, ac imprimi et publicari causavit' [*being an injurious and profane man, and wickedly devising and intending to corrupt the morals of the subjects of this Kingdom and incite them to wickedness, did print and publish, and cause to be printed and published an injurious and obscene book, entitled . . .*], setting forth the several lewd passages 'in malum exemplum' [*to the evil example*], &c. and of this the defendant was found guilty.

And in Trinity Term last, it was moved in arrest of judgment by Mr. Marsh, that however the defendant may be punishable for this in the Spiritual Court as an offence 'contra bonos mores', yet it cannot be a libel for which he is punishable in the Temporal Court. *Libellus* is a diminutive of the word *liber*, and it is *libellus* from its being a book, and not from the matter of its contents. In the Case *De Libellis Famosis*, my Lord Coke says, that it must be against the public, or some private person, to be a libel, and I do not remember ever to have heard this opinion contradicted. Whatever tends to corrupt the morals of the people, ought to be censured in the Spiritual Court, to which properly all such causes belong. What their proceedings are I am a stranger to. But for me it is sufficient to say,

I do not find any case, wherein they were ever prohibited in such a cause. In the reign of King Charles II, there was a filthy run of obscene writings, for which we meet with no prosecution in the Temporal Courts; and since these were things not fit to go unpunished, it is to be supposed that my lords the bishops animadverted upon them in their courts. In the case of the Queen *v.* Read, there was an information for a libel in writing an obscene book, called, *The Fifteen Plagues of a Maidenhead*; and after conviction, it was moved in arrest of judgment, that this was not punishable in the Temporal Courts; and the opinion of Chief Justice Holt was so strong with the objection, that the prosecutor never thought fit to stir it again.

Attorney-General. I do not observe it is pretended there is any other way of punishing the defendant. For if the Spiritual Court had done it, instances might be given; and it is no argument to say, we meet with no prohibitions: such a way of argument would construe them into all sorts of jurisdictions. What I insist upon is, that this is an offence at common law, as it tends to corrupt the morals of the King's subjects, and is against the peace of the King. Peace includes good order and government, and that peace may be broken in many instances without an actual force. 1. If it be an act against the constitution or civil government. 2. If it be against religion. And, 3. If against morality.

1. Under the first head, fall all the cases of seditious words or writings.

2. It is a libel, if it reflects upon religion, that great basis of civil government and liberty; and it may be both a spiritual and temporal offence. In Tremayne's Entries, 226, there is a sentence to have a paper fixed upon the defendant's head, intimating, that he had uttered blasphemous words, tending to the subversion of government. There is one Hall now in custody on a conviction as for a libel, intituled, *A sober Reply to the merry Argument about the Trinity*. And [*Easter Term*] 10 Anne Regina *v.* Clendon, there was a special verdict on a libel about the Trinity, and it was not made a doubt of in that case.

3. As to morality. Destroying the peace of the government; for government is no more than public order, which is

morality. My Lord Chief Justice Holt used to say, Christianity is part of the law. And why not morality too? I do not insist that every immoral act is indictable, such as telling a lie, or the like. But if it is destructive of morality in general; if it does, or may, affect all the King's subjects, it then is an offence of a public nature. And upon this distinction it is, that particular acts of fornication are not punishable in the Temporal Courts, and bawdy houses are. In Sir Charles Sedley's case it was said, that this Court is the *custos morum* of the King's subjects, and upon this foundation there have been many prosecutions against the players for obscene plays, though they have had interest enough to get the proceedings stayed before judgment.

[Sir Charles Sedley was indicted at common law for several misdemeanours against the King's peace, and which were to the great scandal of Christianity; and the cause was, for that he showed his naked body in a balcony in Covent Garden to a great multitude of people, and there did such things, and spoke such words, &c. mentioning some particulars of his misbehaviour, as throwing down bottles (pissed in) *vi et armis* among the people, Keble's *Reports*, I, 620. Fortescue's *Reports*, 99, 100. And this indictment was openly read to him in court; and the justices told him, that notwithstanding there was not then any Star Chamber, yet they would have him know, that the Court of King's Bench was the *custos morum* of all the King's subjects; and that it was then high time to punish such profane actions, committed against all modesty, which were as frequent, as if not only Christianity, but morality also had been neglected. After he had been kept in court by recognisance from Trinity term to the end of Michaelmas term, the Court required him to take his trial at bar: but being advised, he submitted himself to the Court, and confessed the indictment, 15 Charles II, 1663. The Michaelmas term following, the Court considered what judgment to give; and inasmuch as he was a gentleman of a very ancient family, in Kent, and his estate encumbered, not intending his ruin, but his reformation, they fined him only 2,000 marks, and to be imprisoned a week without bail, and to be of good behaviour for three years.

Wood, *Athenae Oxoniensis* p. 1100 reports, with evident incorrectness however, the case of Sir Charles Sedley, as follows:

'In the month of June, 1663, this our author, Sir Charles Sedley, Charles Lord Buckhurst, afterwards Earl of Middlesex,' (more commonly mentioned by his title of Earl of Dorset) 'Sir Thomas Ogle, &c. were at a cook's house at the sign of the Cock in Bow Street, near Covent Garden, within the liberty of Westminster, and being inflamed with strong liquors, they went into the balcony belonging to that house, and putting down their breeches they excrementised in the street: which being done, Sedley stripped himself naked, and with eloquence preached blasphemy to the people; whereupon a riot being raised, the people became very clamorous, and would have forced the door next the street open; but being hindered, the preacher and his company were pelted into their room, and the windows belonging thereunto were broken. This frolic being soon spread abroad, especially by the fanatical party, who aggravated it to the utmost, by making it the most scandalous thing in nature, and nothing more reproachful to religion than that; the said company were summoned to the court of justice in Westminster Hall, where being indicted of a riot before Sir Robert Hyde, Lord Chief Justice of the Common Pleas were all fined, Sir Charles being fined five hundred pounds.'

After relating the insolent and shameless behaviour of Sedley in court, Wood concludes thus:

'The day for payment being appointed, Sir Charles desired Mr. Henry Killigrew, and another gentleman, to apply themselves to His Majesty to get it off; but instead of that, they begged the said sum of His Majesty, and would not abate Sir Charles twopence of the money.'

'Mark,' exlaims Johnson, in his *Life of Dorset*, 'the friendship of the dissolute!'

Sir John Reresby in his Memoirs (A.D. 1675-7) indicates that at that period persons of the highest rank and station were in the habit of begging from the Crown the estates of persons accused of forfeitable offences in anticipation of their conviction: and from his account it seems likely, that false accusations of the most atrocious offences were fabricated in the hope of obtaining such forfeitures. The historians and the records of Scotland, bear ample testimony to the prevalance of practices of this sort in that Kingdom, during the reigns of Charles II and James II.

By statute 21 James I cap. 3, it is declared and enacted, that all commissions, grants, &c. theretofore made or granted, of any grant or promise of the benefit, profit or commodity, of any forfeiture, penalty or sum of money, that is or shall be due by any statute before judgment thereupon had, are altogether contrary to the laws of this realm, in no wise to be put in execution. What was said by the judges in the case of penal statutes will readily be believed; that in their experience such grants made the more violent and undue proceeding against the subject, to the scandal of justice, and offence of many. 'Therefore,' says Lord Coke (*Institutes*, III, 187) 'such beggars are offenders worthy of severe punishment:' and to 'These hunters for blood' he applies the exclamation of Micah, 'They all lie in wait for blood, and every man hunteth his brother to death.' (Our translation says, 'with a net'.)]

Michaelmas 10 William III, Rex *v.* Hill, the defendant was indicted for printing some obscene poems of my Lord Rochester's, tending to the corruption of youth; upon which he went abroad, and was outlawed; which he would not have done, if his counsel had thought it no libel. The Spiritual Courts punish only personal spiritual defamation by words; if it is reduced to writing, it is a temporal offence, and it is punishable as a libel. My Lord Coke in the case *De Libellis Famosis*, had nothing in view but scandalous, defamatory libels. *Libellus* is not always to be taken as a technical word; in this case it may stand as an obscene little book. And as to the case of Read, there was no judgment, but it went off upon the Chief Justice's saying, 'Why don't you go to the Spiritual Court?' Which was giving a false reason for that sudden opinion.

[In the case of the Queen against Read, it was held that a crime that shakes religion as profaneness on the stage, (as to this, see statute 3 James I c. 21) &c. is indictable; but writing an obscene book is not indictable; but punishable only in the Spiritual Court.

This case of the Queen *v.* Read (Fortescue 98,) was an indictment for printing a lascivious and obscene libel, entitled *The Fifteen Plagues of a Maidenhead*. The defendant was tried before Lord Chief Justice Holt, and convicted: and upon motion in arrest of judgment, it appears, that judgment was given by the whole Court for the defendant. And by Holt, C.J. 'There are ecclesiastical courts: why may not this be punished there? If we have no precedent we cannot punish. Show me any precedent.' Powell, J. 'This is for printing bawdy stuff, that reflects on no person: and a libel must be against some particular person or persons, or against the government. It is stuff not fit to be mentioned publicly. If there is no remedy in the Spiritual Court, it does not follow there must be a remedy here. There is no law to punish it: I wish there were; but we cannot make law. It indeed tends to the corruption of good manners, but that is not sufficient for us to punish. As to the case of Sir Charles Sedley, there was something more in that case than showing his naked body in the balcony; for that case was *quod vi et armis* he pissed down upon the people's heads.' And he cited Lady Purbeck's case, which was in the Star Chamber, where they 'quashed the indictment because it was for matters of bawdry.' Holt. 'Who is libelled here? This may be said to be a temptation to incontinence; and therefore why not punishable in the ecclesiastical court? this tends to bawdry, as well as soliciting of chastity; but they do it only to get money.'

Lord Fortescue, at the end of his Report, mentions this case of the King and Curll, 'which' he says 'was an indictment for printing and publishing a libel called, *The Nun in her Smock*; which contained several bawdy expressions, but did contain no libel against any person whatsoever: the Court gave judgment against the defendant, but contrary to my opinion; and I quoted this case. And, indeed, I thought it rather to be published, on purpose to expose the

Romish priests, the father confessors, and Popish religion.'
But since this case of the King *v.* Curll, the Court of
King's Bench without hesitation exercises jurisdiction over
such publications, and over other offences *contra bonos mores*,
which are not attended with breach of the peace.

Upon an attempt (2 George II,) to move an arrest of
judgment in the case of Woolston, who was convicted on four
informations, for his blasphemous *Discourses on the miracles
of our Saviour*, the Court declared they would not suffer it
to be debated, whether to write against Christianity in
general, was not an offence punishable in the Temporal
Courts at common law: it having been settled so to be, in
Taylor's case. And in the case of King *v.* Hall. They desired
it might be taken notice of, that they laid their stress upon
the word 'general' and did not intend to include disputes
between learned men, upon particular controverted points.

In the case of the King against Sir Francis Blake Delaval,
and others, which was a prosecution for a conspiracy to
transfer a female infant apprentice for the purpose of
prostitution, Lord Mansfield said: 'I remember a cause in
the Court of Chancery, wherein it appeared, that a man
had formally[2] assigned his wife over to another man: and
Lord Hardwicke directed a prosecution for that transaction,
as being notoriously and grossly against public decency and
good manners. And so is the present case.—It is true, that
many offences of the incontinent kind fall properly under
the jurisdiction of the ecclesiastical court, and are
appropriated to it. But if you except those appropriated
cases, this Court (King's Bench) is the *custos morum* of the
people, and has the superintendency of offences *contra bonos
mores*: and upon this ground both Sir Charles Sedley and
Curll, who had been guilty of offences against good manners,
were prosecuted here.']

Now it appears there is no instance of the Spiritual Court's inter-
meddling where it is reduced to writing, or in print.

Chief Justice Raymond. I think this is a case of very great
consequence; though, if it was not for the case of the Queen *v.*
Read, I should make no great difficulty in it. Certainly the
Spiritual Court has nothing to do with it, if in writing. And if

it reflects on religion, virtue or morality; if it tends to disturb the civil order of society, I think it is a temporal offence. I do not think *libellus* is always to be taken as a technical word. Would not trover lie 'de quodam libello intitulat the New Testament', and does not the Spiritual Court proceed upon a libel?

Fortescue, J. I own this is a great offence; but I know of no law by which we can punish it. Common law is common usage, and where there is no law there can be no transgression. At common law, drunkenness, or cursing and swearing, were not punishable; and yet I do not find the Spiritual Court took notice of them. This is but a general solicitation of chastity, and not indictable. Lady Purbeck's case was for procuring men and women to meet at her house, and held not indictable, unless there had been particular facts to make it a bawdy-house. To make it indictable there should be a breach of the peace, or something tending to it, of which there is nothing in this case. A libel is a technical word at common law; and I must own the case of the Queen *v.* Read sticks with me, for there was a rule to arrest the judgment *nisi.* And in Sir Charles Sedley's case there was a force, of throwing out bottles upon the people's heads.

Reynolds, J. It is much to be lamented, if this is not punishable. I agree there may be many instances, where acts of immorality are of spiritual cognizance only; but then those are particular acts, where the prosecution is *pro salute animae* of the offender, and not where they are of a general immoral tendency; which I take to be a reasonable distinction. Read's case is indeed a case in point: but I confess I should not have been of that opinion. *Libellus* does not *ex vi terminis* import defamation, but is to be governed by the epithet, which is added to it. This is surely worse than Sir Charles Sedley's case, who only exposed himself to the people then present, (naked,) who might choose whether they would look upon him or not; whereas this book goes all over the Kingdom. Drunkenness and swearing were punishable in the Spiritual Court, before the acts which made them temporal offences, and in which the jurisdiction of the Spiritual Court is saved.

Probyn, J. inclined this to be punishable at common law, as an offence against the peace, intending to weaken the bonds of civil society, virtue, and morality.

But it being a case of great consequence, it was ordered to stand over for a further argument.

And this term *Page, J.* came into the King's Bench, in the room of Justice Fortescue. It was to have been spoke to by Mr. Solicitor-General and myself. But Curll not having attended me[3] in time, I acquainted the Court I was not prepared; and as my want of being ready proceeded from his own neglect, they refused to indulge him to the next term. And in two or three days, they gave it as their unanimous opinion, that this was a temporal offence. They said, it was plain the force used in Sedley's case was but a small ingredient in the judgment of the Court, who fined him 2,000 marks, and if the force was all they went upon, there was no occasion to talk of the Court's being *censor morum* of the King's subjects. They said, if Read's case was to be adjudged, they should rule it otherwise: and therefore, in this case, they gave judgment for the King. And the defendant was afterwards set in the pillory, as he well deserved.

This Edmund Curll stood in the pillory at Charing Cross, but was not pelted, or used ill; for being an artful, cunning, though wicked, fellow, he had contrived to have printed papers dispersed all about Charing Cross, telling the people, he stood there for vindicating the memory of Queen Anne; which had such an effect on the mob, that it would have been dangerous even to have spoken against him: and when he was taken down out of the pillory, the mob carried him off, as it were in triumph, to a neighbouring tavern.

Chapter eight

Henry Sampson Woodfall (1770)

On 19 December 1769 there appeared in the *Public Advertiser*, a paper printed and published by Henry Sampson Woodfall, the most famous of the letters of Junius: the 'Letter to the King'. This was published almost simultaneously by George Robinson in the *Independent Chronicle*; by Henry Baldwin in the *St James Chronicle*, and by John Miller in the *London Evening Post*. On 1 January 1770 the letter was reprinted in the *London Museum of Politics, Miscellanies, and Literature*. The publishers of the three newspapers were prosecuted for seditious libel, as was John Almon who had sold the *London Museum*. The cases ended with varying results. The prosecutions against Baldwin and Robinson were dropped at an early stage and it was only Woodfall, Miller, and Almon who faced trial on the Attorney-General's *ex officio* information. The presiding judge in each case was Lord Chief Justice Mansfield, regarded as the enemy of the opposition press and the advocate of stern measures to be taken against those who sought to use the freedom of unlicensed printing for purposes of political subversion. In 1784, in the Dean of St Asaph's case, he summarized his view on the permissible extent of political press freedom.[1]

> To be free is to live under a government by law. The *liberty of the press* consists in printing without any previous licence, subject to the consequences of law. The *licentiousness* of the press is *Pandora*'s box, the source of every evil.

Mansfield may appear as the dominating, cajoling figure in the trials but an even more important figure was missing: that of Junius himself. The identity of Junius was unknown and has never been conclusively established. His letters were variously attributed to Wilkes, Burke, Gibbon, Chatham, and Shelburne.

Yet the favourite candidate has been Sir Philip Francis, who had been a clerk in both the War Office and the Office of the Secretary of State, two areas of experience reflected in the letters. Moreover the silences of Junius coincided with the absences of Francis from London. On the other hand, Woodfall emphatically denied that Francis was the author. In 1816 John Taylor supported the identification with Francis in his *Identity of Junius*, and after the death of Francis the identification was strengthened for Thomas Creevey by a conversation with Lord Erskine in 1821.[2]

> Before dinner, we had some conversation upon the old
> story whether Francis was Junius, Grey and Erskine both
> expressing their most perfect conviction that he was.
> Erskine mentioned a curious thing, which was confirmed
> by Lord Thanet. It seems they were both dining with Lady
> Francis, since Sir Philip's death, when Erskine asked her
> if Francis ever told her, or whether she ever collected
> from his conversation, that he was the author of Junius. To
> which she answered that he had never mentioned the
> subject, and that the only allusion to it was in a book. So
> she went out of the room, and brought back the little book
> 'Junius Identified', and in the title page was written
> 'Francis', and signed with his name—'I leave this book as
> a legacy to my dear wife.' This I think, considering he never
> would touch the subject or the book of 'Junius Identified',
> affords an additional strong presumption it was he.

Junius's attacks had begun in the *Public Advertiser* in 1769 and among his first targets was the prime minister, the Duke of Grafton. On 29 November Junius denounced him, by no means for the first time, after a prosecution had been brought against Vaughan for trying to buy an office of the Crown, which Grafton had no objection to selling to others.

> By laying in a moderate stock of reputation, you
> undoubtedly meant to provide for the future necessities
> of your character, that with an honourable resistance
> upon record, you might safely indulge your genius, and
> yield to a favourite inclination with security. But you
> have discovered your purposes too soon; and, instead of the

modest reserve of virtue, have shown us the termagant chastity of a prude, who gratifies her passions with distinction, and prosecutes one lover for a rape, while she solicits the lewd embraces of another.

When Grafton fell from power, Junius commented on 14 February 1770, 'The condition you are reduced to would disarm a private enemy of his resentment, and leave no consolation to the most vindictive spirit, but that such an object as you are would disgrace the dignity of revenge.'

The attacks on Grafton passed without any attempt at prosecution but Junius's 'Letter to the King' could hardly be ignored. In fact, it was directed to the king only by innuendo, being entitled 'Letter to the ****'. In the letter itself 'king' appears as 'k—g'; 'House of Commons' as 'H— of C—'; 'England' as 'E–gl—d', and so on. Yet the meaning and purpose of the letter are clear enough from the following extracts.

Your subjects, sir, wish for nothing but that as they are reasonable and affectionate enough to separate your person from your government, so you in your turn should distinguish between the conduct which becomes the permanent dignity of a k—g, and that which serves only to promote the temporary interest and miserable ambition of a minister.

But if the English people should no longer confine their resentment to a submissive representation of their wrongs; if following the glorious example of their ancestors, they should no longer appeal to the creature of the constitution, but to that high Being who gave them the rights of humanity, whose gifts it were sacrilege to surrender, let me ask you, sir, upon what part of your subjects would you rely for assistance?

The people of I—l—d have been uniformly plundered and oppressed. In return, they give you every day fresh marks of their resentment. They despise the miserable governor you have sent them, because he is the creature of Lord Bute; nor is it from any natural confusion in their ideas that they are so ready to confound the original of a k—g with the disgraceful representation of him.

The distance of the colonies would make it impossible

for them to take an active interest in your affairs, if they
were as well affected to your government as they once
pretended to be to your person. . . . They consider you as
united with your servants against A—r—a, and know how
to distinguish the s—n and a venal p—t on one side, from
the real sentiments of the English people on the other. . . .
They left their native land in search of freedom, and found
it in a desert Divided as they are into a thousand forms
of policy and religion, there is one point in which they all
agree: they equally detest the pageantry of a k—g, and
the supercilious hypocrisy of a bishop.

The name of Stuart of itself, is only contemptible;—armed
with the sovereign authority, their principles are
formidable. The prince who imitates their conduct should
be warned by their example; and while he plumes himself
upon the security of his title to the Crown, should remember
that as it was acquired by one revolution, it may be
lost by another.

The charges of seditious libel brought against Woodfall
and the other defendants were not sanctioned by any grand
jury. The Attorney-General, William de Grey, exercised his
right to lay *ex officio* informations against them. To many
publishers in the eighteenth and nineteenth centuries this
seemed an intolerable abuse of power, since the Attorney-
General held a political appointment and might use *ex officio*
informations to intimidate or bankrupt the opposition press,
even without necessarily bringing all the cases to trial. Moreover,
cases of seditious libel were among those for which the Attorney-
General, until 1825, had the right to request a special jury,
chosen from a list of special jurors whose qualifications, in
terms of wealth or social rank, were greater than those of
ordinary jurors. Publishers accused of seditious libel naturally
objected to this, on the grounds that such special juries were the
most likely to condemn the accused of acting against the
political *status quo*. Special jurors were a select group and there
was considerable alarm in 1817 when it was revealed that they
had had to act with injudicious frequency. In the previous
year, 100 special jurors of the City of London had tried 274
cases between them. Forty of them had been summoned more

than twenty times, and another fifty of them more than ten times. A few had made a regular guinea a week as special jurors.

Until the Libel Act of 1792 jurors in such cases as Woodfall's were allowed to decide only on the two questions of fact: whether the defendant had published the alleged libel, and whether the 'innuendoes' (the Crown's interpretation of the meaning of passages cited) in the indictment were correct. So if Woodfall was the publisher and such blanks as 'k—g' or 'p—t' meant 'king' and parliament', he was guilty. It was then up to the defence to move in arrest of judgment on the grounds that the publication was not seditious, and that question of law would be decided by the King's Bench judges. Not even special juries were content to have their powers curtailed in this way and they were increasingly inclined to return verdicts, as in Woodfall's case, which were far from unqualified convictions and which would, therefore, require either a new trial or the acquittal of the defendant.

In the Junius prosecutions John Almon was tried first, on 2 June 1770. Though he had merely sold copies of the *London Museum* containing the 'Letter to the King', he was convicted, fined ten marks, and required to provide sureties for his good behaviour for two years. His counsel moved unsuccessfully for a new trial. In Woodfall's case, on 13 June, the jury returned its doubtful verdict, and on 18 July a third jury acquitted John Miller. There was a formal attempt to put Woodfall on trial again, though the Crown offered no evidence. It is said that at the first trial, when the copy of the *Public Advertiser* containing the libel was passed to the jury, the foreman of the jury, who was sympathetic to Woodfall, unobtrusively pocketed the paper. The Attorney-General was unable to offer evidence at a second trial because, without the paper, he could no longer offer technical proof of publication.

The account of Woodfall's trial reprinted here is taken from the *London Museum*, itself the subject of a prosecution for re-printing Junius's letter. It is far from being an impartial account though it remains a good example of trial reporting as political propaganda, a weapon used increasingly by the radical press and culminating in the reports of the trials of men like William Hone in 1817 or Richard Carlile in 1819. By that time, defendants and spectators had turned the trials themselves into political events to such an extent that even the most factual report was potential propaganda.

The case of HENRY SAMPSON WOODFALL, on an Information filed by the Attorney-General for publishing Junius's Letter to the King: 10 GEORGE III. A.D. 1770. (*London Museum*).

[The report here given is the fullest which I have seen of this trial. I have therefore inserted it, notwithstanding the flippancy and partiality of its manner.]

13 June

This day came on at Guildhall, before Lord Chief Justice Mansfield, the trial of an information filed by Mr. Attorney-General *ex officio*, against Henry Sampson Woodfall, for printing and publishing a letter signed 'Junius', in the *Public Advertiser* of the 19th of December 1769.

Only seven of the Special Jury attended, as follows:

William Bond, of Walbrook.
Peter Cazalet, Swithin's Lane.
Alexander Peter Allan, Mark Lane.
Frederick Cumerell, Mincing Lane.
Haman Meyer, ditto.
John Thomas, ditto.
Barnington Buggin, Philpot Lane.

To which were added the following five talesmen:[3]

William Halyard.
Paul Varges, carpenter, Distaff Lane.
William Sibley.
William Willet, plasterer, Distaff Lane.
William Davis.

After Mr. Walker had opened the cause by reading the letter signed 'Junius,' &c. with the innuendoes of the information,

Mr. Attorney-General (De Grey) began, exactly at ten o'clock, by saying that nothing had ever raised a juster indignation in the mind of every man who wishes the continuance of our excellent constitution, than this letter of Junius. He then addressed himself to the passions and interest of the jurors, by telling them that they were more than any other men concerned to bring such offenders to justice, because anything that tended to public confusion was more especially fatal to commerce, and to those who hazard large fortunes in trade. He said that this letter of Junius tended to public confusion. He then harangued with great seeming zeal on the glorious liberty of the press, which he acknowledged ought to be encouraged and exercised, as far as could possibly consist with the very being of society. But he said that the abuse of the liberty of the press is more fatal than any other, and therefore entreated them not to suffer that liberty, intended for our salvation, to be turned to sedition, to our perdition. He said the jury would be instructed from the bench,—that is,—a—a—he must believe they would be instructed from the bench, that the only two things for their consideration were

1. Whether the blanks in the printed paper were fairly filled up in the information: and

2. Whether there were sufficient evidence for the publication of the paper by Woodfall.

Mr. Attorney-General then said he thought it proper to explain his own conduct, because he was not merely an advocate in these matters but officially answerable. This Letter of Junius, he assured the jury, had given universal offence. He had therefore in hand six other prosecutions of different publishers for the same offence. He thought it his duty to prosecute them, and had therefore demanded the names of the publishers because he, Mr. Attorney-General, does not read newspapers. In the objects of prosecution he endeavoured to make a distinction and to pass by those who were poor or had large families of children, &c. He declared upon his honour, as a man, that he had no motive to urge him against any particular publisher but merely the execution of his office. That he could have wished to have tried Mr. What's-His-Name?—Woodfall, ay, Mr. Woodfall, the original publisher, first. Because as for who was the author of Junius, that he could by no means discover, that remained an impenetrable secret.

After this defence of himself, Mr. Attorney-General returned again to the cause in hand, by repeating to the jury that if, first, the blanks in the *Public Advertiser* were fairly filled up by the innuendoes of the information; and if, secondly, the publication was proved, the jury must find Mr. Woodfall guilty.

Crowder, the first witness, was then called at twenty minutes after ten, and examined by Mr. Thurlow, Solicitor-General.

Crowder deposed, that it is his office and employment to buy up the publications of every day for the Treasury. On Almon's trial, the same witness, Crowder, called himself an assistant to the Messenger of the Press. That he bought the *Public Advertiser* in question of one Colford, whom he supposes to be Mr. Woodfall's man. He bought it in Mr. Woodfall's publishing room. He bought twelve of them. He had bought the *Public Advertiser* every day at Mr. Woodfall's for a year past.

The Letter of Junius was then read from the paper.

The second witness, Robert Harris, was sworn, and examined by Mr. Morton. He said he was the register of the stamps.[4] He produced his book, in which the newspaper of each day is kept, for an account of the advertisements which are paid for. He said the account for the *Public Advertiser* is kept in the name of Mr. Woodfall: that receipts are made out to him: that his servant generally attends monthly to settle accounts for the duty on the advertisements in that paper, but that sometimes Mr. Woodfall had attended in person.

The third witness (*Lee*) was sworn and examined by Mr. Wallace. He said he was a servant to Sir John Fielding: that he had often carried advertisements from his master to Mr. Woodfall, had sometimes seen Mr. Woodfall and delivered them to him, but very rarely: that he had one receipt for advertisements in the *Public Advertiser*, signed by Mr. Woodfall.

Here ended the evidence and pleading on the side of the prosecution.

Mr. Serjeant Glynn said he agreed with Mr. Attorney-General as to the excellence of a London jury, and doubted not the liberties of the people were sufficiently safe while there were trials by jury. He told the jury that if they were of opinion that the sense put upon Junius's Letter in the information was the true sense; if it was clear that it was a false, scandalous, and seditious libel; if they thought his client published it with a professed intention, a premeditated design, of abusing and aspersing the King; if the defendant meant or wished to alienate the affections of His Majesty's subjects; if it appeared to them that his end in printing it was to stir up rebellion and commotion; as honest men they ought, and undoubtedly would, bring his client in guilty. But if, on the contrary, the temper of the times was such that the people needed that kind of information contained in the letter; if the facts could be proved; if the acts of government in which the King, as a part of government, was necessarily and virtually concerned, highly demanded public reprehension; and the printer published it with the truly laudable motive of informing his fellow-subjects; if, so far from containing any personal abuse of the King, it was written with an honest but guarded freedom; the author and publisher would, by all worthy, all sensible men, be considered as having acted the parts of good subjects and good citizens. He informed the jury that the counsel for the Crown had not gone upon the subject-matter of the Letter. They did not even attempt to prove it a libel, notwithstanding the epithets bestowed upon it in the information; and that the paper in which it was first printed was not by any means set apart solely to canvass for party or faction but was equally open to all. He admitted that private personal abuse was wrong but the public acts of government often demanded public scrutiny; that many, very many of the highest rank, as well as from the highest to the lowest in the opposition, had been scandalously traduced and vilified in the public papers with impunity; that if the defendant was brought in guilty, the hands of every publisher would be tied and the gentlemen not in office might, by the ministerial scribblers, be abused to the grossest degree, as it would be dangerous to answer them if, upon the appearance of every free answer, informations were to be filed and the printers convicted and punished. The liberty of the press was immediately concerned. The stroke was levelled at it in this prosecution, but he did not doubt the jury would maturely, deliberately, and attentively consider the matter, read over the Letter with care and circumspection; and if they found it was not written with intent to vilify the person of the King, but freely to canvass the acts of government, they would consider the publisher as having done his fellow-subjects essential service, and acquit him.

Mr. Lee, the other counsel for the defendant, then got up, and began with observing that after the very learned and able speech made by Mr. Serjeant Glynn, little remained for him to say, but he particularly urged the jury to consider the intention of the printer in publishing it, and to remember how peculiarly necessary it was, at this juncture, that the press should be open to all political discussion. He defended the paper on the same principles as Mr. Glynn, and made a very eloquent and judicious harangue, concluding with declaring that as no intention could be proved, they ought not to find his client guilty.

Mr. Attorney-General affected a kind of surprise. He said the counsel for the defendant had stated points of law to the jury; that he believed he had a right to reply, notwithstanding they had not examined witnesses; and he believed so, he said, because they had stated points of law which he did not allow.

Lord Mansfield told him that, as Attorney-General, he might reply, notwithstanding the defendant had not examined witnesses: that the Solicitor-General, indeed, or any other counsel, could not, but that the Attorney-General might.

Mr. Attorney-General doubted about his right to reply; said, however, he believed he had a right; but that he would not be particular, that he would not reply—yet all the while he still kept making a reply, such as it was—at length finished with saying, 'The bench will reply on those points to the defendant's counsel, and instruct the jury properly.'

Mr. Attorney-General was not mistaken in his former belief and in his latter declaration of what the bench would do and say, for Lord Mansfield then gave his charge to the jury according to Mr. Attorney-General's anticipation.

Lord Mansfield told the jury that there were only two points on which they were sworn to give their verdict.

[The following is the report of Lord Mansfield's direction to the jury, given in the preface to Mr. G. Woodfall's edition of Junius.

'Lord Mansfield, in his charge, told the jury that there were only two points for their consideration: the first the printing and publishing the paper in question, the second the sense and meaning of it: that as to the charges of its being malicious, seditious &c. they were inferences in law about which no evidence need be given, any more than that part of an indictment need be proved by evidence which charges a man with being moved by the instigation of the devil: that therefore the printing and sense of the paper were alone what the jury had to consider of, and that if the paper should really contain no breach of the law, that was a matter which might afterwards be moved in arrest of judgment. That he had no evidence to sum up to them, as the defendant's counsel admitted the printing and publication to be well proved. That as to the sense, they had not called in doubt the manner in which the dashes in the paper were filled up in the record, by giving any other sense to the passages. If they had, the jury would have been to consider which application was the true one, that charged in the information or suggested by the defendant. That the jury might now compare the paper with the information. That if they did not find the application wrong, they must find the defendant guilty, and if they did find it wrong, they must acquit him. That this was not the time for alleviation or aggravation, that being for future consideration. That every subject was under the control of the law, and had a right to expect from it protection for his person, his property, and his good name. That if any man offended the laws, he was amenable to them, and was not to be censured or punished but in a legal course. That any person libelled had a right either to bring a civil or a criminal prosecution. That in the latter, which is by information or indictment, it is immaterial whether the publication be false or true. That it is no defence to say it is true, because it is a breach of the peace, and therefore criminal, but in a civil prosecution it is a defence to say the charges in the publication are true, because the plaintiff there sues only for a pecuniary satisfaction to himself, and that this is the distinction as to that nature of defence. His lordship said he was afraid it was too true that few characters in the Kingdom escaped libels. That many were very injuriously treated, and, if so, that the best way to prevent it was by an application to the law, which is open to every man. That the liberty of the press consisted in every man having the power to publish his sentiments without first applying for a licence to anyone, but if any man published what was against law, he did it at his peril and was answerable for it in the same manner as he who suffers his hand to commit an assault or his tongue to utter blasphemy.']

There were only two points on which, according to their oath, they must determine. That as for the intention, the malice, sedition, or any other still harder words, which might be given in informations for libels, whether public or private, they were mere formal words, mere words of course, mere inference of law, with which the jury were not to concern themselves; that they were words which signify nothing, just as when it is said in bills of indictment for murder, 'instigated by the devil,' &c., that the two points mentioned were the only things for the consideration of the jury.

[In the 'Letter from Candour to the *Public Advertiser*,' it is mentioned that in the trial of the printers of the *North Briton*, No. 45, in 1764, Lord Mansfield in a very masterly manner interrupted the counsel and informed them, and afterwards in an elaborate discourse clearly instructed the jury, that the words in the information, charging the paper to have been published with the most wicked intent, in order to excite His Majesty's dutiful subjects to sedition, and charging it to be a false, scandalous, and seditious libel, were words of course, like 'corrupt' in an indictment for perjury, or like those in an indictment for murder, charging the murder to have been committed at the instigation of the devil, and that the jury ought not to regard them at all. The author of the letter, after making this statement, and comparing the language so ascribed to Lord Mansfield with that of [*Lord Chief Justice*] Jeffreys in the case of Sir Samuel Barnardiston [*1684*], remarks upon the concurrence of the two chief justices not only in sentiment but in expression.[5]]

That if there was indeed nothing criminal in Junius's Letter, the verdict of guilty would do no harm, would be attended with no consequences. The Court would consider of that, the Court were the only judges of that. If that is made appear to the Court, the Court will arrest judgment. He said, 'My brother Glynn has admitted that the truth or falsehood of a libel, whether public or private, however prosecuted, is out of the question.'

At this assertion of Lord Mansfield every man in court was shocked. Serjeant Glynn was astonished, and on application made to him instantly by several of the counsel and his friends to contradict Lord Mansfield's assertion, Mr. Glynn with that honest diffidence natural to him, asked them, 'Good God! Did I admit anything like what Lord Mansfield says? Did I, by any incorrectness in the expression, or by any mistake, use words that could be so misunderstood or misinterpreted?' Every gentleman near him assured him that he had not. Whereupon, Serjeant Glynn rose, and very modestly assured his lordship that he had never admitted what his lordship supposed. Lord Mansfield begged Mr. Glynn's pardon, and turned it off with great dexterity, just saying slightly, 'Oh! I find I was mistaken. Well then, my brother Glynn is of a different opinion.' And then instantly proceeded: 'As you have been told these are the only two points for your decision; if, indeed, you think that the blanks in Junius's Letter can have another application than that put upon them by the information, that is a matter for your judgment: but you must observe that even the counsel for the defendant have not pretended to put any other meaning to the blanks. If you think the evidence for the publication not sufficient, that is likewise a matter for your consideration, but you must observe that even the counsel for the defendant have admitted the publication.' Lord Mansfield then observed that the laws and proceedings in regard to libels were perfectly equal, equally advantageous to high and to low: for that the low might prosecute for a libel, if they were defamed, as well as the rich, and would be sure to have justice done them by the law. He said that it was not then the proper time for aggravation or alleviation, or consideration of the matter of the Letter, or of Mr. Woodfall's intention. To be sure, the Court would consider all that when they should come to pass sentence. 'As for the liberty of the press,' said he, 'I will tell you what that is. The liberty of the press is that a man may print what he pleases without a licenser. As long as it remains so, the liberty of the press is not restrained. It is the same thing as in all other actions. A man may use his arm, but he must not strike his neighbour. A man may use his tongue, but he must not speak blasphemy.' At the word 'blasphemy' so lugged in, there was a general whisper ran through the Court, for everyone perceived the aim of it, Mr. Wilkes sitting so very near the Chief Justice.

About twelve the jury withdrew. At half an hour after three Lord Mansfield began to whisper with Serjeant Davy, who had been out of court and returned, with the Attorney-General, with Mr. Wallace, and the other Crown lawyers. In the space of a quarter of an hour he sent three times to the jury to know if they were not agreed in their verdict. He said he would not sit longer than four, if the other business of the Court should be over. The jury not returning, Lord Mansfield proposed to Mr. Lee that he should sign an agreement with Mr. Attorney-General that the jury might give their verdict to Lord Mansfield privately at Lord Mansfield's house. After some time and persuasion from Lord Mansfield, Mr. Lee consented and signed such agreement. After which, Lord Mansfield pulled off his hat and said, 'Mr. Lee, you have done right to consent.' Lord Mansfield then adjourned the Court, and retired. The jury continued undetermined until near ten at night, when they agreed upon their verdict, and went in hackney coaches from Guildhall to Lord Mansfield's house in Bloomsbury Square, and gave their verdict in these words, 'Guilty of printing and publishing only.'

Lord Mansfield stood at his parlour door, and made the jury give their verdict in his hall where the footmen were, and when they had given it he withdrew, without saying a word.

Chapter nine

John Horne (1777)

Of all the defendants whose cases are recorded in *State Trials*, John Horne, *alias* John Horne Tooke, has perhaps the best claim to the title of advocate and jurist *manqué*. Born in 1736, he was educated at Westminster, Eton, and by private tutors. It says something for his inclination to argument that he lost the sight of one eye in a fight with a schoolfellow who happened to be armed with a knife. His record at St John's College, Cambridge, was distinguished and he entered the Inner Temple in 1756. But John Horne was destined for the Church and, despite his innate talent, was never called to the Bar.

He entered political controversy as a supporter of John Wilkes, publishing *The Petition of an Englishman* in 1765 and supporting Wilkes in the famous Middlesex election three years later. But another supporter of Wilkes, George Onslow, became a Lord of the Treasury in 1769 and in the *Public Advertiser* of 14 July 1769 Horne accused him of gaining 'a thousand pounds in a very common and usual manner', later specified as 'his interest for a certain lucrative post in America'. This emerged as an accusation that Onslow had sold the collectorship of taxes for Piscataway in New Hampshire. Onslow sued Horne for libel, the case being heard before Mr Justice Blackstone at Surrey Assizes in April 1770. Onslow claimed £10,000 in damages but was nonsuited because of an error in the indictment. The case was retried before Lord Mansfield at the next assizes but Onslow still lost on a technicality. His taste in fashionable lawyers to plead his case was said to have cost him £1,500 on this occasion. 'I know Mr Onslow perfectly,' wrote Junius, 'He is a false silly fellow. Depend upon it, he will get nothing but shame by contending with Horne.'

In 1769 Horne was involved in the foundation of the Society

for the Defence of the Bill of Rights, an organization stimulated into being by the government's treatment of Wilkes. Yet within a year or two Horne began to fear that this Society would never achieve any worthwhile political object, since it appeared to exist for no purpose but that of paying Wilkes's expenses. Wilkes had come well out of the *North Briton* affair while others, including the printer William Bingley, still remained in prison and in debt. To his credit, Horne supported Bingley against Wilkes, persuading the society to vote £500 to the printer's aid. Horne ended his alliance with Wilkes and attempted to dissolve the Society. The proposal was defeated by twenty-six votes to twenty-four, whereupon the minority withdrew and formed the Constitutional Society.

The rift between Horne and Wilkes lasted for some years. In 1771 Horne unsuccessfully supported Richard Oliver against Wilkes in the election for Sheriff of the City of London, drawing upon himself the anger of government and opposition alike. In the same year, by encouraging certain newspapers to publish parliamentary proceedings, he managed to involve Wilkes and the City of London in a legal battle with the House of Commons over the right to publish reports of parliamentary debates. Then Horne resigned his living and retired to Brentford to study law and philology.

This retirement was brief. One of his supporters, William Tooke, had an estate near Purley which was threatened by the Enclosure Bill of 1774, a problem which Horne dealt with by a violent attack in the *Public Advertiser* on Sir Fletcher Norton, Speaker of the House of Commons. Woodfall, the printer, and Horne were summoned to the Bar of the House, where Horne refused to give any material evidence and was finally discharged. The next year, with the outbreak of the War of Independence in America, Horne was active in the Constitutional Society, supporting the American colonists and accusing the British government and army of murder. On 7 June 1775 the Constitutional Society met at the King's Arms Tavern. After the meeting was over, Horne drew up an advertisement, which was to be the subject of the prosecution for seditious libel reprinted in this collection.

At a special meeting this day of several members of the Constitutional Society, during an adjournment, a gentleman proposed that a subscription should be immediately entered into by such of the members present who might approve the purpose, for raising the sum of 100*l.* to be applied to the relief of the widows, orphans, and aged parents of our beloved American fellow-subjects, who, faithful to the character of Englishmen, preferring death to slavery, were for that reason only inhumanly murdered by the King's troops at or near Lexington and Concord, in the province of Massachusetts, on the 19th of last April; which sum being immediately collected, it was thereupon resolved that Mr. Horne do pay tomorrow into the hands of Messrs. Brownes and Collinson, on account of Dr. Franklin, the said sum of 100*l.* and that Dr. Franklin be requested to apply the same to the above-mentioned purpose.

John Horne.

In 1775 Benjamin Franklin was still in England, fearing, as he said, that he would be 'taken up' if the New England colonists should come to blows with the British troops. Horne's advertisement appeared in the *Public Advertiser* of 9 June 1775 and in seven other periodicals, against whose publishers the Attorney-General laid *ex officio* informations. Convictions were obtained against those who printed and published the advertisement in the *Public Ledger*, the *St James Chronicle*, and the *London Chronicle*, but the energies of the Attorney-General, Sir Edward Thurlow, were concentrated against Horne himself. The case, like Woodfall's in 1770, was tried by a special jury on an *ex officio* information, two privileges of the Attorney-General which Horne found time to impugn during his defence. Like some radical publishers in the early nineteenth century, Horne was determined to defend himself and to treat both Lord Mansfield and Thurlow as if they were his opponents at the hustings. He bandied insults with Thurlow, while Thurlow sneered at political scribblers and insisted that neither a fine (which might be paid by subscription) nor imprisonment (which was little hardship to a man of sedentary occupation) could be a substitute for making Horne face his opponents through the pillory. At least one of Horne's political enemies disagreed. 'I hope they did not put the dog in the pillory for his libel,' said Samuel Johnson, 'He has too much literature for that.'

Lord Mansfield, like Thurlow, was one of Horne's targets, though no doubt some of Horne's indignation was stimulated by the sight of that former radical, John Wilkes, sitting on the bench with the judge. So Horne argued with Mansfield on points of law and imparted a due share of innuendo and insult. Under the existing system there could only have been one outcome to the case but Horne fought tenaciously.

It is some consolation to know that his time in the King's Bench prison was not unbearably arduous. He lived in a house within the prison rules and continued to meet his friends, some of them at a weekly dinner at the Dog and Duck. The trial of Huggins and the fate of Horne show that, inside prison no less than in the rest of eighteenth-century England, there was one law for the rich and another for the poor. When gaol fever threatened, Horne drank large quantities of claret, which saved him from the fever but left him prone to gout. During his imprisonment he published *A Letter to Dunning*, a discussion of legal points which soon became an examination of the rôle of prepositions and conjunctions in English grammar.

On his release, he acquired a small estate near Huntingdon and tried a number of experiments in agriculture but when these were unsuccessful he returned to London and lived in Dean Street with Mary and Charlotte Hart, his illegitimate daughters. It was at this time that he changed his name to John Horne Tooke, in expectation of becoming William Tooke's heir.

Horne Tooke's enthusiasm for philology led to the major literary work of his life, *ΕΠΕΑ ΠΤΕΡΟΕΝΤΑ* or, *The Diversions of Purley*, the first part of which appeared in 1786 and won him a considerable reputation as a pioneer in the study of Norse, Gothic, and Old English. Yet his political enthusiasm remained undiminished and, as a supporter of Pitt, he stood against Charles James Fox in the Westminster election of 1790. On losing by a substantial number of votes, he petitioned the House of Commons to declare the election invalid because of the riotous behaviour of the electorate. The petition failed and he was then successfully sued by Fox for the costs of the case.

In 1794 Horne Tooke was one of those tried for high treason, at a time when the government sought to suppress the

Corresponding Societies, for fear that they might introduce the doctrines and methods of revolutionary France into English politics. Like Thomas Hardy and the other defendants, Horne Tooke was acquitted. It is said that he deliberately engaged in conversation with a government spy to provoke a prosecution of himself, knowing that he would be acquitted and that his acquittal would be a victory against the government. If true, his conduct shows a remarkable lack of any sense of self-preservation, given the prevalent fear at that time of invasion from without and treason from within. As it happened, Horne Tooke approved of only one style of revolution, not the type which had occurred in France in 1789 but the English variety of a century earlier.

He stood as candidate for Westminster a second time in 1796, and lost again. In 1801, however, Lord Camelford gave him a seat for the rotten borough of Old Sarum. No sooner was Horne Tooke in Parliament than a Bill was passed by both Houses declaring that, for the future, the clergy would be ineligible for election. It was a short and hard-earned parliamentary career.

William Tooke died in 1802 but left Horne Tooke only £500, which led to prolonged litigation with no satisfactory results. In 1805, however, Horne Tooke published the second part of *The Diversions of Purley*, which was reputed to have earned him several thousand pounds. The remaining years, until his death in 1812, were spent in retirement, though his dinner parties, which were remarkable for their quantity of food as well as drink, remained a feature of his life. He had won drinking bouts against both Boswell and Richard Porson, Regius Professor of Greek at Cambridge, no small victory in the light of other stories about Porson, who was said, in a desperate moment, to have drunk the spirit for his landlady's lamps on finding nothing better available. Among Horne Tooke's other guests were Thomas Paine, Bentham, Coleridge, Thomas Erskine, and most improbably, Lord Thurlow, the Attorney-General who had prosecuted him in 1777.

Horne Tooke was not, like many radical publishers and pamphleteers of his time, a poor or self-educated man. Nor did he ever, like Wilkes, change from a leader of revolt to an upholder of established order. He failed to become a lawyer but he was often an impressive advocate. His ability to find a quarrel with political associates hardly diminished his reputation for conviviality. In the last years of the eighteenth century there were enough men ready to support either the constitution unaltered or a revolution on the French pattern. As usual, it was Horne Tooke's fortune to fall out with both parties. His aptitude seemed to be for whatever course of action ran contrary to his own best interest, yet in an age whose inhabitants are all too glibly docketed as eccentrics or exhibitionists, Horne Tooke was unquestionably an original.

Proceedings against JOHN HORNE, Clerk, on an Information in the King's Bench by the Attorney-General, for a Libel: 17 GEORGE III. A.D. 1777.

Friday 4 July 1777.

As soon as the court was opened, the special jury were called over: eleven only appearing, Mr. Attorney-General prayed a tales.[1] The box containing the names of the common jury standing open upon the table, the Associate took out a paper and, showing it to Mr. Horne, asked if he had any objection to that man's being sworn on the jury. Mr. Horne replied, 'I object to that name, and for this reason. I desire that the box may be shut and shaken, and when that is done I shall have no objection to any name.' The box was accordingly shut and shaken, and a name drawn out, but another of the special jury coming into court the talesman was not sworn.

The following special jury were sworn:
Joseph Dalmer, Cursitor Street, merchant.
Philip Bulkley, Fleet Street, druggist.
James Brant, Cheapside, silkman.
David Buffar, Cheapside, woollen draper.
William Watts, Fore Street, goldsmith.
Nathaniel Lucas, Fore Street, merchant.
William Abdy, Oat Lane, goldsmith.

Thomas Smith, Milk Street, merchant.
Thomas Brooks, Cateaton Street, linen draper.
M. Stanton, Aldermanbury, warehouseman.
William Lloyd, Christ Church, woollen draper.
Henry Morris, Fleet Street, silversmith.
Then the information was opened by Mr. Buller.

Mr. Horne. My lord, with your lordship's permission, I believe it is proper for me, at this time, before Mr. Attorney-General proceeds, to make an objection, and to request your lordship's decision concerning a point of practice in the proceeding of this trial. Have I your lordship's leave?

Lord Mansfield. Certainly.

Mr. Horne. Gentlemen of the jury . . .

Lord Mansfield. No. Not to the jury. If you make an objection to the irregularity of the proceedings, you must address me.

Mr. Horne. I am well aware of it: and I hope that your lordship will, upon this and other occasions, hear me before you suppose me to be in the wrong. I was not going to address my argument nor my objection to the jury, if your lordship will only permit me to request their attention, because I have frequently observed upon trials that in all cases almost when application has been made to the judge to decide upon any objection, the jury have been generally supposed to be in a manner out of court: and I therefore now address myself to the jury only to request their attention and for no other purpose.

Lord Mansfield. Very well. Go on.

Mr. Horne. Gentlemen of the jury, what I have said to his lordship, if you heard it, may perhaps make it unnecessary for me to address you. Gentlemen, though what I am going to say to his lordship respects a matter of law and practice of the Court, yet I meant to request your attention because you may find perhaps that the decision may concern you to hear it. My lord, I understand, and I think I see good reasons why it should be so, that it is the usual practice and wholesome custom of the Court in trials of this kind that unless the defendant examines witnesses in his defence, the defendant's answer closes the pleading: and it is not the practice in that case that the counsel for the prosecution should reply. But, my lord, in the late trials of the printers for printing and publishing the advertisement now in question, I observed that

Mr. Attorney-General claimed and exercised the peculiar privilege of replying, notwithstanding that no witnesses had been called for the defendant. My lord, with your lordship's permission, I mean to submit my reasons to your lordship in support of my objection to this claim of Mr. Attorney-General in the present trial.

Lord Mansfield. You come too early for the objection, because the objection, if there is any foundation in it, should be when he gets up to reply.

Mr. Horne. My lord, I own I did expect that Mr. Attorney-General would urge something of that kind against what I have said. I stopped, expecting that answer from him; because, my lord, he may very likely imagine it to be a part of the duty of his office to baffle me in any manner, and to take all advantages which he can, whether fair or unfair, against me, and to obtain a verdict against me by any means—there are reasons why he should attempt to do so; and therefore I own I expected that the Attorney-General would have urged that against me. But, my lord, I apprehend, with great submission, that this, and this only, is the proper moment . . .

Lord Mansfield. Mr. Horne, I will do so far for you. If the defence that you are to make may in any manner be guided or governed by a knowledge whether the Attorney-General has or has not a right to reply, if Mr. Attorney-General acquiesces in it, I have no objection to your being apprised how it stands beforehand, because otherwise it would come after you had made your defence. And if you mean to calculate your defence in some way differently, upon the expectation of his having or his not having a right to reply, I will willingly—I dare say the Attorney-General makes no objection to it—hear you upon that point now.

Attorney-General. None in the world.

Mr. Horne. Your lordship has hit upon one of the very reasons that I was going to lay before you. But, my lord, I had rather that this had come as a matter of justice than as an acquiescence from the Attorney-General, because I suppose that every defendant who shall hereafter stand in my situation will have the same right. And if it comes as a matter of favour from the Attorney-General, those for whom I am much more concerned than myself, may not perhaps meet with that genteel

acquiescence. However, I thank the Attorney-General. I shall
beg then, my lord, at present to make my objection. I am sure
I should have been permitted to make it, because the
arguments which I had to use would have been such as would
more particularly have affected your lordship's mind. If then
I am permitted, I suppose that I am now to object to the right
of reply.

Lord Mansfield. You are now to object to the right of reply.

Mr. Horne. My lord, if I should forget anything upon this
occasion, so new to me, and make any mistakes, I shall beg
leave to refresh my memory with what I have written down.
My lord, I have been taught by the best authorities that the
established practice and approved rules of the Court are so
only because they are reason, and reason approved by long
experience, and they obtain as rules and practice only for that
cause. My lord, I believe I shall not be contradicted by your
lordship when I aver that it is the established practice and
approved rule of the Court, in trials of this kind—where the
Attorney-General does not prosecute—that if the evidence
brought for the prosecution is not controverted by any other
evidence on the part of the defendant but the fact, as far as it
depends upon testimony, taken as the prosecutor's evidence
left it, that then the defendant's answer closes the pleading.
And this, my lord, has obtained and been established as the
approved rule and practice of the Court, because it is
supposed the method best calculated for the obtaining of
justice, that is for the conviction of the guilty and the acquittal
of the innocent, for both are to be regarded. And when that is
done, then only, I suppose, is justice done. Now, my lord, the
reason of this practice is not, like some others, so covered over
by the rust of ages, or disguised by the change of circumstances
as that it should be difficult now to discover it. On the
contrary, it is, to my understanding and apprehension, as
plain and evident now as it was the first day that it was
introduced. But that is no part of my business to enter into.
The reason of the practice it does not belong to me to give.
It is sufficient for me to say that such is the practice, and
being the practice it must be supposed the best method of
obtaining justice. Then, my lord, I humbly submit it to your
lordship, that if this is the best method for obtaining of justice,

a contrary method must be attempted for some other end.
And that end must be injustice or the conviction of the
accused by any means. My lord, the practice and this
exemption from it, which Mr. Attorney-General claims,
cannot both stand. One or the other must be given up,
because they cannot both be the best method and most likely
means for the obtaining of justice. Now, my lord, that the
King, or that the Attorney-General in his name, should be
permitted to pursue any other method or practice than that
established method which is best calculated for the obtaining
of justice, seems to me completely absurd. For the King, such
as the law and such as reason conceive him, can have no
other interest but in the obtaining of justice, impartial justice.
And if it was possible, my lord, to conceive a king even with a
leaning or an inclination on either side, it must rather be that
his subjects should be found innocent than guilty. But this claim
of Mr. Attorney-General, my lord, absurdly supposes the
contrary, and that the King has an interest in their being
convicted, and that therefore easier and readier means and
greater means are to be allowed to the King for obtaining a
conviction than are allowed to any other person, my equal or
my inferior. And yet, my lord, I must acknowledge that the
claim which I am now objecting to is not a new one. My lord,
in the reign of James II, that man—for he never was for one
moment a King—claimed the peculiar right, prerogative, and
power of dispensing with the laws of the land. Sir Edward
Herbert, the Chief Justice of those days, and the other judges
decided in favour of that claim. Thank God, my lord, the
Glorious Revolution—and I call it so: it shall not have less
praise from me because it is now grown uncourtly—the
Glorious Revolution put an end to that iniquity.
Unfortunately for this country, the principles which produced
that and many other iniquities are now again revived and
fostered, and amongst many other most shameful doctrines,
this doctrine of a dispensing power is now revived again—
under another shape and form indeed, but it is the same
power. It is now a prerogative to dispense with the rules and
methods of proceeding. That is, my lord, to dispense with the
laws: for the rules and methods of proceeding—and I have
heard your lordship say it in other cases—are parts of the laws

of the land. My lord, I have been told—and that by a greater authority than any almost that now lives—that 'the methods and forms of justice are essential to justice itself.' And, my lord, the forms and methods of proceeding are particularly tender in that part of the laws which is calculated for the protection of innocence. My lord, the penal laws are made to bring criminals and offenders to justice, but the forms and methods of proceeding of the courts of justice are appointed singly to distinguish the innocent from the guilty, and to protect them against exorbitant power. My lord, in the case of this particular privilege which the Attorney-General claims, I think I could spend a day in showing how many received legal maxims and truths it violates. For truth is of such a nature that it has a thousand branches issuing from it, and falsehood, let it be as careful as it can, will run against some one or other of them.

*   *   *

Lord Mansfield. There is no occasion for Mr. Attorney-General to say anything. I am most clear that the Attorney-General has a right to reply if he thinks fit, and that I cannot deprive him of it. And there is no such rule that in no case a private prosecutor or private plaintiff shall not reply, if new matter is urged which calls for a reply; new questions of law, new observations, or any matter that makes a reply necessary. No authority at law has been quoted to the contrary. A party that begins has a right to reply. There is not a State Trial where the Solicitor-General or the Attorney-General have not replied, and I know of no law that says in any case the prosecutor may not reply.

*   *   *

Mr. Horne. Your lordship must be very sensible how untoward is my situation in this case. This is only a repetition of what happened before, if your lordship will thus do the business of Mr. Attorney-General for him. My lord, you now take from me what you give to him. You take from me that right of reply which by the practice of the Court I have, whilst you give to him that right of reply which by the practice of the Court he has not. I have a right to reply to the Attorney-

General's answer to my objection, but I have no right to reply upon the judge. I beg the Attorney-General may do his own business. He is full of reason and argument. He smiles. Indeed he well may. My lord, he can surely prove the justice of his claim himself, if there is any in it. My lord . . .

Lord Mansfield. Sir—hear. Your proper reply to the judgment I have given is a motion to the Court. I never here decide. It is speaking to no purpose to persuade me where I have no doubt. The Attorney-General here will be of the same opinion with me. But your proper reply to me is a motion to the Court. And if the suffering him to reply is against law, it is an irregularity in the trial, for which the verdict will be set aside. You will have a remedy.

Mr. Horne. O, my lord, I have already suffered under your lordship's directing me to remedies. The most cruel of all poisoners are those who poison our remedies. Has your lordship forgotten? I am sure you have not forgotten that I have once before in my life had the honour to be tried before your lordship for a pretended libel. My lord, this matter of reply I know so well to be the practice, not only from the intelligence I have had upon that subject, but from that very trial at Guildford, on the action brought against me by the present Lord Onslow. My lord, I could then have contradicted his evidence. I will just mention two or three particulars in this case. It was the most scandalous one that ever came before a court. Your lordship cannot forget the particulars in that trial. I was prosecuted by him for a libel. On the first action which he brought I obtained a nonsuit. Upon that, a fresh action was brought. To that fresh action—in order to try it in Surrey where the plaintiff had his influence—in that fresh action, words spoken a year or two before were added, words of a different nature and upon a different subject. We came to trial before your lordship and I do remember some very strong cases—which indeed I intended to have published—of your lordship's practice in that trial. But, my lord, however impatient I may be thought to be, I am very patient under personal injuries. I have never complained of the practices used against me on that trial, nor of the mistakes—to speak gently—which your lordship made. Your lordship then told me, as now, that I should have a remedy . . .

John Horne

Attorney-General. I beg leave to object to this way of proceeding in a
trial. What can it be to the issue that is joined in this cause,
any part of the history of what related to the trial at Guildford?

Lord Mansfield. If I remember right, you had a remedy there, for
it was determined not to be actionable.

Mr. Horne. True, my lord, but it cost me 200*l*. The remedy was
almost as bad as the verdict would have been.

Lord Mansfield. There must be an end.

Mr. Horne. Not of this objection.

Lord Mansfield. No. An end of going out of the cause. You must
behave decently and properly.

Mr. Horne. I will surely behave properly.

Lord Mansfield. This is over. I tell you beforehand, I apprise you
of it, which is going out of the way, that it is not in my power
to deprive the prosecutor of replying, if he sees cause to desire
it.

Mr. Horne. Now, then, my lord, I entreat you to let me decently
tell you of the situation you put me into. When I offer to
prove by argument the right which I have to make my
objection at this time, your lordship kindly stops me and takes
it for granted. Then afterwards, it seems, it is you who
apprised me. You tell me you have, out of the rule, apprised
me. Yet because I accepted that which I knew to be my right,
as an apprisal which you were willing to give me, not meaning
however to preclude myself from the argument, your lordship
makes use of my acceptance of this apprisal to defeat my
objection. First, your lordship interferes to save Mr. Attorney-
General from attempting to give a reason, which you both
know he cannot give. And then Mr. Attorney-General gets up
to save your lordship in his turn, and to stop me from
explaining your lordship's conduct. Thus between your
lordship and Mr. Attorney-General, a defendant is in a blessed
situation. (*Here some promiscuous altercation ensued, after which Mr.
Horne proceeded.*) What I was speaking of was merely this, that
the practice . . . (*Here again some interruption.*) I was going to
show your lordship—in answer to what fell from you, and not
distinct from this cause, nor from what your lordship had
said—I was going, and decently going, to show your lordship
that it was the practice of the Court that the prosecutor
should not reply unless evidence is called for the defendant.

I was going to show it to your lordship from my own particular
case before your lordship at Guildford, and that I suffered
under it considerably, and I mentioned the instance.
[*Horne repeated his objection but his argument was finally cut short
by Lord Mansfield.*]
Lord Mansfield. (To the Attorney-General) Go on with the trial.
Mr. Horne. I shall hear no reason then from either of you? Well!
If so, I must submit under it.
Attorney-General. My lord, and gentlemen of the jury, there is
nothing in this case, unless the behaviour of the defendant
should constitute that something, that can make it at all
different from the most ordinary case of a plain delinquent
in a most gross offence being brought before a court of
justice. I have looked round with a degree of examination to
see if I could see whether there was one amongst the numerous
bystanders that I saw here who had conceived a favourable
impression from so extraordinary an interposition as one has
heard today. I certainly should not rise to take off or repel
loose slander scattered about without being pointed at any
one individual particularly, much less should I take notice
of that sort of slander which, affecting to point itself, only
disgraced itself in the manner of that affectation.

*　　*　　*

This is an information brought against Mr. Horne for being the
author and the original publisher of this libel. The crime that
I put most upon is that which I stated last, that he was the
original publisher of this libel. It is in that respect that his
crime appears to me to differ most from those that have been
called into justice before. The circumstance of his name being
printed at the bottom of the libel was an additional aggravation
in this respect, because it seemed to imply a bolder insult
upon manners and decency, and the laws of the country than
a simple publication of a libel without that name would have
been. It *seemed* to imply this because while that name lay hid
behind the printer of the paper, the stoutest champion for
sedition could not have defied the laws with greater security.
For though it stood in capitals upon the front of many
thousand pages, yet it was as inscrutable and impossible for
me to follow as if the name had not appeared upon the paper

at all. For the rest of it, I put it upon the publication, chiefly
because that seems to be the whole object and drift of the
composer of the libel, for as a composition it is absolutely
nothing. I do not mean to speak of it by way of derogation
from the parts and talents of the ingenious gentleman, whose
parts and talents I never heard so much of as I have done
today. I do not mean to speak it in derogation of them. No
doubt but he could have writ a better thing, but his
understanding was industriously let down and suppressed, and
the very purpose of this writing was to make it ribaldry and
trash. For the intention of it was, as it appears to me, the
intention of it was nothing more than to defy the laws and
justice of the country, proclaiming as it were thus. Either
punish this libel or confess that there are no laws in the
country by which a libel can be punished. Others have
entertained sufficient malice against this country. Others have
been anxious enough to excite sedition, but this is written
chiefly with the purpose of telling mankind, 'Thus I dare do!
I dare insult the laws without having any earthly thing to
state to the public, except an insult upon the laws.' Sometimes
a libel is covered, though thinly covered enough, with the
pretence of informing mankind, or of discussing public subjects
for the use of mankind. Here is not even the affectation of
giving information. Here is not even the affectation of
discussion, but the writer tells you in so many blunt words, of
no kind of meaning in the world but to convey reproach and
scandal, that the persons who were employed by the
government are guilty of murder, and the persons who
employed them consequently involved in the same guilt.

*   *   *

Murdered by the King's troops! What kind of palliation—
justification it is absurd and nonsense to talk of—but what
kind of palliation can be given to the charging men with the
crime of murder by writing against them in a newspaper? Is
it to be laid down for law, or a thing to be tolerated in a
civilised country, that crimes of the most heinous sort shall be
imputed to men by a public reviler in a newspaper, who yet
dares not stand forth as an accuser? Is that to be tolerated in
a civilised country—the writing against men that they are

guilty of murder who are not to be accused of that crime?
Is it to be tolerated in a country where an orderly government
prevails, and while the form of government subsists, to write
against the transactions of that government, as if stained with
all the crimes under heaven, and calculated for no earthly
purpose but of committing those crimes? To suppress liberty
—the only object for which government is or ought to be
erected—to suppress that liberty by the means of murder is
imputed to the transactions of the government of the freest
country now under heaven! And it is called liberty to do that!
Whereas men must be short-sighted indeed, a man must be
drivelling like an idiot that does not see that the maintaining
of regular government is the true, the only means of
maintaining liberty. Is it liberty to put the characters of
persons, the properties of every individual, under the
tyrannous hand of anarchy, and of every man that thinks
proper to seize them uncontrolled by law? Is that liberty?
And is there any one bystander of the most ordinary
understanding that hears me now speak, that has so gross an
understanding as to imagine that he would be more free if it
were in the power of any man that thought proper to revile
his character—which is the question which is now immediately
subjected to you—or to injure him in his person or fortune, or
in any other manner whatever? This therefore is not to be
coloured, as far as I can foresee, by any kind of argument
whatever. The nature of the libel is too gross to be commented
upon; it does no honour to anybody that has been concerned
in making it.

I shall content myself with proving the fact of this paper
having been written, of this paper having been published
originally by Mr. Horne, and the conclusion to be made upon
that is too obvious a one, and too broad a one, for me to
foresee at least any kind of difficulty about it. It was my duty
to lay it before you. I, charged with the duty of my office,
have brought it here: it is your duty to judge of it. You,
charged by the oath that you have taken, are to determine
upon it. If you can be of opinion that this licentiousness is fit to
be tolerated, according to the old and established laws of this
country; if you are of opinion that the fact is not proved upon
the defendant in the manner in which it is stated by the

witnesses; it will be your duty, your oaths will bind you, to acquit him. But if the fact should be proved, if it should stand as clear as to my judgment and apprehension it now stands, you will be constrained by the same necessity of duty, and by the additional sanction of an oath, to entertain exactly the opinion of it which I have found myself constrained to entertain. I have no wish—I did not know Mr. Horne—I have no wish to prosecute any one individual, nor have I been desired, if I had such a wish, to prosecute him. And I hope I may add that no desire could have compelled me to prosecute a man whom I myself had not thought guilty, notwithstanding anything that has been said on the contrary side. I go upon the evidence as it is in my possession. I go upon the evidence as it is in my power to produce it. If there be any evidence on the other side, and if that is sufficient to refute the imputation which the evidence that I have to produce lays upon him, I shall be as ready to examine that with exactly the same degree of candour and, I hope, of uprightness, as I have done the present. My duty is done by laying the matter before you. Your duty, I am sure, will be done to your own honour and the support of public justice by the verdict you will give upon the occasion.

Evidence for the Prosecution

Thomas Wilson sworn. Examined by Mr. Solicitor-General.
[Alexander Wedderburn, afterwards Earl of Rosslyn, and successively Chief Justice of Common Pleas and Lord Chancellor [*as Lord Loughborough*].]
Solicitor-General. Look at those papers. (*The several manuscripts from which the advertisements were printed in the newspapers. The witness inspects them.*)
Do you know whose handwriting those papers are? —They look like Mr. Horne's handwriting.
Do you know Mr. Horne?—I have seen him write.
Do you take these to be his handwriting?—They are like his handwriting. I will not upon my oath say that they are his handwriting. I believe that they are.
The manuscripts of the two advertisements read in court.
Henry Sampson Woodfall sworn. Examined by Mr. Wallace.
What business are you?—A printer.

Do you print any newspaper?—Yes.

What paper?—*The Public Advertiser.*

Mr. Wallace. Look at these two papers. (*Showing the witness the manuscripts of the advertisements. The witness inspects the manuscripts.*)

Have you ever seen these papers before?—Yes.

When did you see the first of them?—About the 7th of June 1775, as near as I can recollect.

By what means did you come by the sight of it?—Mr. Horne, the defendant, gave it me.

For what purpose?—To publish in the *Public Advertiser.*

Did you accordingly publish it?—I did.

Had you any other directions from Mr. Horne?—Yes. He desired me to send it to several other papers, which I did.

Do you recollect the names of any of them?—The whole, I believe, of them. I cannot exactly recollect.

Did you follow his directions?—I did.

Was anything paid for it?—Yes. Mr. Horne paid the bill.

For the publication?—Yes.

Mr. Wallace. Look at those newspapers. (*Showing the witness the* Public Advertiser *of June the 9th, and of July the 14th, 1775. The witness inspects newspapers.*)

Are those papers published by you?—I print that paper, and I suppose they are.

Cross-examined by the defendant.

Mr. Horne. I am very glad to see you, Mr. Woodfall. I desire to ask you some questions. Pray what was your motive for inserting that advertisement?—Your desire.

Had you no other motive?—I was paid for it, as the advertisement is paid for.

Pray was it by accident or by my desire that there should be witnesses to see me write that advertisement?—By your desire.

And did I, or did I not, formally, before that witness, when called in, deliver that paper as my act and deed, as if it had been a bond?—Yes.

It is true, I did. Did I not always direct you, if called upon, to furnish the fullest proof that you could give?—You did, sir.

Now then, sir, if you please, say whether I have ever written anything in your newspaper before.—Yes, frequently.

How many years ago, do you think?—The first remarkable thing
that I remember was something about Sir John Gibbons, about
his mistaking Easter for a feast or a fast.

How long ago is that?—About the year 1768, about the election
time.

That is about nine years ago?—Yes.

Have I at any time desired you to screen me from the laws?—
No.

Has not the method of my transactions with you at all times been
that you should at all times, for your own sake, if called upon,
give me up to justice?—Certainly. That has always been your
desire.

Pray, sir, were you not once called upon by the House of Commons
for something that I wrote in your paper?—Yes, sir.

Do you remember that I did or did not, when I took care to
furnish such full proof of this advertisement, give you the
reason for it?—I cannot say I recollect the reason.

I will mention it. Whether was this the reason? That in the last
transaction before the House of Commons it was pretended
they let me off because they could not get full evidence. Do
you remember whether I rehearsed that or not, and said that
if they now chose to take notice of this advertisement, they
should not want full evidence?—I do recollect that
conversation.

You remember that was the reason I gave?—I do.

Will you please to look at these newspapers? (*Showing several papers
of the* Public Advertiser *to the witness. The witness inspects them.*)

Do you know these newsapers?—I do.

Do you believe that you published them?—I do.

Look at the dates. I will call them over to you from a list. May
the 30th and the 31st; June the 6th, the 9th, the 10th, the
12th, the 15th, and the 16th, 1775.—I have looked at the
papers. They are all of my publication. The date of one of
them I cannot make out, it is June something.

We will go on. June the 21st and the 27th, 1775. Then there is
January the 11th, February the 8th, February the 7th, the
11th, June the 2nd, and June the 30th, 1777.—They are likewise of my publishing.

Pray, sir, do you recollect the contents of the paper of May the
30th, 1775?—No, upon my soul, I do not.

You are upon your oath.—I know that indeed.

Read that part. (*Pointing a part out.*) Read from, 'In provincial congress, April 26, 1774,' down to that part. (*Pointing it out.*)

Mr. Wallace. The officer should read it, though not now. You will be entitled to read it when you come to your defence.

Mr. Horne. Pray do you know Mr. Arthur Lee?—Yes.

Did you ever receive any account from him relative to the persons who were killed at Lexington and Concord?—I really do not recollect.

Do you recollect that you ever published his name to an account? —I think I did, relating to his agency for some colony.

Look at that and see whether you remember that, and how you received it. (*Witness inspects* Public Advertiser of *May 31, 1775.*) —Yes. I think I received this from Mr. Arthur Lee.

Pray who was Mr. Arthur Lee?—He is of the bar. I have seen him in Westminster Hall. He was there at the trial of Mr. Wright the printer upon this very affair. I believe he was retained there.

Pray was he retained in your cause when you were to be prosecuted for this advertisement?—He was.

And why did you retain him? Had you any particular reason? —I presumed he knew more of the subject of the advertisement than I did.

Did he ever tell you anything upon the subject?—We have had private conversation together as a matter of news.

Did he ever tell you he had lodged affidavits with the Lord Mayor of London?—He did.

Sir, did you ever tell me so?—I do not recollect.

Pray when had you, for the first time, any notice of a prosecution for the publishing of this advertisement?—About two years ago.

Pray did that prosecution go on?—No.

Do you know why?—Yes. I let judgment go by default.

The first time?—I was never called upon till last January.

It began two years ago, and you were never called forward upon it till last January?—I think that was about the month.

As near as you can recollect?—Yes.

When were you first applied to, or were you ever applied to, to be a witness in this cause?—I was not.

You never were?—No.

How came you to be an evidence?—I heard that if I could produce my author, matters might be better for me: and as you had no sort of objection, which you told me at the time, I did of course produce those copies that appeared there to Messrs. Chamberlayne and White, the Solicitors for the Treasury.

Should you at any time, if you had been called upon, have declared that I was the author of that advertisement?—Most certainly, for you desired it.

And would have given your evidence?—Yes.

Whom was the application made by?—It was no sort of application at all. I heard of it.

By whom?—My brother.

You never refused to furnish evidence against the author?—No.

You never were applied to, to do it?—No, I was not.

You have said that I never desired you to conceal me from the law for anything you published from me. Did you ever receive any letter or message from Sir Thomas Mills in your life?—A private letter I have.

But did not that private letter relate to the public paper?—Never.

Did you never receive any message not to insert anything in your paper about Lord Mansfield's earldom?—No.

Upon your oath?—Upon my oath, to the best of my recollection, I never did.

From any quarter?—No.

Sir, were you ever sent for by Lord Bute?—No, I never saw him.

Were you not sent for for inserting a paragraph about the King's marriage?—No, I am not consulted by the higher powers, I assure you.

If I had thought you were, I never should have trusted you. I do not think you are.—I am much obliged to you for your good opinion.

Mr. Horne. I will give you no more trouble.

William Woodfall sworn. Examined by Mr. Wallace.

Please to look at that paper. (*Showing the witness the manuscript of the advertisement. The witness inspects it.*)

Have you seen that paper before?—I have.

When did you first see it?—Mr. Horne delivered it into my hands in my brother's counting house on the 8th of June, to be inserted in the *London Packet* and *Morning Chronicle*, both which papers I print.

Was it accordingly inserted in those papers?—It was.

Look at those papers. (*Showing the witness several papers of the* Morning Chronicle *and* London Packet. *The witness inspects them.*)

Are those papers published by you?—They are.

Cross-examined by the defendant.

Mr. Horne. Mr William Woodfall, I will not repeat all the same questions to you. Did you ever receive any application?—No.

Your answer is of the quickest. Had you not better hear the question?—I presume you meant to ask the same question you put to my brother, as you laid an emphasis upon the word 'you'.

Did you ever receive any letter, or message, or desire, or request, of any kind, in any manner, not to insert anything in your paper relative to Lord Mansfield's earldom, on your oath?— On my oath, I never received any letter.

Message, or request, of any kind, in any manner, sir, from Sir Thomas Mills, I ask you?—No, I think not.

You must be a little more positive, because my question will not admit of a 'think'.—I do not recollect I did.

Then take a little time.—I don't recollect that I did. I know very well that some person or other once mentioned it to me.

That is an application. To mention it to you is a stronger application than a letter.—I had some conversation about it. I don't recollect that I was desired not to publish it.

Was it to request you not to insert squibs or anything?—I recollect I did insert it.

What?—Lord Mansfield's promotion to an earldom.

What was that application? That you 'would' insert paragraphs about it, or 'would not'?—It was a conversation, not of the nature of business, nor any express desire to me, some conversation as might be between two friends.

Upon your oath, you had never any application to omit inserting anything of that kind?—Upon my oath, I don't recollect that I had.

Nor have you ever said that you had?—If I don't recollect that I received any application to keep out anything relative to it, I consequently cannot have spoken of it.

Did you, or did you not, ever speak of it?—Not that I am aware of.
But you will not swear positively you never did?—I had no
direct application to me to keep out anything.
'Direct.' My question was 'direct' or 'indirect', or of any kind.—
I mean to answer 'direct'. I don't recollect that I was ever
applied to, to keep out anything, or that I ever said I was
applied to, to keep out anything.
More than that you cannot recollect?—No.
*The Associate read the advertisements in the several papers that had been
proved and put into court on the part of the prosecution.*
Attorney-General. My lord, we have done.
Mr. Horne. Gentlemen of the jury, I am much happier, gentlemen,
in addressing myself to you, and I hope and believe I shall be
much more fortunate as well as happy, than in addressing
myself to the judge. I have been betrayed, gentlemen, I hope,
into no unseemly warmth, but yet into some warmth. I have
felt myself like a man first put into hot water, but I have now
been long enough in it to be perfectly cool. And, gentlemen,
some small allowances might have been made for me by my
judge, who presides upon this cause, when he considers the
peculiar disadvantages in which I stand here before him.
Gentlemen, I am an absolute novice in these matters, and yet
opposed to gentlemen some of the most eminent in their
profession, and some of the most conversant in practice. But
that is not all, I have a farther disadvantage. I stand here,
gentlemen, before you, a culprit as well as a pleader, personally
and very materially interested in the issue of the cause which I
have to defend. And every gentleman in the court must know
—some perhaps by their own experience, all by the reason of
the thing—how very different is the sportful combat with
foils from that which is seriously disputed with unbated
swords, and how frequently the fluttering of the heart in the
latter situation has been known to enfeeble the steadiest wrist,
and to dazzle the clearest and most quick-sighted eye.

[*Horne began to denounce the power of the Attorney-General to initiate
press prosecutions by his own* ex officio *information without
requiring the sanction of a grand jury, as in other cases.*]

Gentlemen, it is true that the Court of King's Bench has
also assumed a power of accusing men. They say they may

safely be trusted with it. I believe their claim illegal, but I have nothing to do with it, and I acknowledge that it is much safer there than in the hands of an Attorney-General, who is whipped in and whipped out just as the minister, whose friend he is, goes in or out.

But that is not all. The Court of King's Bench cannot grant an information without an affidavit, without an accusation upon oath. No one of the judges of the Court of King's Bench can do it, and yet they are a little more independent— they have fewer hopes, and therefore fewer fears—than the Attorney-General. Yet no one of the judges of the court can accuse a man. It must be the whole court, and they must do it in consequence of an oath. If I am wrong, you will have the pleasure of contradicting it. (*Turning to the Attorney-General.*) But the Attorney-General accuses men neither upon the oath of others, nor yet upon his own oath. If he believes the matter of the accusation true, it is but the belief of one man, and he a prejudiced man, and the most improper man in the Kingdom for his authority to be taken in such a case. But, gentlemen, what is much worse, it frequently happens that no man whatever avows the accusation, or believes it. No, not the Attorney-General himself who files the information. I will prove it by and by, even in the case of the Attorney-General who filed this declaration. Gentlemen, I shall desire by and by, for your satisfaction and mine, to find out whether there is one man in the country that believes me guilty of the crime laid to my charge; a crime of that nature that is to have a punishment which is called by the law a temporary death, an exclusion from society, imprisonment. The apparent object of this prosecution is to take what little money out of my pocket I may have there, and to imprison me, and so exclude me from that society of which I have rendered myself unworthy. However, I have the pleasure to see that there sits a gentleman by the judge who is now trying me, who, as well as myself, has charged the King's troops with murder, a charge which at that time excited great abhorrence and detestation against him. The judge and that gentleman have been laughing all the time of this trial, they have enjoyed each other's company exceedingly. (*A great laugh, for some minutes, of the whole audience.*) Well, gentlemen, (*turning towards Lord Mansfield and*

Mr. Wilkes) I have caused another laugh between the
gentlemen, but it gives me pleasure to think that if ever I am
to come out of prison again—if you are so kind as to put me
there—I too may have the honour, if it be one, of sitting
cheek by cheek with the judge and laughing at some other
libeller. I said, if I come out again—because if it is possible
that I should be put there for this charge, I believe that will
never happen. I will never cease repeating the charge I have
made till those men are legally tried and acquitted who are
guilty of what I call murder. I will not be contented with one,
nor with two, nor with twenty juries. I will repeat the charge
of murder upon the troops, every day, if this doctrine gets so
far even as to a doubt: and I call upon the Attorney-General
now, if he may, if he can, if he will venture without the
permission of those ministers whose humble servant alone he
is; if he may venture, I call upon him to pledge himself to
bring an information for a seditious libel against the King and
the government every time I charge the troops with murder.
I promise him I will give him business enough, and I hope he
will, if he may venture to do it, promise to file an information
every time I charge them with murder when they commit it.

[*Horne went on to attack the Special Jury system, whereby such
cases as his were tried by those men of substantial wealth and social
rank who qualified as special jurors.*]

The sheriff's officer stands by, the Solicitor of the Treasury,
his clerk, and so forth. And whilst the names are taken, if
a name—for they know their distinction—if a name which
they do not like occurs and turns up, the sheriff's officer
says, 'Oh, sir, he is dead.' The defendant, who does not know
all the world, and cannot know all the names in that book,
does not desire a dead man for his juryman. 'Sir, that man
has retired.' 'That man does not live any longer where he
did.' 'Sir, that man is too old.' 'Sir, this man has failed
and become a bankrupt.' 'Sir, this man will not attend.'
'Oh,' it is said very reasonably, 'let us have men that will
attend, otherwise the purpose of a special jury is defeated.'

It seemed very extraordinary to me, I wrote down the
names, and two of them which the officer objected to I saved.
I begged him not to kill men thus without remorse, as they

have done in America, merely because he understood them to be friends to liberty. That it was very true, we shall see them alive again next week and happy, but let them be alive to this cause. The first name I took notice of was Mr. Sainsbury, a tobacconist on Ludgate Hill. The sheriff's officer said he had been dead seven months. That struck me. I am a snuff-taker, and buy my snuff at his shop, therefore I knew Mr. Sainsbury was not so long dead. I asked him strictly if he was sure Mr. Sainsbury was dead, and how long he had been dead. 'Six or seven months.' 'Why, I read his name today. He must then be dead within a day or two, for I saw in the newspapers that Mr. Sainsbury was appointed by the City of London one of the committee,' it happened to be the very same day, 'to receive the toll of the Thames navigation.' And as the City of London does not often appoint dead men for these purposes, I concluded that the sheriff's officer was mistaken, and Mr. Sainsbury was permitted to be put down amongst you, gentlemen, appointed for this special jury.

*　　*　　*

There is something more unfortunate in the case of a special jury. The special jurymen, if they fail to attend that trial for which they are appointed, are never censured, fined, nor punished by the judge. In the trial of one of the printers only four of the special jury attended. This is kind in the Chief Justice, but it has a very unkind consequence to the defendant, especially in a trial of this nature, for I will tell you what the consequence is. The best men and the worst men are sure to attend upon a special jury where the Crown is concerned: the best men from a nice sense of their duty, the worst men from a sense of their interest. The best men are known by the Solicitor of the Treasury. Such a one cannot be in above one or two verdicts: he tries no more causes for the Crown. There is a good sort of a man, who is indeed the most proper to try all this kind of causes, an impartial, moderate, prudent man, who meddles with no opinions. That man will not attend, for why should he get into a scrape? He need not attend, he is sure not to be censured, why should he attend? The consequence follows that frequently only four or five men attend, and those such as particularly ought not to attend in a

Crown cause. I do not say that it happens now. Not that I care, I do not mean to coax you, gentlemen, I have nothing to fear. You have more to fear in the verdict than I have, because your consciences are at stake in the verdict. I will do my duty, not for the sake of the verdict. Now what follows this permission to special jurymen to attend or not, as they like best? Why, every man that is gaping for a contract, or who has one, is sure to show his eagerness and zeal.

It happened so in the trial of the first cause for this advertisement. The printer showed me the list. Amongst them, one of the first I observed was Sir James Esdaile, Alderman of London, and a contractor for the army—there were several others, I do not mention the gentlemen's names. He would have struck him out. I said, 'No. There are so many bad that ought to be struck out, leave in Sir James. It is impossible that a magistrate of London! with so much business! a contractor under the Crown! if he has any modesty! he cannot, an Alderman of London! go down to be a special juryman in Middlesex!'—He was the foreman of the jury. He was sure to attend. And so they got the first verdict, in order to give them this influence upon men's minds. 'We have got a verdict. This question has been determined by a jury.'

*   *   *

But, gentlemen, I will show you what is not the motive of this prosecution. The motive of this prosecution is not to prevent the evil tendency of this wicked libel, of this horrid charge against the King's troops of murder, against soldiers who never commit it, who are not likely to commit it. I am sorry to read to you any paper. I did indeed intend to have read many, but the time I see will be too long. I will only read one or two to you, just to satisfy you of some things which you perhaps are not aware of. Here is the *Public Advertiser* of May the 30th, 1775. You will find in it a very serious, very particular, very sharp accusation against the King's troops of murder; the whole circumstances at length; and murder, murder, murder in every line. But it is so long that I will not read it to you now, because you can all remember to look at it hereafter. The papers are 30 May and 31 May. The government then, I mean the minister—I make an improper use of the word 'government'—the minister desires the public, upon this charge of murder against the troops, to suspend their belief. What follows? This paper which I have proved. 'As a doubt of the authenticity of the account from Salem, touching an engagement between the King's troops and the provincials in Massachusetts Bay, &c. I desire to inform all those who wish to see the original affidavits which confirm that account, that they are deposited at the Mansion House with the Right Hon. the Lord Mayor for their inspection. Arthur Lee.'

Then come the copies of the affidavits, all the particulars at length, murder is not spared at all. Then, amongst the rest, comes an affidavit, which I shall prove to you presently more authentically than this, though it is enough for me that it was published. But you know, gentlemen, I am not the original author of the charge. The gentleman has been talking of the original author of the charge. He thinks he may tell you so now, two years afterwards, but if he had told you so at the time of this advertisement, every man in the court would have laughed at it. Here is the original charge, signed by the agent of the province where the murders were committed, and the original affidavits confirming it are here said to be lodged with the Lord Mayor for inspection. It is very lucky for Mr. Lee that his receiving them, and causing them to be advertised has caused no prosecution against him. We shall know presently whether this affidavit be a forgery or not. The gentleman for whose it is given attends here by my subpoena to prove or to disprove it.

'I, Edward Thoroton Gould, of His Majesty's Own Regiment of Foot, being of lawful age, do testify and declare that on the evening of the 18th instant, under the orders of General Gage, I embarked with the light infantry and grenadiers of the line, commanded by Colonel Smith, and landed on the marshes of Cambridge, from whence we proceeded to Lexington. On our arrival at the place we saw a body of provincial troops armed, to the number of about sixty or seventy men. On our approach they dispersed, and soon after firing began, but which party fired first I cannot exactly say, as our troops rushed on shouting and huzzaing previous to the firing, which was continued by our troops so long as any of the provincials were to be seen. From thence we

marched to Concord. On a hill near the entrance of the town
we saw another body of the provincials assembled. The light
infantry companies were ordered up the hill to disperse them.
On our approach they retreated towards Concord. The
grenadiers continued the road under the hill towards the town.
Six companies of light infantry were ordered down to take
possession of the bridge, which the provincials retreated over.
The company I commanded was one. Three companies of the
above detachment went forward about two miles. In the
meantime the provincial troops returned, to the number of
about three or four hundred. We drew up on the Concord side
of the bridge. The provincials came down upon us, upon
which we engaged and gave the first fire. This was the first
engagement after the one at Lexington. A continued firing
from both parties lasted through the whole day. I myself was
wounded at the attack of the bridge, and am now treated
with the greatest humanity, and taken all possible care of by
the provincials at Medford.   *Signed*, Edward Thoroton
Gould.'

   When first I heard of this prosecution, and not before, I
began to consider with myself whether I had indeed made use
of any such expression or word as distinguished what I had
said from the case of many other persons. Not a day passed
but I found some newspaper with the same charge, containing
the same word 'murder'. I need not read any of them to you,
you can all recollect. Go to the papers that are published
today, to those published before this charge was brought
against me and since, and see if you don't constantly find in
them this charge of murder against the King's troops. I took
extracts from them till I was tired, and not only from the
newspapers, but several other publications; from that
honourable gentleman's publication and others, which are of
more consequence than fugitive pieces in a newspaper. These
all prove the Attorney-General's nice sense of honour and
integrity, and regard to the public good, who prosecutes this
advertisement. Now, that men may not be misled by it, after
suffering them to run wild for two years, and be misled without
any control! But, gentlemen, so far from that being the motive
of this prosecution, the papers are all full of the same charge
and will continue full, I have no doubt. I protest upon my

honour, they are none of them made by me. I have been dumb ever since. I meant to do good by it when I made the charge, and I have been dumb ever since because I could not see that any good was to be produced. If then you see what is not the motive for this prosecution of me, at this distant time, that will lead your minds to conclude what is the motive.

Gentlemen, the language of the Attorney-General forces me to say a few words upon a subject which is the most disagreeable for a man to speak of, unless indeed it is when he appears as I do, a defendant. I thought when the Attorney-General opened his charge upon this prosecution that he would have taken a different line from that which he repeatedly pursued in the trials of the printers. He knew that I had heard him talk against 'indecency, a flood of obscenity, and scandalous publications'. I had already heard him charge that advertisement to be full of 'ribaldry, Billingsgate, scurrility, balderdash, and impudence'. I have not used a word that he did not use. All these I knew he had charged upon that poor advertisement. I thought that upon this prosecution he would not give me such an advantage as to say the same things or take the same line that he took before. It is true he gained a verdict by that line before, and therefore perhaps thought he might this time. I own I did think that he would have paid me the compliment of something a little new, but he says he never knew so much of my talents and learning as at this time. The gentleman's memory is short. I would have forgot it, if he had not. He represents me to you in the light of a scurrilous, ribald, balderdash, Billingsgate, impudent fellow. That boldness with which I defend the right of the subject will not, with any man who has a regard for the right of the subject, pass for impudence. Those who know anything of me must judge whether I am impudent upon other occasions.

*   *   *

Mr. Horne having concluded, the Attorney-General began to address the jury by way of reply, upon which Mr. Horne rose and spoke to Lord Mansfield as follows:

Mr. Horne. My lord, I don't mean to interrupt the Attorney-General but, my lord, my haste and the shame I feel for having made any defence to such a kind of charge made me forget to examine my witnesses. The Attorney-General has not proceeded far in his reply, and I hope I shall be at liberty to call them now.

Attorney-General. You will not examine witnesses to justify a libel? My lord, I object to his calling witnesses, except he had opened to what points he meant to call them.

Lord Mansfield. You had better not object, Mr. Attorney-General. You had better hear his witnesses.

Mr. Horne. My lord, if Mr. Attorney-General make an objection, I will endeavour to obviate his objection.

Lord Mansfield. Call your witnesses.

Mr. Horne. I call the Attorney-General.

Lord Mansfield. Oh! You can't examine the Attorney-General.

Mr. Horne. Does your lordship deliver that as the law? My lord, I call the Attorney-General, and desire that the book may be given to him.

Lord Mansfield. You must state then what questions you mean to ask him, for he has a right to demur to the questions, and take the opinion of the Court.

Mr. Horne. If I do that, it will be more than he was directed by your lordship to do with any of the witnesses he examined.

Lord Mansfield. They were called of common course: the Attorney-General may demur to it.

Mr. Horne. If I ask him an improper question, he may then object to it, if he can.

Lord Mansfield. If you call the Attorney-General in any cause, if you don't state the question, he may demur.

Mr. Horne. Can he before he is sworn?

Lord Mansfield. He may demur to being examined at all.

Mr. Horne. Yes, and I dare say he will.

Lord Mansfield. You might as well call a common attorney or an advocate employed against you in a cause.

Mr. Horne. But this, my lord, differs widely. In what I shall call Mr. Attorney-General to, he acts neither as attorney nor as advocate.

Lord Mansfield. State the question.

Mr. Horne. My lord, I have many questions to ask him. He has paraded upon his honour, his conscience, and his duty. He is not acting as an attorney or an advocate in the cause. When he files an information he is then acting as a judge or a jury;

and if he has not acted in it with that integrity with which
he would have done upon oath, so much the worse for him.
One chief reason why I desire to examine him is to obtain this:
that I may point out a means by which an accusation in future
shall not be brought against a man without an oath, at least
from somebody. My lord, one question I mean to ask him is
concerning that accusation which he has now brought, how it
came to be brought, how it came to be dropped, and some
other circumstances attending it. He has talked so much of the
fairness, and the conscience, and the integrity of his motives in
doing it, that I am sure it will look very comical if he refuses
to swear to those declarations. If he will not swear to these
motives, without his oath I cannot believe it: and if, contrary
to my expectations, he does swear to it, after his oath I shall be
left to exercise my own judgment.

Attorney-General. To any matter so impertinent as that! If that
gentleman had had any question of fact to have asked me
relative to his defence, I would not have objected to have
sworn to it, although I stand in the place of prosecutor in this
cause, where in point of form I might. But I put myself upon
this, that I will not be examined to questions so impertinent
as those that have been now proposed.

Mr. Horne. My lord, the gentlemen of the jury will please to
observe then, that here is an accusation without an accuser.
Your lordship smiles! Upon my word, my lord, I do not think
it a thing to be laughed at. If I had the honour to be talking
with your lordship over a table, I should speak of it with the
same seriousness, and not as a quibble. I hope the gentleman
will upon oath justify that information, for the integrity of
which he has been haranguing.—He will not!—Well, then, I
must do without the evidence of the Attorney-General.

Lord Mansfield. I cannot force him to be examined.

Mr. Horne. No, my lord, nor do I believe anybody else could.
Please to call Lord George Germaine.

Lord George Germaine was called by the Crier but did not appear.

Mr. Horne. He is gone to Germany too, I suppose, with General
Gage.

Mr. Alderman Oliver sworn. Examined by Mr. Horne.

Mr. Horne. My lord, I call this witness to prove the truth of the
assertions contained in the advertisement.

Sir, I must desire you first to speak to the particulars of a meeting
called, during an adjournment of the Constitutional Society, in
the year 1775. Was there a meeting called by you in June
1775?—I believe there was, upon your application.

Are you sure of it?—I am.

Did you know the purpose for which it was called before it met?
—Yes, I did.

Did you approve of that purpose?—I did.

Was a proposal made to subscribe any money, and for the
purposes mentioned?—Yes it was, and by you.

A sum of money was subscribed?—There was.

Did you contribute part of it?—I did.

Was such a direction, as in the advertisement, given to me?—
There was.

There is another advertisement of 50*l*. I believe I need not read it,
it is well understood. Did I receive that 50*l*. from you in the
name of an unknown contributor?—Through me.

Was that 50*l*. given for the purposes mentioned?—It was.

By whom?—Sir Stephen Theodore Janssen. I was also a
subscriber to the same purpose.

I mentioned in the course of my defence what may otherwise
perhaps be represented as not true. Did I send by you, upon
a relation from you of a motion made for an Act of Parliament
to take away the right of appeal from the subjects in cases of
murder, did I, or not, send that message which you heard me
represent in my defence?—You sent a message by me, and I
dare say, from your accuracy of memory and your truth, you
did deliver a message for the Attorney-General. Whether I
thought that it would be of the same effect,—I did mention to
Mr. Rose Fuller the determination of Mr. Horne to go all
lengths in opposition to that Act which was to destroy the
right of appeal in cases of murder. And I do believe in my
conscience his application prevented any further steps being
taken upon it.

The fact, as I represented it, the witness says is true.—Certainly so.

*William Lacey sworn. Examined by Mr. Horne. A receipt for 100*l.
shown to the witness.

Is that your handwriting?—It is.

Do you recollect that 100*l*. for which that is your receipt, being
paid in at your house?—I do.

In the name of Dr. Franklin?—On his account.

Do you know by whom that was paid?—I have it in my book in the name of Mr. Horne.

Do you recollect me to have paid it myself?—I do not, but it was paid.

Do you know of any other sum paid?—No. I have got a copy as it stands in my book here.

Is there anything besides the 100*l.* put in?—No.

No 50*l.*?—No.

Where is Mr. Chetham?—He is in Ireland.

He is a clerk in your house?—He was.

And used to receive money occasionally?—Yes.

Do you know his handwriting?—I believe I should.

Look at that receipt.

A receipt for 50l. was shown to the witness.

Lacey. I believe that to be his writing.

Mr. Horne. Call Mr. Gould.

Mr. Edward Thoroton Gould sworn. Examined by Mr. Horne.

Did you in the year 1775 serve in a regiment of foot belonging to His Majesty?—I did.

Were you present at Lexington and Concord on the 19th of April 1775?—I was.

How came you to be there?—As a subaltern officer, ordered there.

Ordered by whom?—General Gage.

At what time did you receive those orders?—I don't recollect immediately the time.

Was it on the 19th, 18th, or 17th of April?—I believe it was on the 18th in the evening.

Did you receive them personally from General Gage?—No such thing.

Whom then?—From the adjutant of the regiment.

When did you set out from Boston for Lexington?—I cannot exactly say the time in the morning, but it was very early, two or three o'clock.

That is in the night in April. Was it dark?—It was.

Did you march with drums beating?—No, we did not.

Did you march as silently as you could?—There were not any particular orders given for silence.

Was it observed?—Nor it was not observed, not particularly by me.

Were you taken prisoner at Lexington or Concord, or either of them?—At the place called Monottama, in my return from Lexington.

I shall ask you no questions that you dislike. Give me a hint if there is any one you wish to decline. Did you make any affidavit?—Yes, I did.

Will you please to read that? (*Giving the witness the* Public Advertiser, *31 May 1775.*)—I believe that to be the exact substance of the affidavit that I made.

Lord Mansfield. It cannot be read without the Attorney-General consents to it.

Attorney-General. I don't consent.

Lord Mansfield. If he consents to it, I have no objection.

Mr. Horne. May I give it to the jury?

Lord Mansfield. No. I suppose they have all read it years ago.

Mr. Horne. My lord, that is my misfortune that it is so long ago.

Mr. Horne begins to read it.

Lord Mansfield. You must not read it.

Mr. Horne. I have proved the publication by the printer.

Lord Mansfield. It will have a different consequence if you only mean to prove that there was such an affidavit published. If you mean to make that use of it, then you may produce the affidavit or have it read. If you mean to prove the contents of it, they must come from the witness, and then you will have a right to have it read.

Mr. Horne. I mean both to prove the contents true, and the publication of the affidavit: that, indeed, I have already proved.

Lord Mansfield. Then you may read the affidavit, if you make use of the publication of it.

Mr. Horne. I make use of both; that it was so published, and charged, and that it is true.

'*The Public Advertiser*, Wednesday 31 May 1775.'

The affidavit read.

Are the contents of that affidavit true?—[*Gould.*] They are. It was made at the time I was wounded and taken prisoner.

Pray, do you know that the Americans upon that occasion scalped any of our troops?—I heard they did, but I did not see them.

You saw none?—I did not.

From whom did you hear it?—From a captain that advanced up the country.

Were you, at the time when the orders were given to you to go to Lexington and Concord, apprehensive of any attack by those Americans against whom you went?—We were as soon as we saw them. We found them armed.

Before you went from Boston?—That day we did.

How many miles is Lexington or Concord from Boston?—The farther is about twenty-five miles, the nearer is about twelve.

Did you know, had you any intelligence that the Americans of Lexington and Concord were, at that time, marching, or intending to march to attack you at Boston?—We supposed that they were marching to attack us, from a continued firing of alarm guns, cannon, or they appeared to be such from the report.

Lord Mansfield. Did you say cannon?—Cannon.

Lord Mansfield. When was that?—As soon as we began the march, very early in the morning.

Mr. Horne. But did you hear those alarm guns before your orders for the march were given, or before your march began?—No.

But after you had begun your march?—Yes. After we began our march the alarm guns began firing.

Did you suppose those alarm guns to be in consequence of your having begun the march?—I cannot say.

I will not desire you to suppose, (though the gentleman has supposed that they were coming to attack him) but do you know of any intelligence whether the persons who fired the alarm guns, whether those were the persons who were killed at Lexington and Concord?—No, I do not.

Mr. Horne. How those orders came you cannot tell, therefore I do not mean to examine to it.

One of the Jury. Pray who did the alarm guns belong to, to the Americans or our corps?—From the provincials.

Mr. Horne. What do you mean by an alarm gun? Alarm may be misunderstood.—[*Gould.*] That is, what they term in the country an alarm gun. It is a notice given to assemble the country.

After you had begun your march, you heard these alarm guns?—Yes.

Mr. Horne. My Lord Percy, I thank your lordship for your

attendance. I will not trouble your lordship with any
questions. I shall not ask your lordship those questions I
intended, since General Gage has not thought proper to
attend. He is gone to Germany, I understand, and will not be
back, I suppose, these three or four days!

Lord Mansfield. Then you have done?

Mr. Horne. Yes.

REPLY

Attorney-General. May it please your lordship, and gentlemen of
the jury.

The gentleman has chosen to take the conduct of his defence
himself, and in the course of the conduct of it, he has
proceeded in as singular a way as I believe ever any cause
was conducted that was ever tried in any court of justice. He
certainly has done more than the wisdom, than the propriety,
than the decency of any counsel would have permitted him to
do on a similar occasion. And if I conjecture his aim aright,
from the manner in which he has attempted the defence, he
has more cast about to be stopped in a great variety of parts,
for the sake of making it a topic of complaint, than seriously
stated them, as hoping they could be deemed by any
by-stander—and more particularly by you that are to judge of
them—at all pertinent to his defence. I did not recollect on
the outset that I had so totally passed over the terms of this
charge, much less that I had so profusely enlarged upon
subjects foreign and impertinent to that charge, as to lay me
open to any reflections upon that account. It is not to my
purpose, and therefore I will trouble you with no reflections
upon those various stories—histories of various adventures in
many parts of the world—with which he has thought proper
to interlard the speech he has made to you upon this subject;
which before I sit down I hope I shall be perfectly justified in
having stated to you as one of the plainest, and clearest, and
shortest propositions that ever was laid before a jury.
Gentlemen, it is certainly true, the charge in the information
consists in this, that he did write and publish, and cause and
procure to be written and published, a certain false, wicked,
malicious, scandalous, and seditious libel. I was afraid when
my speech was loaded with the imputation of having thrown
out invectives in the terms of the information, that the

information had not been sufficiently explicit upon the true
nature and quality of the libel which it offered to bring before
you. I admit that the information is explicit, that it is direct,
and that it perfectly and justly qualifies the nature of the
charge that is brought before you of scandalous and seditious.
It is likewise inferred that this is concerning His Majesty's
government, and the employment of his troops. The
information has therefore undertaken to say that the scurrilous
matter which follows was delivered in writing, concerning the
King's government, and concerning the employment of the
troops. If it was delivered concerning either, it is sufficient.
That it was delivered concerning both, I take now, by this
time at least, to be perfectly clear.

*   *   *

What is the rest of his defence? It consists in abusing me; the
judge; the jury; the Crown Office; the law as it now stands;
the counsel that appeared for the printers who were convicted
of the same crime before, because they did not do enough and
act to his mind; and the Solicitor of the Treasury! That is the
nature of the defence made in this cause! I have chosen to
separate it from the case, and yet I believe I shall be forgiven
if I say a few words upon the rest of the subject. The learned
gentleman thinks proper to state to you that this is a
prosecution of two years old, because the offence was
committed on the 9th of June 1775, and because you are
now trying it in July 1777. Now if he could have made
anything of the observation, it would have been just as
handsome to himself—it is nothing to me, for I despise all
those things—it would have been as handsome to himself, if he
had thought proper to state the facts precisely as they were.
This information was filed in Michaelmas term 1776, and it
was not my fault, but his fault, that it was not brought on to
trial in the Hilary term following. But still there is between
the 9th of June 1775 and Michaelmas 1776 some time,
though not two years; a year and something more. Then he
complains that I thought proper to file my information against
the printers first, although I might have applied to those
printers in order to have obtained evidence against him. In
the first place, I have made it a rule to myself not to apply to

any printers in any other way than by charging them for their delinquency, and bringing them before a jury to be tried. That is the application that I make and always will make to the printer of a libel. In the second place, if I had though proper to apply, as he calls it, to the printer, I might have had a fictitious conversation put upon me, in order to prove that I had practised with them to get Mr. Horne delivered up. Now in the third place, it is a matter of perfect indifference to me whether I prosecute the printer or the author. And I will tell you why. My notion with regard to authors are [*sic*] that most of them are generated by printers, at least more authors are produced by printers than printers by authors: and if the press was never to go till the good sense of some author set it to work, it would prevent a great deal of the groaning of the press upon publications and subjects much too frivolous to be regretted if they were lost, and I believe authors have grown more from the press than the press has grown from authorship. If I stop the publication of libels, I think I do an essential good to the country. I know if they are printed and published ostensibly, where to apply to stop them: but I never did, nor ever will, stop them by applying to the printers.

*   *   *

I have gone very much out of my way, and very contrary to the turn of my temper, when I have embarked so far in a defence of myself at all, but when facts are stated I thought it necessary to restate and explain these facts. Beyond that, let general and loose reflections take what place they please. I put myself upon my public conduct for my justification, without boasting of that conduct either one way or the other. If I am wrong in that conduct, let it condemn me: if I am right in that conduct, let it approve me. It is upon that only that I desire to rest it, without boasting or without disclaiming either on one side or the other. I will say no more upon that subject but refer it to you to determine what ought to be done upon a charge thus stated, and thus industriously proved upon the part of the defendant, if any proof had been wanting to support it upon the part of the prosecutor.

Lord Mansfield. Gentlemen of the jury, if ever there was a question, the true merits of which lay in a very narrow compass, it is the present. This is an information against the defendant for writing and composing, and printing and publishing, or causing to be printed and published, that is, for being the author and publisher of a paper, which the information charges as a seditious libel. If it be a seditious libel in its own nature, there is no justification attempted. Why then, there are but two points for you to satisfy yourselves in, in order to the forming of your verdict.

Did he compose and publish it? That is, was he the author and publisher of it? Upon this occasion, that is entirely out of the case, for it is admitted. As to the excuse of ignorance, or being imposed upon, which is a topic in the case of printers and others, it is out of this case because it is avowed to be done deliberately; and it is now avowed, and the contents of it. Why then there remains nothing more but that which reading the paper must enable you to form a judgment upon, superior to all the arguments in the world, and that is:

Is the sense of this paper that arraignment of the government, and the employment of the troops, upon the occasion of Lexington mentioned in that paper? Read! You will form the conclusion yourselves. What is it? Why, it is this: that our beloved American fellow-subjects—therefore innocent men—[are] in rebellion against the state. They are our fellow subjects, but not so absolutely beloved without exception! Beloved to many purposes. Beloved to be reclaimed. Beloved to be forgiven. Beloved to have good done to them. But not beloved so as to be abetted in their rebellion! And therefore that certainly conveys an idea that they are innocent. But farther it says that they were inhumanly murdered at Lexington by the King's troops, merely on account of their acting like Englishmen and preferring liberty to slavery! The information charges the libel to relate to the King's government and the employment of his troops. Read it, and see whether it does relate to them. If it does, what is the employment they are ordered upon? What is the employment that they execute? To murder, the paper says, innocent subjects, because they act like Englishmen, and prefer liberty to slavery! Why, then, what are they who gave the orders? What are they who execute them? Draw the conclusion. It don't stand upon argument. If any man dares to give orders to murder a subject, or to execute those orders, or to make any subject a slave, he is as high a criminal as can exist in this state.

* * *

You will judge whether it conveys a harmless, innocent proposition for the good and welfare of this Kingdom, the support of the legislative government, and the King's authority according to law, or whether it is not denying the government and legislative authority of England, and justifying the Americans; averring that they are totally innocent; that they only desire not to be slaves; not disputing to be subjects, but they desire only not to be slaves; and that the use that is made of the King's troops upon this occasion—for you will carry your mind back to the time when this paper was wrote—was to reduce them to slavery. And if it was intended to convey that meaning, there can be little doubt whether that is an arraignment of the government and of the troops employed by them or not. But that is a matter for your judgment. You will judge of the meaning of it. You will judge of the subject to which it is applied, and connect them together. And if it is a criminal arraignment of these troops, acting under the orders of the officers employed by the government of this country, to charge them with murdering innocent subjects, because they would not be slaves, you will find your verdict one way. But if you are of opinion that the contest is to reduce innocent subjects to slavery, and that they were all murdered—like the cases of undoubted murders, of Glencoe, and twenty other massacres that might be named—why then you may form a different conclusion with regard to the meaning and application of this paper.

[Mansfield concluded his summing-up with a defence of the Attorney-General's right of reply, which had been challenged by Horne at the opening of the case.]

The jury withdrew about five o'clock, and returned into court about half an hour after six, and gave in their verdict that the defendant was guilty.

[Four months later, on 19 November 1777, the Attorney-General moved for judgment against John Horne in the Court of King's

John Horne

*Bench. Both men argued their cases before Lord Mansfield and the
hearing was eventually adjourned until 24 November. When the
hearing was resumed on that day, the Attorney-General outlined the
various types of punishment which the Court might impose on Horne
and he argued with some enthusiasm for a form of corporal
punishment, preferably the pillory.]*

Attorney-General. My lord, the punishments to be inflicted upon
misdemeanours of this sort, have usually been of three different
kinds: fine, corporal punishment by imprisonment, and infamy
by the judgment of the pillory. With regard to the fine, it is
impossible for justice to make this sort of punishment, however
the infamy will, always fall upon the offender. Because it is
well known that men who have more wealth, who have better
and more respectful situations and reputations to be watchful
over, employ men in desperate situations both of circumstances
and characters, in order to do that which serves their party
purposes. And when the punishment comes to be inflicted,
this Court must have regard to the apparent situation and
circumstances of the man employed, that is, of the man
convicted, with regard to the punishment.

With regard to imprisonment, that is a species of punishment
not to be considered alike in all cases, but varies with the
person who is to be the object of it: and so varies with the
person that it would be proper for the judgment of the Court
to state circumstances which will make the imprisonment fall
lighter or heavier, as the truth is, upon the person presented
to the Court. I say, my lord, that would be proper, if I had not
been spared all trouble upon that account by hearing it
solemnly avowed in your lordship's presence, by the defendant
himself, that imprisonment was no kind of inconvenience to
him: for that certain employments, which he did not state,
would occasion his confinement in so close a way, that it was
mere matter of circumstance whether it happened in one
place or another; and that the longest imprisonment which
this Court could inflict for punishment was not beyond the
reach of accommodation which those occasions rendered
necessary to him. In this respect, therefore, imprisonment
is not only as with respect to the person not an adequate
punishment to the offence, but the public are told, and told by

a pamphlet which bears the reverend gentleman's name—
may be his name may have been forged to it, but by a
pamphlet that bears that name—that it will be no punishment.
And your lordships—according to the usual style with which
he has affected to treat justice, from the beginning to the end
—are told that you cannot punish him in that way. And
therefore, if that is a species of punishment which cannot affect
him, as your lordship has been before told in a manner to be
relied upon, he has made it manifest that your lordships'
judgment in that part of the punishment operates nothing with
respect to him personally; and consequently that it will lose
its whole force and efficacy as with respect to that example
which the public justice ought to hold out to the world.

I stated in the third place to your lordships the pillory to
have been the usual punishment for this species of offence. I
apprehend it to have been so in this case for above two
hundred years before the time when prosecutions grew rank
in the Star Chamber, and to those degrees which made that
court properly to be abolished. The punishment of the pillory
was inflicted not only during the time that such prosecutions
were rank in the Star Chamber but it also continued to be
inflicted upon this sort of crime, and that by the best authority,
after the time of the abolishing the Star Chamber, after the time
of the Revolution, and while my Lord Chief Justice Holt sat in
this court. In looking over precedents for the sake of the other
question, I observed that Mr. Tutchin, an author of some
eminence in his day, was angry with Holt, the Lord Chief
Justice, for transferring, as he called it, the punishment of
bakers to authors.[2] That was upon a personal conceit, which
such an author as Tutchin thought himself entitled to
entertain of the superior dignity of that character all along.
He thought that the falsifying of weights and measures was a
more mechanical employment than the forging of lies, and that
it was less gentleman-like to rob men of their money than of
their good name. But that is a peculiarity which belongs to the
little vanity that inspires an author. I trust therefore, when I
speak of Lord Chief Justice Holt, and of the time in which he
lived, I speak—for all, but particularly for this—of as great an
authority as ever sat in judgment upon any case whatever.
His name was held high during his life, and has been held in

reverence in all subsequent times. He deserved popularity by doing that which was right upon great, trying, and important occasions. He obtained popularity because he despised all other means of aiming at it, but that of doing right upon all occasions. From the temper of those times, from the vehemence and designs of that faction that opposed him, Sir John Holt would have been reviled, if the revilers of that day had not observed in the greatness of his spirit and character, that it was impossible to reach him. And he has preserved a name which was highly honoured during his life, and which will live as long as the English constitution lives. Citing him, therefore, in support of this as a proper punishment to be inflicted upon this sort of offence, is giving in my apprehension, the greatest authority for it.

[*Judgment against John Horne was pronounced by Mr Justice Aston, who sat with Lord Mansfield on this occasion. He concluded with the sentence of the Court.*]

Mr Justice Aston. The Court have considered of the punishment fit to be inflicted upon you for this offence, and the sentence of the Court is, that you do pay a fine to the King of 200*l.*, that you be imprisoned for the space of twelve months, and until that fine be paid, and that upon the determination of your imprisonment you do find sureties for your good behaviour for three years, yourself in 400*l.* and two sureties in 200*l.* each.

Mr. Horne. My lord, I am not at all aware of what is meant by finding sureties for the good behaviour for three years. It is that part of the sentence that perhaps I shall find most difficult to comply with, because I don't understand it. If I am not irregular in entreating your lordship to explain it to me— your lordships, I suppose, would choose to have your sentences plainly understood, and I know not the nature of this suretyship.

Lord Mansfield. It is a common addition.

Mr. Horne. And, it may be, a common hardship.

Mr. Justice Aston. Not to repeat offences of this sort.

Mr. Horne. Of this sort?

Lord Mansfield. Any misdemeanour.

Mr. Justice Aston. Whatever shall be construed bad behaviour.

Mr. Horne. If your lordships would imprison me for these three years, I should be safer, because I can't foresee but that the most meritorious action of my life may be construed to be of the same nature.

Lord Mansfield. You must be tried by a jury, by your country, and be convicted. You know it is a most constant addition. You know that yourself very well.—Where are the tipstaffs?

[In May 1778 Horne attempted to reverse the judgment against him by bringing a writ of error in Parliament, on the grounds that the charge of seditious libel had not been explicitly enough made against him in the indictment. However, after legal argument, the indictment, the verdict of the jury, and the judgment of the Court were held to be justified and the sentence upon Horne was affirmed.]

Chapter ten

John Hatchard (1817)

In 1807 the advocates of the abolition of slavery, including William Wilberforce, formed the African Institution to press for such intermediate measures as the registration of all slaves and to issue information and propaganda whose aim was to be the total abolition of slavery. The Duke of Gloucester consented to be President, while Lord Grenville, Lord Howick and Spencer Perceval were among the more prominent members. No less promising was the first anniversary celebration on 25 March 1808, which Wilberforce described as 'a magnificent day, between five and six hundred people, ten or twelve noblemen, and forty or more M.P.s—the Duke of Gloucester in the chair. We were afraid beforehand, and doubted about putting it off.'[1]

Like so many associations for the improvement of human conditions in the early nineteenth century, the African Institution issued an annual report, which like many other reports of its kind was published or retailed by John Hatchard (1769–1849). Hatchard, whose bookshop has remained a feature of Piccadilly ever since, first set up business at 173 Piccadilly but later transferred to 187. His first publication, *Reform or Ruin*, appeared in 1797 and he was the publisher of the *Christian Observer* from its first issue in 1802 until his retirement in 1846. He was also responsible for issuing the publications of such bodies as the Society for Bettering the Conditions of the Poor, and the Philanthropic Society.

In 1816 there appeared the *Tenth Annual Report of the Directors of the African Institution*, which included an account from Antigua of the case of an aide-de-camp to the Governor, Sir James Leith. The aide-de-camp had flogged a female slave who was pregnant. The young woman complained to the Governor, who reprimanded his aide-de-camp, who, in turn, flogged the woman again. The Governor dismissed his aide-de-camp from his service and the aide-de-camp returned his uniform by dressing up one of his negro boys in it and sending him to the Governor on a donkey. The Governor then ordered an indictment of the aide-de-camp to be presented to the grand jury of the island, who refused to sanction a prosecution. Such was the story circulated by the African Institution and supplied to them by a previously reliable correspondent in Antigua, whom Wilberforce refers to as 'Dr H.'

Unfortunately, the story as presented was not corroborated by the judicial records of the island. Moreover, Antigua, which had been colonized by the British in 1632, had a population small enough for such an incident to have been general gossip. At the command of the island's legislature, an action was brought against John Hatchard for a libel on the eight aides-de-camp of Antigua (individually and collectively), and on the administration of justice in the island.

'We, of course, shall prevent his suffering,'[2] said Wilberforce of Hatchard but, as the prosecution insisted, the case against Hatchard would only be dropped if the identity of the African Institution's informant were to be revealed. Wilberforce described the meeting of the institution over this matter on 1 April 1817. 'African Institution meeting to settle whether to give up Dr. H.'s name, which the Duke and others supported. Brougham argued powerfully, as I urged also, that it would be positively wrong as well as inexpedient.'[3]

The name was not revealed and, to the abolitionists, it was Hatchard rather than Dr H. who became the hero of the incident. Of Dr H., Wilberforce wrote irritably, 'He seems rather querulous, and a little disposed to regard himself as a saint in our calendar, though poor Hatchard has been the martyr.'[4]

The case was presented in the form of general arguments on both sides. The African Institution had got the story of the aide-de-camp wrong, either in whole or in part. Yet such barbaric treatment of pregnant slaves was a common practice and was confirmed, for instance, in the *Journal of a Residence on a Georgian Plantation* by the actress Fanny Kemble in 1838–9. Above the legal argument rolled the moral declamations of the contending parties. The prosecution case was supported by the hypothesis that if the slaves suspected that their masters were under attack from Europe, the lives of the settlers might be in danger. The prosecution, of course, did not support slavery in principle, but the freedom of the slaves must not be bought at the expense of their masters. Emancipation was an admirable ideal but in the existing economic difficulties of Great Britain it was unrealistic to assume that the government could compensate the slave-owners for the loss of their human property, which emancipation would entail. It was the voice of 'realism' at its least attractive.

In the best tradition of *State Trials*, John Hatchard's case is less remarkable for its legal implications than for its portrayal of two factions in English society in the early nineteenth century. It is certainly instructive to see that the abolitionists were not always above reproach in their conduct. According to the *Quarterly Review*, this was not the only occasion on which the African Institution had been responsible for issuing such details without verifying their accuracy.[5] On the other side, it is no less instructive to see men appearing, not as advocates of a monstrous tyranny but as reasonable men of goodwill, eager for humane and idealistic courses of action, yet owing a higher allegiance to the realities of legal and economic requirements.

Proceedings on the Trial of JOHN HATCHARD for a Libel, published in *The Tenth Report of the Directors of the African Institution*; tried in the Court of King's Bench, by a Special Jury, before the Hon. Sir Charles Abbott, Knight, one of the Justices of His Majesty's said Court, February 17th; 57 GEORGE III. A.D. 1817.

Counsel for the Prosecution

Mr. Serjeant Best (afterwards a Judge of the King's Bench)
Mr. Marryat
Mr. Curwood
Mr. Fitzgerald

Solicitors

Messrs. Martineau and Malton

Counsel for the Defendant

Mr. Attorney-General (Sir William Garrow, afterwards a Baron of the Exchequer)

Mr. Scarlett

Mr. Richardson (afterwards a Judge of the Common Pleas)

Solicitors

Messrs. Lambert and Son

The indictment was opened by Mr. Fitzgerald.

[*Each of the ten counts of the indictment cited the same passage from* The Tenth Report of the Directors of the African Institution.

'*The Directors are also informed that about a year ago the following circumstance took place in the island of Antigua. A gentleman who held the situation of aide-de-camp to the Governor Sir James Leith, having severely cart-whipped a negro woman of his own, who was pregnant, she laid her complaint before the Governor, who humanely attended to her story, and dismissed her with some money for herself and a note to her owner. Instead, however, of taking His Excellency's interference in good part, the gentleman gave the unfortunate woman an additional number of lashes, and dispatched a note to Sir James Leith, who in consequence ordered his secretary to inform the writer that Sir James had no further occasion for his services. On the receipt of this information, the gentleman dressed up one of his negro boys in his own uniform, and mounting him upon an ass, dispatched him with an insolent note to the Governor. He was afterwards indicted for cruelty at the express order of the Governor, but the grand jury refused to find the bill.*'

The first count of the indictment charged this as a libel on all eight of Sir James Leith's aides-de-camp: Thomas Norbury Kirby; Langford Lovell Hodge; Samuel Warner; John Horsford; Paul Horsford; William Gunthorpe; Nicholas Nugent, and George Ottley. Counts two to nine, inclusive, charged the passage as libelling individual aides-de-camp, each count, in turn, naming one of the eight. The tenth count charged the passage as a libel on the grand jury of Antigua and, incidentally, on the administration of criminal justice in the island.

No single aide-de-camp had been specified in the alleged libel but the first nine counts of the indictment had been drawn up to cover the contingency that they had been libelled collectively or that at least one of them must have been libelled individually.]

Mr. Serjeant Best. Gentlemen of the jury, the present prosecution has been directed by the legislature of the island of Antigua, for the purpose of protecting the characters of a most respectable class of men, the colonial aides-de-camp of the Governor of that island, and, which is still more important, the administration of justice there, from the slanders which form the subject of this indictment. And, I might add, for the purpose of protecting the lives of all the white inhabitants of that settlement, for I do not hesitate to assert that, unless the Institution from which this libel has proceeded shall be prevented from promulgating unfounded and exaggerated statements of supposed occurrences in the West Indies, there can be no security for those of our countrymen whose destiny it is to live in the midst of a negro population which has been rendered, by events in Europe, most sensitive to everything that relates to their condition, and which inhales disaffection and insubordination from every calumny upon their masters.

Do not imagine that I design to attribute any *ill intentions* to the society from which this libel has emanated. I know that some of the most respectable, honourable, and estimable men in this country are enrolled amongst its members, but, on that account, the slanders of which I complain are the more dangerous, because anything appearing to come from such persons—for I do not attribute to the respectable portion of this association the circulation of anything so false and malignant as this report—instantly receives from every class of society the most implicit credit. It is not therefore in resentment but in self-defence that the prosecutors now come forward. Long have they been anxious to meet, in this temple of truth and justice, those who have, without even the slightest foundation, imputed to the great body of slave-proprietors the most heinous crimes. But, until the present moment, the distance of the place where the crimes have been alleged to have been committed, and the difficulty of bringing witnesses hither, have prevented them from preferring their just complaints.

My learned friend, by reading the indictment, has informed
you that the libel therein set forth attacks the characters
of the colonial aides-de-camp to Sir James Leith, at that
time Governor of Antigua and the other Leeward Islands,
and severely reflects upon the grand jury of that settlement.
It is a part of what is called *The Tenth Report of the Directors
of the African Institution*. It runs thus. 'The Directors are also
informed that about a year ago the following circumstance
took place in the island of Antigua. A gentleman who held
the situation of aide-de-camp to the Governor, Sir James
Leith, having severely cart-whipped a negro woman of his
own, who was pregnant, she laid her complaint before the
Governor, who humanely attended to her story, and
dismissed her with some money for herself, and a note to
her owner.'

This aide-de-camp is represented to be such an inhuman
monster as to cart-whip a poor woman who was in that
state which would restrain any man, even though approaching
to a brute, from treating her with cruelty. 'Instead, however,
of taking His Excellency's interference in good part, the
gentleman gave the unfortunate woman an additional
number of lashes, and dispatched a note to Sir James Leith,
who in consequence ordered his secretary;' the contents of
the note are not stated, but we are to presume that it
asserted the right to treat with unbounded inhumanity any
unfortunate wretch in a state of slavery 'to inform the writer
that Sir James Leith had no further occasion for his services.
On the receipt of this information,' it is not enough therefore
to represent that a pregnant woman was cart-whipped, that
in consequence of her complaining she was treated with the
same cruelty a second time, and that her master was
dismissed and punished for his misconduct, but it is added
'the gentleman dressed up one of his negro boys in his own
uniform, and mounting him upon an ass, dispatched him with
an insolent note to the Governor.' This slander applies solely
to the aide-de-camp, but you will by what follows discover
that the real object of the writer is to cause it to be believed
that negro slaves in the West Indies receive no protection
from the colonial judicatures, and that they are in a situation
of unexampled wretchedness. 'He,' meaning the aide-de-camp,

'was afterwards indicted for cruelty at the express order of the
Governor, but the grand jury refused to find the bill.' Which
means that the grand jury were so deaf to the calls of
humanity, so corrupt, and so wicked, as to refuse to find this
bill, although the appeal of the unfortunate negro was
sanctioned by the support of the Governor, the protector of
all the oppressed in that island.

This libel does not merely state a single fact which might
have been mistaken or misunderstood by the writer, but it
relates a series of events in which different persons were
engaged. It is impossible that such a narration could have
originated in accident or in misconception of any story which
had been told in any part of the West Indies. It is a false,
scandalous, and malignant fabrication, invented for the wicked
purpose of holding out to the British public and to the negro
population of the West India islands—in the centre of which
be it remembered that the inhabitants of one large island
have thrown off the white yoke and established a negro
republic[6]— that those who in the situation of grand jurymen
are called to administer justice, are so debased by the horrid
tyranny in which a system of slavery allows them to indulge
that no negro can, under any possible circumstances, obtain
redress at their hands.

If this were true, ought such a system to be endured for a
moment? Could a Christian nation permit, for an instant,
a government to exist under which such things can happen?
And can there be a more wicked libel than such a malignant
misrepresentation, which must have been invented for the
purpose of beating down by false charges a cause which cannot
be subdued by fair argument? But it may be said, 'You have
not brought forward the *author* but only the printer.' That is
not the fault of the prosecutors, for immediately upon the libel
reaching the West Indies, my respectable and honourable
friend who sits behind me, and who holds the situation of
agent for Antigua, was directed by the two houses of
legislature of that island to call upon Mr. Hatchard to deliver
up his author. Mr. Hatchard told us that he had published
the report for the African Institution, and to them he must
refer us for the author. In consequence of this, we called upon
the African Institution. We desired them to deliver up, that

we might prosecute, the man who has dared to circulate through the world this most unfounded, infamous, and cruel slander. They, in their wisdom, thought proper to reply, 'You may go on against the printer, we shall not give up the author.' I am sure, if the respectable individuals whose names I have seen in the list of members of that society had been present, such an answer would not have been sent. It could only have proceeded from some persons of that respectable body who were influenced more by zeal than discretion in promoting the measures which that society has undertaken to advocate.

Can there be any good reason for this conduct? It occurs to me that the reason to be given may be this. 'The man who furnished this information is now in the island of Antigua, and by giving his name the Institution would surrender him to the vengeance of the British residents.' Is he there? If he be in the island of Antigua, he ought instantly to be driven from it, because he must be aware that not one scintilla of what he has stated in this paper ever existed in point of fact. He is therefore too wicked and mischievous a man to be permitted to remain for a single hour in that or in any other colony in the West Indies. If he be in this country, there cannot be any reasonable objection to giving him up. If given up, we should have proceeded against him in such a way as would have afforded him an opportunity of proving at the bar of a British court of justice the truth of what he has written. If he could have done so, the consequence would have been a call upon the legislature to provide, at any expense, the means by which the system of slavery under which human beings were thus maltreated should be abolished. But the African Society have thought proper not to disclose the author's name, and therefore I am driven to the necessity of indicting the printer, he being the only person against whom I have any means of proceeding.

Notwithstanding what the gentlemen slandered have suffered, notwithstanding the apprehensions which the inhabitants of Antigua have entertained from the circulation of these libels, I assure you that this prosecution is not instituted in any spirit of hostility. I assure you, gentlemen, that if charity constitutes a part of Christianity, there are as good Christians on the other side of the Atlantic as on this.

Injured although they have been, they seek not indemnity for the past, but security for the future. They fear nothing which can be said of them *with truth*. They do not desire to prevent their opponents from urging any arguments which their united talents can bring forward. In the fair field of argument, the freedom of the press, happily established in this country, will protect them. My clients merely desire that when their opponents hazard assertions, they will take care to be correctly informed as to their facts. Let them bear in mind that the only protection for the European inhabitants of our West Indian islands, surrounded as they are by a negro population, consists in the conviction entertained by the negroes, that the authority of their masters will be upheld by the mother country. If the negroes are to be told that the British settlers have not the protection of Great Britain, but that on the contrary a society, in which are to be found the highest names, is disseminating through the world papers showing that the European inhabitants of the West Indies must be held in detestation at home, and are ready to be delivered up to the vengeance of those negroes, is it possible that the spirit of insurrection can be controlled?

I never have been an advocate for slavery. On the contrary, I have always thought—and, I believe, those who send me here think—that if slavery could be put an end to consistently with justice to the interests of the great body of West Indian proprietors, it ought to be abolished. But let us not, in the eager pursuit of one object, lose sight of every other. Let us remember that if we owe humanity to the negroes, we also owe it to the white population. Let us remember that to abolish slavery, we must either send to the West Indies such a force as would be sufficient to protect the Europeans from the emancipated negroes, or we must bring home and indemnify the colonists, who upon the assurance of protection from the British government, have embarked their property in the cultivation of these settlements. If Great Britain is prepared to offer either alternative, I can venture to say that there is not an inhabitant in the West Indian islands who would not rejoice as much as any gentleman whom I have the honour of addressing, that this system should be overturned. I am afraid, however, that neither

alternative would be justified by the present state of our
finances, and since our countrymen must remain in the
plantations, let us not endanger their security by vilifying
that character which is their best protection. When a spirit
of insurrection is excited amongst the negroes, what means
have the African Institution to allay it? What power to shelter
its victims from its fury? The stoutest hearts will surely
tremble at dangers which they can neither resist nor share.

That this paper is a libel, I am sure there cannot be the
least doubt. It will be, however, for his lordship to say whether
my opinion be correct. It will be his lordship's duty—and
no one can discharge it better than the learned judge in
whose presence I have the honour to address you—to tell
you whether this paper be a libel or not. If his lordship shall
be of opinion that it is not a libel, whatever these respectable
gentlemen may have suffered, this prosecution must fail. If
his lordship shall be of opinion that it is a libel—and I cannot
doubt that that opinion will be delivered by his lordship—
there cannot be any defence for Mr. Hatchard. The defendant
has certainly selected an advocate—my learned friend the
Attorney-General—who, if it be possible for any talents to
offer a defence or to suggest a palliation of the guilt of this paper,
will offer it, but it appears to me to be altogether
indefensible. When you shall have received the rule of law from
his lordship, you will have no difficulty in this case, and the
result must be a verdict of guilty.

*   *   *

The remainder is a question of law, which, however, under a
late Act of Parliament, you are to decide, for the jury are
now judges of the law in cases of libel. But upon that
question you are directed by the same Act to receive the
assistance of his lordship, and I am convinced that whatever
opinion his lordship shall pronounce to you, you will follow.
But I should have no hesitation in leaving that question
to you, even if his lordship had not been directed to give
you his assistance, for can any man living doubt that to say
of a grand jury that a bill has been presented to them which
they have refused to find, accompanied with an insinuation
that they so refused because they chose to countenance the

crime of cart-whipping a pregnant woman, is a libel upon
that grand jury?

If, which is impossible, you should pronounce a verdict
of acquittal, and anybody were to publish in Antigua that
the jury who tried this cause found a verdict of not guilty
because they were enemies to the slave trade, and therefore
would not convict any person who had attacked the slave
trade, could any man doubt that this would be a libel?
The cases are precisely similar, and if juries were to allow
themselves to say that they would not act upon those
principles of law under which papers of this sort have been
long holden to be libels, and to adopt unknown rules for their
guidance, such conduct would destroy the liberty of the
press, and indeed all other liberty. Unless courts of justice
act upon known established rules, no man can know what
is libel, or indeed any other offence, and we should be in
the worst state of slavery—a total ignorance of the rules
by which to regulate our conduct. It is established that he
who calumniates either an individual or a public body, by
any writing, is a libeller. Individuals in high public stations,
and the grand inquest of Antigua, are by this paper greatly
slandered. The grand juries in the island of Antigua necessarily
require the same protection that the grand juries in this
country require, and I am sure they will receive it from you.

I have now laid the case before you, and have stated, as
distinctly as I can, the motives which have led to this
prosecution. I shall add but one circumstance more, and shall
then leave the case in your hands. Even at this moment, if
the African Institution, or Mr. Hatchard the defendant, whom
I consider as identified with them, will give up to us the
author of this libel, I will offer to you no evidence. I will
suffer a verdict of acquittal to be recorded. If that is done—
if it is not done, it is absolutely necessary that I should press
for a conviction here. For unless a conviction can be obtained
in such a case as this, the legislature, the grand jury, the
public functionaries in the island of Antigua have no
protection in the laws of that country from which they all
spring, and to which they have the strongest possible right to
look back for protection.

John Hatchard

EVIDENCE FOR THE PROSECUTION

Paul Horsford, Esq. sworn. Examined by Mr. Marryat.

Are you generally a resident in the island of Antigua?—I am generally a resident in the island of Antigua.

Of what government does the island of Antigua form a part?—Of the Leeward Island government.

Of the Leeward Islands, of what description?—The islands composing the Leeward Islands are Antigua, Montserrat, Tortola, and Nevis—there are two or three smaller islands of no signification.

Are they all in the West Indies?—Yes.

Mr. Justice Abbott. Are these called the Leeward Caribee Islands?—They are.

Mr. Marryat. Were you present when Sir James Leith came out and was sworn in as Governor?—I was.

About what time was that?—As far as my memory will serve me, I think it was about the month of June in 1814. I am not perfectly clear as to the month: the year I am certain of, and it was long before the month of August.

Was he Governor before the 1st of January 1815?—Certainly.

Had he in his capacity of Governor any colonial aides-de-camp in the island of Antigua?—He had.

Were you one of them?—I was.

How many others had he?—Seven others.

Will you favour us with the names of your co-aides-de-camp?—Mr. Thomas Norbury Kirby, Mr. Langford Lovell Hodge, Samuel Warner, John Horsford, myself, William Gunthorpe, Nicholas Nugent, and George Ottley.

Were those gentlemen residing in the island of Antigua, who were appointed as aides-de-camp for that colony?—They were.

Were they, generally speaking, proprietors of slaves in that island?—All of them.

Did those gentlemen, the eight you have named, continue as aides-de-camp while you remained in the island?—They did.

Till you left it?—Yes.

When did you leave it?—I left it on the 22nd of April in the last year.

Mr. Marryat. That, my lord, is a time subsequent to the publication of the report. I believe you are in the practice of the law yourself in the island?

Horsford. I am.

Is there a grand jury in the island, or for the island?—There is
a grand jury for the island.

Is it a grand jury for the whole island, or for a district or
division of the island?—For the whole island.

What situation do you hold in the profession of the law there?—
At present I hold the situation of Attorney-General.

I do not know whether you have terms or sessions there.—Sessions.

Which are held generally for the whole island?—Yes.

Is there a grand jury convened to each of those sessions for the
finding of bills?—There is.

How often?—Twice a year.

You have two sessions a year?—Yes.

Would it have been incident to your situation as Attorney-
General to have known of any prosecution directed by the
Governor of that island?—Certainly.

Were you at any time made acquainted with any prosecution
directed or intended by the Governor of that island against
either of his aides-de-camp?—I was not.

Was any bill preferred, to your knowledge, against either of
Sir James Leith's aides-de-camp during his government?—
There was not.

Could such a bill have been preferred without your knowing it?—
Impossible.

Mr. Justice Abbott. I take you to say that no bill was preferred
against either of them, nor could have been without your
knowledge?—I conceive so.

Mr. Justice Abbott. Is it part of your official duty as Attorney-
General to be made acquainted with every prosecution? I
know in many cases it is so. In Wales, at the great sessions,
the Attorney-General of the circuit is acquainted with all
prosecutions.—In all cases where the King's name is used, the
Attorney-General appears for the King.

Mr. Attorney-General. It is so in Scotland likewise.

Mr. Justice Abbott. Yes, the Lord Advocate there appears for the
King in all prosecutions.

Mr. Marryat. From the date you have given us of your leaving
the island of Antigua, I do not know whether the *Tenth
Report of the African Institution* had reached that island.—Not
that I know of.

During your residence there, were you cognisant of any such transaction as is alluded to in this prosecution, of any complaint made by a woman to the Governor against either of his aides-de-camp, for cruelty to her?—None.

Was any aide-de-camp dismissed during that time?—No.

Were his aides-de-camp residing much with him, until you left the island?—Occasionally with him; never residing in the house with him.

Never residing in the Government House with him?—No, they attended him on duty but did not make the Government House the place of their residence.

Were you acquainted with any misunderstanding between him and any of his aides-de-camp, on any subject of complaint which had come before him?—None that ever came to my knowledge.

Mr. Justice Abbott. No complaint against any of the aides-de-camp came to your knowledge?—No.

Paul Horsford, Esq. cross-examined by Mr. Attorney-General.

I perceive that in your two very respectable situations in the island, if there had been such a thing you must have known it, either as Attorney-General instituting such prosecution, or as aide-de-camp to the Governor. Therefore, you are, as I am, quite unable to point this to any particular person. Whatever it may have originated in, whether a publication or anything else, it does not point to any of those gentlemen?— Certainly.

Doubtless you were consulted before the indictment was framed. You have named everybody who at that time came under the description of colonial aide-de-camp to the Governor. Those eight gentlemen were all to whom that description applied?— Yes.

Mr. Justice Abbott. You said that it did not apply to any one of those gentlemen. What did you mean to say did not apply to any of those gentlemen?—The statement which has been made as composing the libel.

Mr. Justice Abbott. You mean that the facts there stated do not apply to them?—No.

Mr. Justice Abbott. Do you mean that the matter itself does not apply?—I cannot say as to the matter, the facts, it appears to me, can apply to nobody else.

Mr. Marryat. You know no matter of fact to point this publication to either?—I do not.

Mr. Justice Abbott. You say the facts do not apply to either of the aides-de-camp but the matter can apply to no one else but one of them?—Just so.

Mr. Philip Martineau sworn. Examined by Mr. Curwood.

I believe you are attorney for the prosecution?—I am.

Do you know Mr. Hatchard's shop?—Yes, I do.

In Piccadilly?—Yes.

Did you, on the 30th of October last, buy the book you hold in your hand, at that shop?—Yes, I did.

Was it sold by one of his servants?—Mr. Hatchard was in the shop at the time.

Mr. Justice Abbott. Where is his shop?—In Piccadilly.

Does that purport to be the *Tenth Report of the African Institution*?—Yes, it does.

Mr. Philip Martineau cross-examined by Mr. Scarlett.

Do you know of the publication of any other *Tenth Report* since that?—Yes, I do. I have had it sent me by Mr. Lambert, the attorney on the other side.

You know that a new edition was published?—Yes, I do.

In which this passage . . .

Mr. Serjeant Best. I object to that.

Mr. Attorney-General. I apprehend my learned friend is not founded in his objection. Indeed, I ought to beg Mr. Scarlett's pardon, he would support his question better than I can, but I rise to sustain my learned friend's question, to which it does not appear to me there is any objection.

Mr. Justice Abbott. It will be more regular to hear the objection first. You will then know better how to point your answer to it.

Mr. Attorney-General. I will state what the question is, and then my learned friend may point out his objection. Whether in the new edition sent to him, this passage was not entirely omitted?

Mr. Serjeant Best. I submit to your lordship that that question cannot be asked, because, as I apprehend, the *Tenth Report* itself must be produced in order to see whether it does contain it or not.

Mr. Attorney-General. This is not the time for me to observe upon the topics which have been urged—not but that I thought we might have been in the next cause long ago. I am here to show that there was no malicious intention, for that the moment the defendant was apprised of this, he cut out all that was charged to be offensive, and sent forth to the world a new and harmless edition, and not only that but marking it as having omitted something that was not substantiated.

Mr. Justice Abbott. The contents of the written paper must appear by the production of the paper itself. He says a copy of a new edition has been sent to him. I should think, if you wish to put it in, you may show it to him and give it in evidence, if you think fit.

Mr. Scarlett. My lord, I was not asking a word about the contents. I only ask as to the fact, whether a new edition has been published?—Yes, there has.

Mr. Justice Abbott. I have it down that a new edition of the *Tenth Report* has been since sent to him.

Mr. Scarlett. And that is not the copy you now produce?—That is not.

Mr. Curwood. At what time did you receive this second edition?— It was after Michaelmas term. I think in the month of December.

After you had threatened a prosecution?—After the bill was found.

Mr. Justice Abbott. Why should you go into that? Is it not sufficient that when that is produced, the contents of it will appear?

Mr. Serjeant Best. Certainly, my lord.

[*The allegedly libellous passage, cited in the indictment, was then read out.*]

Mr. Marryat. Just read what the pamphlet purports by its title to be, whether it purports to be the *Tenth Report of the Directors of the African Institution*, read at the Annual General Meeting held on the 27th day of March 1816.

Mr. Law. It does.

Mr. Marryat. It is so stated in the indictment.

Mr. Serjeant Best. That is the case on the part of the prosecution.

[*After some legal argument on the method of setting out dates in the indictment and on the requirement of proof that Sir James Leith was Governor of Antigua, the Attorney-General opened the case for the defence.*]

Mr. Attorney-General. Gentlemen of the jury, I rise to endeavour to perform my duty to Mr. Hatchard under circumstances which are certainly rather novel, and not remarkably agreeable to the person who has to perform it. The course which my learned friend—whose avocations have called him elsewhere, not retiring while he had anything to do, but having performed all the duty which he today owes to those who, to use his expression, have sent him here—has pursued, is an extraordinary, and I think rather an alarming one. For he tells you that he has been sent here by the command of the legislative body of the island of Antigua. That legislative body send my learned friend here as the prosecutor of an alleged libel upon some individual, who formerly constituted a part of the community of that island! I will venture to say, in the hearing and subject to the correction of as learned and as well informed a magistrate as ever presided in the seat of justice, that this thing is done now for the first time. I know that persons who have formerly, much to their own honour and to the advantage of the country, filled the office which—unworthily compared to them—I have now the honour to fill, have been repeatedly ordered by the Commons House of Parliament to institute proceedings in certain cases of libel, but in no case for libels upon private individuals, to whom and to each and every of whom, the courts of our country are open to receive their individual complaints, and who ought, at least in this sacred sanctuary of justice, to meet those whom they would accuse without any extraordinary or unnatural influence. The only case in which anything is admitted that in the slightest degree differs from that which I state to be the condition of all English subjects, is where for the protection of the whole community a branch of the legislature commands its officer to institute a prosecution for something that affects the security of the state, but this is the first time, in the course of a longer experience in this place than—considering that our days pass away, and that one is hastening forward to the conclusion of them, one has a pleasure to recollect—after a long experience in this place, it

is the first time that my mind has been afflicted by hearing
that any prosecution against which I have had to contend
was instituted by the order of any legislative body. If my
learned friend were, by the rules of the court, in a condition
to reply to me upon this topic, I know perfectly well the
fertility and the resources of his mind, and that he would
have something that might, at least for a moment, serve by
way of answer to the observation, but when it comes to be
examined, it vanishes into air.

*   *   *

What! The eight colonial aides-de-camp of the deceased Sir
James Leith are to have the whole weight of the legislative
body of Antigua to bear down a London bookseller, who is
supposed to have committed an offence against them! But
my learned friend—for it would have been much too bold
merely to have stated that in an English court of justice—
adds that this forsooth is a libel on the administration of
justice. On some of the various objects which he states to
belong to the prosecution, it will be my painful duty to make
a few remarks to you. One of them was to preserve the
administration of justice in His Majesty's West India islands
pure, and to protect the characters of those who are assembled
for the purpose of giving purity to that administration, and it
is supposed that the *Tenth Report of the African Institution* is a
libel upon the grand jury of the island of Antigua.

Gentlemen, it is a stalking-horse in order to captivate and
to run away with you, to talk of this being a libel upon the
grand jury of the island of Antigua. What is it that is said of
the grand jury? I pass by the rest of the case to return to it
presently—to dismiss this, which I state to be an attempt to
carry away unfairly your sober judgments, and to make you
believe you are called upon to do that today which you would
do readily and willingly on any occasion—to protect the pure
administration of justice in the most remote part of His
Majesty's dominions. What is said here? That a complaint
was presented to the grand jury of the island, and that they
refused to find a bill. To which my learned friend, without
the least alteration of the tone of his voice, adds because in
the West India islands every man who constitutes one of the

grand jury keeps slaves—every man there has an interest in holding up everything which his neighbours do in the treatment of slaves, and therefore when you present a bill to the grand jury, even by order of the Governor, a thing better spared than practised, you cannot obtain justice if the matter be the ill treatment of a slave. Why, gentlemen, if that had found its way into the report of the African Institution, I should have found the labours of today much more severe than they are. If the reporter had said the grand jury of the island of Antigua refused to interfere, however plain the question before them; if they had viewed the dead body of a slave, who at an advanced period of her pregnancy had had that which, thank God, we know only by the reports of the treatment, which it is supposed has sometimes obtained in these scenes of melancholy inflictions—I say, supposed to have sometimes obtained—if it had been said that, upon a view of a dead body and a charge of murder against a white master, the grand jury had passed on to other matters, and had refused to find a bill, they would not have heard from me that it was not a libel upon them. But is it a libel upon them to say merely they refused to find a bill? Look to the tables before Parliament, and see how persons accused before magistrates in this, our country, are dealt with, and you will find that the number of those against whom bills are presented before grand juries, and who are put upon trial, is every year much smaller than that of the persons who have been accused before magistrates. I think I could venture to say that there is not a year in which there are not very many scores—I should think some hundreds in London and Middlesex alone—against whom complaints have been made before magistrates on oath for the commission of felonies, which charges notwithstanding, the grand juries returned, saying—not that there is no foundation for the charge, and that the party is innocent— no, but saying, 'Ignoramus—we do not find the bill.' Now, all that is said against this grand jury of the island of Antigua is that a bill of indictment was ordered by the Governor to be presented to the grand jury but that it was not found. This is charged as a libel. Mr. Hatchard is a mere scapegoat, to whom in the beginning, the middle, and the end of my learned friend's speech, there was an invitation that he should

make his peace on very cheap terms, if terms could be cheap
which involved a dereliction of his character and his honour.
And the African Institution might receive their deliverance
upon very cheap terms, if baseness were consistent with those
principles on which they have acted in the administration
of that Institution. My learned friend has thrown out that
upon these cheap terms, even if they do not appear to men of
honour to be extremely cheap, Mr. Hatchard may today go
free.

*   *   *

I will not mention the name, but I remember very early in
my professional life, before I was called to the bar, being
present when one of the most illustrious characters of the
period in which we have lived—who very soon left us to
serve his country in a most distinguished station, and most
difficult in which his country could require those services—
I mean Mr. Pitt—and another great man, a friend of mine,
the present Lord Erskine, being concerned for a person
charged with a libel, the description of the prosecutor was
that he was tall and proud. A witness was called into the box
to say that was of and concerning the prosecutor, and the
witness was cross-examined. 'Do you mean to say that Mr.
A. B. the prosecutor,' I choose to call him so to avoid the
name, 'is tall and proud?' 'Why, you will agree with me he
is tall.' 'Yes, yes, but will you say he is proud?' That was a
difficult question to the friend of the man described as proud,
but the witness felt no difficulty. He said, 'To people in
general I have no doubt that the person of whom you are
speaking is considered to be proud. His manners are retired
with respect to strangers. I who have been honoured by his
acquaintance and intimacy, know that he is a very affable
and a very kind man, but I have reason to believe that those
who do not know him so well consider him as proud.' There
are two qualities, one which does belong to him eminently, for
he is tall; and the other, which the world ascribes, that he is
proud. Now, to apply that, suppose among the aides-de-camp
of Sir James Leith there had been any gentleman remarkable,
not for that for which I have no doubt in the world the
learned and respectable person who has been called as a
witness, the gentleman to whom the island had to look for

advice as Attorney-General, was remarkable. Suppose he had
been distinguished for some extraordinary absurdity of
manners, or some extreme deformity of person, and a person
had said, 'That soldier, that remarkable aide-de-camp of
Sir James Leith, that man who was always dancing about
like a Merry Andrew.' Suppose he had St. Vitus's Dance, or
any malady which made him unsteady in his gait, or without
putting that which might give anybody offence, describing some
personal remarkable circumstance about him, and then it
had been said, 'Why, he cart-whipped his slave four months
gone with child. This was represented to the Governor, the
Governor reprimanded the gentleman for it, gave the woman
some money, and told the gentleman he had no further
occasion for his services. Upon which, this dancing gentleman,'
following up the description I have supposed, 'took offence,
dressed up one of his slave boys in his own uniform, and sent
him with an insulting message to the Governor.' Suppose the
gentleman's brother had been called, and asked, 'Whom do
you understand to be represented by this aide-de-camp, who
was reprimanded by the Governor?' He would say, 'My
brother, the Attorney-General, because he is described by a
circumstances which belongs to him. He has a complaint which
makes him unsteady in his walk, and I am sure by his being
described as dancing about everybody so understood it.' If that
had been charged as a libel of and concerning this gentleman,
it would have been a question to be left to you, whether the
libel was not meant to apply to the gentleman to whom it was
stated to allude. Not that I mean to put any case disrespectful
to the learned gentleman who has been called. In all I say, I
mean to treat him with the greatest possible respect.

But let us now come to the libel in question and see
whether there is a possibility, whilst the law of England
continues as it is, that Mr. Hatchard or anybody else can be
said to be within the present indictment. The libel itself
speaks of one individual, and one individual alone: not of
eight, not of any number exceeding one, but one individual
alone, and without anything to separate him from the other
seven aides-de-camp, who were equally colonial aides-de-camp
to Sir James Leith at the time to which it has reference.
What is the evidence we have upon the subject? Is there any

application of it to any one of them? The learned Attorney-General tells you there were but eight aides-de-camp in the island.

Mr. Richardson. The indictment charges it to be a libel of and concerning some one of the eight.

Mr. Attorney-General. Gentlemen, I was speaking of the evidence, and what my learned friend has suggested to me is convenient, because this is the proper place to call your attention to it. The libel is of and concerning some one of eight persons. You cannot say by your verdict, 'We are of opinion Mr. Hatchard has published a libel of and concerning some one of eight persons.' It would be a bad verdict. You must say, upon your oaths, 'We are of opinion, upon the evidence before us, that the defendant is guilty of publishing a libel against A.B.'—or C.D., or any other of the two combined letters in the alphabet describing Christian and surnames— 'He is guilty of publishing this of and concerning one particular individual.' Let us see whom you can say. Was it the Attorney-General, Mr. Horsford? I asked the witness. He says, 'No, there is nothing that points to me particularly. It would be easy to point to me.' If he meant to apply this to him, he might say, 'A man holding one of the highest legal situations in the island.' Nobody after that would have doubted that he meant Mr. Paul Horsford, the Attorney-General. But he goes on and tells you it is impossible for any man alive to single out any one of these persons to whom it is supposed to apply, more than another. For as to all of them it is false. 'I had the means of knowing,' he says, 'if any such complaint was made to the Governor, I must have known if any indictment was preferred, and the draft of it must have had my signature to authorise its going to the grand jury. I must have known of the reprimand of the Governor, and the dismissal of the aide-de-camp, and I cannot give you anyone by conjecture, imagination, or guess, on whom you can affix this. And if you called not only me, but if you called the whole white population, there is not a man who could tell you what name you could insert in a special verdict, as that of the individual of and concerning whom Mr. Hatchard was guilty of publishing this statement.'

*   *   *

Now what is the character of that on which you are called on today to decide? And what is the object of those who have sent my learned friend here, under their legislative order, to make these the subjects of discussion, knowing that what passes here will be read in Antigua? And it is the knowing that which makes me acquit myself of the duty I owe Mr. Hatchard with little satisfaction to myself. I am ill at ease, God knows. I do the best things badly, but I am far short of feeling satisfaction here. When I am about to submit a sentiment to you, I am pulled back by the spectre of the consequences that would arise. I feel that however causelessly this is brought here by those who have sent my learned friend, I must endeavour to do my duty as a good citizen to the state, as a friend to the black population of the West Indies, and no less a friend to the white. For where in Britain can be found a man who can feel a disposition to be an enemy to the white population? I hope they have not got the length of saying every white man must be an enemy to the whites in the West Indies, who wishes to increase the security, and exalt the character of those who constitute that population by exterminating abuses which in every community are unfortunately to be found. Unless such men must necessarily be the enemies of the white population of the West Indies, there is no person who feels an interest on my side of the case who is not only not an enemy to them but who does not show in every moment, and does not feel in every pulsation of his heart, that he is the kindest friend of that population. My learned friend talks of numbers and physical strength, and of the comparative condition of this part of the community and the other. This I will say, if anybody thinks it worthwhile to remember what I say, that the best protection is kindness and Christian affection to those placed under their authority, and that those who have laboured to bring forward this reformed and improved condition are the best friends of both.

Mr. Hatchard, the bookseller, wants no introduction in this place. He is one of the most respectable tradesmen in the metropolis. He has been carrying on a business, always attended with peril and danger, in such a manner as to exempt him—until the legislative body of Antigua have ordered him to be prosecuted—not only from prosecution but from reproach. Look at the shelves of his warehouse, the contents of them are calculated to promote and increase science and useful knowledge; to enlarge the sphere of the moral fitness of mankind; and I will venture to say that no purchaser who leaves his shop can make a selection which has not the object of making him a better man than he was before the purchase. This is the man today brought before you for publishing a libel on the grand jury of the island of Antigua, and on an unnamed and undesignated, a not-to-be-found individual. I am obliged to take liberties with language, to describe the anomalous condition of men not-to-be-found. This man of virtue and integrity is supposed to have published this, with a view to traduce the character either of the grand jury in its aggregate character, or some one of eight individuals who fill the offices of aides-de-camp of Sir James Leith.

Well, but my learned friend is not ordered by this supreme authority to consider that Mr. Hatchard meant anything wrong—he did not tell you so—he does not state it if he had been, and I am sure he would tell you he believes Mr. Hatchard never read the *Tenth Report* till after the prosecution. Still, a bookseller who sells a book must be taken to have read it. I am not attempting to deceive you. But Mr. Hatchard, by my learned friend, is considered so innocent that you could not fail to observe how concerned he was to let him walk away and tell his family, 'Oh, it was but a summer's cloud, there is no interruption to our happiness, nobody believed I was malignant! I was the instrument of doing something that brought me within the scope of an indictment, but there is no harm done and I go free.' Upon what terms? 'Why,' says my learned friend, 'Only give up your author, that is all we want of you.' And then my learned friend's own mind immediately suggested to him the probable condition of the author. 'He is in Antigua,' says my learned friend. Is he in Antigua? 'Give up your author.' He knows that Mr. Hatchard cannot give up his author.

Well, but then the African Institution, what will you do about them? Why, I have told you already, they have not desired me to conceal it, in their title page it is stated to be the Tenth Report of that African Institution. Why, I think we might as well have had an indictment against them. My learned friend gave us a hint at the persons composing that body. It would have been a very good indictment, on the precedent of the present, to have said that all the African Institution, or some one of them—I have seen such indictments, where they know very little about indictments— that all or some one of the African Institution published this, and therefore you, the jury, be so good as find out some one. I will give the names of all, and as it is published in their names, find out one whom you can say you will find guilty of having published it. Well, but the African Institution published this with a malicious intent to injure either the grand jury or some of these individuals, the aides-de-camp of Sir James Leith. The African Institution consists of persons who I hope will be spared, by the providence of God, long to add to the blessings they have for many years been conferring on their country in various forms and shapes. And if it should please God now to terminate their useful career, we shall, as to some of them in particular, find their characters in the page of history amongst the most illustrious benefactors of mankind. They have been labouring incessantly to break the chains of bondage, and to prevent the scenes of horror, desolation, and bloodshed, which tore parents from their children, and children from their parents, and took them to a foreign shore, to endure great hardships in the voyage, their lives not being mended after that transatlantic voyage—they have for twenty years been labouring, with splendid co-adjutors, who are gone to their silent graves—and have found still much to be done. I repeat it again, they have done it for the benefit of the black population, and at the same time for the benefit of the whites, by whom they are surrounded.

In their anxious desire of doing this, they communicate to each other and, by the press, to the public, the reports of the transactions of the Institution of which they are distinguished members. They cannot record the transactions in the West Indies as eye-witnesses, but they have established the means of intercourse and correspondence with some of the most respectable persons to be found there, from whom they receive what experience has taught them to be authentic, correct, and fair representations of scenes they think it necessary to communicate. May it not happen—must it not happen, in the state of things in which we mortals are placed, that into all such transactions error occasionally may creep? May it not happen that a humane and benevolent person, known to be corresponding with the Institution for bettering the condition of the people of Africa, may be imposed upon by benevolent persons who wish to promote their object, who are themselves imposed upon as to the fact they narrate, and perhaps in too glowing colours observe upon it? Is it quite inconsistent with our experience to believe that those who are anxious to make these subjects, subjects of public and popular discussion, to have them made the subject of tract upon tract, and treatise upon treatise, till we are tired of the postman bringing them to our door—is it quite inconsistent with our experience to know that persons may be found in the community of the West Indies who will send what they know to be false to a person who they know is likely to communicate it to those whom he corresponds with at home, to draw their reports into disgrace, and make them afraid of going on with the work, to bring them into disrepute?

* * *

SUMMING-UP

Mr. Justice Abbott. Gentlemen of the jury, this is an indictment against John Hatchard for the publication of a supposed libel. By the indictment, two distinct characters are given to this publication. One is that it has a tendency, and is calculated, to defame the several persons who filled the situation of aide-de-camp to Sir James Leith, who was the Governor-General of the Leeward Islands at the period alluded to in the publication. The other is that it has a tendency to, and that it is published therefore with the intention of bringing the criminal justice of the island of Antigua into disrepute, by representing that criminal justice there was not duly administered on the behalf of slaves. These two characters, you see, are perfectly distinct, and I shall by and by request the favour of your opinion on each of them.

* * *

This publication and your verdict have nothing at all to do
with any general question relating to the slave-trade or its
abolition, or with the manner in which persons in that
unfortunate situation are or ought to be treated. No general
question at all is involved in your verdict, neither is it of
any importance whether the prosecution in question has been
instituted under the direction of the legislative body of the
island of Antigua, or not. It is quite immaterial to a jury, who
are to pass a verdict of guilty or not guilty on an individual,
who or what his prosecutor may be. It has been said that the
object of this prosecution was not so much to punish Mr.
Hatchard, the publisher, as by the medium of a prosecution
against him to compel a disclosure of the original author of
this slander. With that you seem to me to have as little to do
as with the other topics. There is no doubt that by the law
of this country, and of all other civilised countries, a printer
or bookseller is answerable criminally as well as civilly, for
the contents of the books he publishes, no less than the author
of them. If, indeed, the law should be otherwise, reputation,
the protection of which is one of the greatest objects of the law,
as much as the protection of property, and scarcely less than
the protection of life itself, would be wholly unprotected. For
if publishers were not answerable, as the authors are generally
unknown, slanders might be circulated to any extent, and on
any subject, without any possible means of prevention or
punishment. It was not indeed pretended by the advocate
for the defendant that Mr. Hatchard is not answerable for
this publication, if in your opinion it should turn out to be
criminal. As little have you to do with the question whether
there has been a second edition, or what may be its contents.
A person cannot relieve himself from a charge of libel by
publishing a contradiction, even on the next day. That is
matter for consideration at another time and place, but does
not lead to an acquittal of the original charge.

Gentlemen, you all know very well that the injury that
is done to the reputation of a particular person by a
publication of today cannot be remedied by a retraction
tomorrow. Many of those who see the original may never live
or be in the way to see the contradiction of it: and in the
meantime if they see it, great mischief must be done,

irreparable injury may be suffered. As little have you to do
with the body by whom this publication is sent into the world.
I mean the African Institution. Because however high and
honourable the individuals who compose it may be, however
laudable and praiseworthy their general views, yet if in the
prosecution of those views, laudable as they may be, they put
forth to the world slanders upon an individual, or upon any
body of individuals, or upon the administration of justice in
any particular place, they are as much amenable to the law
for such an act as the meanest subject of the country.

*   *   *

I have been invited to give my opinion on the contents of this
paper, and it is probably my duty to do so. But you are not
to be governed by my opinion, or give any greater weight
to it than in the exercise of your own judgment and reason
you think it entitled to. For the character of the paper is to
be determined by your opinion, and not by mine. I am of
opinion that this publication, ambiguously as it is expressed
as to the individual, and false as it is in all its parts, has a
tendency to bring all the persons who hold the situations of
aides-de-camp of Sir James Leith into suspicion and disgrace,
and is therefore a libel in the first view in which I put it. I
am also of opinion, that, taking the whole together, the
expression at the close, "but the grand jury refused to find
the bill," does mean to impute an improper refusal. That is
my opinion upon the two questions, but I request you to
exercise your judgment, and found your verdict upon the
result of that judgment.

*The jury immediately found the defendant guilty upon the first and last
counts.*

[*On 10 May 1817 Serjeant Best moved for judgment against John
Hatchard in the Court of King's Bench. Various affidavits were read
on Hatchard's behalf, including evidence of good character from
Sir Robert Peel and Lord Grantham. Another affidavit described
the reaction of the African Institution to two letters, from Sir
James Leith and the Hon. Thomas Norbury Kirby, published
in the* Courier, The Times, *and the* Morning Chronicle *on 4
October 1816, denying the truth of the libel. A meeting of the*

Directors of the African Institution was held and a report published in the same three newspapers.

'At a special meeting of the Directors of the African Institution, held at the Westminster Library on Saturday the 12th of October 1816. On reading in the Courier *newspaper of the 4th instant, two letters published by order of the Council and Assembly of Antigua, the one from the Hon. Thomas Norbury Kirby, of that island, addressed to Sir James Leith, late Governor of the Leeward Islands, and now Governor of Barbados; and the other, in answer thereto, from the said Governor, to the said Mr. Kirby, contradicting a statement in the* Tenth Report *of this Institution, and on reading a letter of the 8th day of April, 1815, addressed to the Secretary of this Institution, by a correspondent in the West Indies, in which the statement referred to in the preceding letters was originally communicated to this Institution: Resolved, that it appears from the said letters of the Hon. Thomas N. Kirby, and Sir James Leith (of the authenticity of which the Directors see no reason to doubt), that the statement referred to, though communicated by a gentleman on whose accuracy they reasonably relied, has been contradicted from the highest authority. That the Directors have in this instance strong ground for believing that their informant was persuaded of the truth of the facts which we reported, because they have had experience of his veracity and correctness in former and subsequent cases, and because it is impossible to impute to him any motive for the inventing such a story, or propagating it, knowing it to be false. He had nothing to gain by deceiving the Institution, but had to lose by it the good opinion, which by his benevolent efforts to promote its objects he had previously acquired, and the public nature of the facts represented made the speedy detection of the imposture unavoidable: Resolved, that the Secretary do write to the said correspondent by the first conveyance, in the name of the Board, enclosing a copy of these resolutions, and requesting that he will immediately transmit the necessary explanations on the subject: Resolved, that copies of these resolutions be immediately published in all the London newspapers, in which the publication of the Council and Assembly of Antigua has appeared: By order of the Board, Thomas Harrison, Secretary.'*

Between his trial and the motion for judgment against him, Hatchard had written to the African Institution and asked whether the Directors would be prepared to make available to him the letter from their unnamed correspondent in the West Indies. He received a reply from the Secretary, which was included in another affidavit at the time of the judgment.

'*African Institution, 29th April, 1817.*

'*Sir, Your application has been submitted to the Directors of the African Institution, at a meeting assembled for that purpose, and I am directed to return the following answer. The Directors would be far from desiring to screen from merited punishment any person who had sent them false information, if they could fairly ascribe to him an intention to deceive; but in the present instance they have every reason to conclude that he believed the erroneous information which he sent them to be true, and they therefore do not feel themselves at liberty to violate the obligation arising from the confidence reposed in them by the writer of the letter for which you ask. The Directors, therefore, while they deeply regret that you should be exposed to any ill consequences from an act in which there was certainly, on your part, nothing intentionally wrong or inconsistent with the respectable character you have always maintained, are of opinion that they cannot, without injustice to a third person, relieve you from that hardship by communicating to you his letter. They, however, entertain a hope that the prosecutors will not think it a good reason for acting towards you with a harshness from which they were willing, in consideration of your innocence, to abstain, that you do not comply with a condition which it is out of your power to perform. I have the honour to be, Sir, your obedient servant, Thomas Harrison, Sec. A.I.*'

After legal representations on both sides, judgment against Hatchard was pronounced by Mr. Justice Bayley. What follows is the conclusion of his speech.]

Mr. *Justice Bayley.* That somebody is very highly criminal in this case, no one who has read the publication can at all doubt; that it has originated in wilful and wicked fabrication, no man alive can doubt. That it is defeating the purposes of justice to withhold that information by which the wicked criminality might be traced up to the original author, is obvious. However, the Court does not feel itself warranted in visiting upon you that which is not your offence, satisfied as they are that you have done everything in your power to discover who the author is, and they feel that they have no right to add to your punishment because you have not given up that author, whom you really are absolutely incapable of giving up. At the same time, every person who publishes a libel is answerable for that libel, and if no other is forthcoming to the hands of justice, the person by whom the publication is made is the person who must, to a certain extent at least, answer. Not that there is the same degree of criminality in, and consequently there ought not to be the same degree of punishment inflicted upon, the person who stands merely in the character of a bookseller, selling for other persons under circumstances which imply no want of caution on his part. You did not receive it from suspicious characters, you received it from persons upon whom you thought you might with propriety and confidence rely.

Taking all the circumstances of the case into consideration, taking the character which has been given you into consideration, and taking into consideration that you are a sacrifice to other persons, that this has not originated with you, and that you are not able to give up the real author, this Court doth order and adjudge that for this your offence you do pay to the King a fine of 100*l*., and that you be imprisoned in the custody of the Marshal of the Marshalsea until that fine is paid.

The defendant immediately paid the fine, and was discharged.

Notes

Introduction

1 *Hours in a Library*, 1892, vol. 3, p. 307.
2 *Ibid.*
3 1 *State Trials*, p. xix.
4 *Ibid.*, p. xxi.
5 *History of England*, 1849–61, vol. 1, p. 3.
6 *Narratives of State Trials in the Nineteenth Century*, 1882, vol. 1, p. v.
7 *Ibid.*, vol. 1, p. x.
8 British Museum Add. MSS., 5880 f. 198b.
9 1 *State Trials*, p. xlvii.
10 *Ibid.*, p. xxii.
11 *Ibid.*, p. xxii.
12 *Ibid.*, p. li.
13 *Life and Adventures of Peter Porcupine*, 1796, p. 22.
14 *Ibid.*, pp. 22–3.
15 *The Progress of a Plough-Boy to a Seat in Parliament*, ed. William Reitzel, 1933, p. 138.
16 Advertisement leaf in 22 *State Trials*.
17 *Biographical, Literary, and Political Anecdotes of the Most Eminent Persons of the Present Age*, 1797, vol. 1, p. 235.
18 1 Vent. 293.

Salmon's Preface

1 John Rushworth, *Historical Collections*, 1659–1701.

One   Sir Thomas More

1 *The Mirror of Virtue in Worldly Greatness: or, The Life of Sir Thomas More*, 1626. The quotation is from S. W. Singer's modernized text.
2 *Op cit.*
3 *Op. cit.*
4 This account of More's trial is drawn from three sources: Edward Hall, *Chronicle*, 1542; Lord Herbert of Cherbury, *Life and Reign of Henry VIII*, 1649; Cressacre More, *Life and Death of Sir Thomas More*, 1631.

Three   Colonel John Penruddock

1 *Mercurius Politicus* 15–22 March 1655. Quoted in Margaret James and Maureen Weinstock, *England during the Interregnum*, 1935, pp. 94–5.
2 Sir John Glynne (1603–66), formerly Recorder of London. Of his

conduct in Penruddock's case, Samuel Butler wrote in the 1674 edition of *Hudibras*:

> Did not the learned Glynne and Maynard
> To make good subjects traitors strain hard?

3 A defendant convicted of treason was liable to forfeit his estate as well as his life. If he refused to plead and was pressed to death, his estate might be saved for his heirs.

4 William Steele (d. 1680), Glynne's successor as Recorder of London.

5 *History of the Rebellion*, ed. W. Dunn Macray, 1888, vol. 5, pp. 373–9.

Four   Theobald Wolfe Tone

1 William Jackson was tried and convicted of treason in Dublin in 1794–5. He died in court before being sentenced. *Cf.* 25 *State Trials*, pp. 783–890.

2 Tadeusz Andrzej Bonawentura Kosciuszko (1746–1817) was a Polish soldier and statesman who served under Washington in the American War of Independence. In 1794 he led a Polish army in an unsuccessful attempt to establish an independent Polish republic on the American model.

3 Charette de la Contrie (1763–96) and Charles-Eugène-Gabriel Virot de Sombreuil (1769–95) were both executed by firing squads after unsuccessful attempts to overthrow the revolutionary régime in France.

Five   John Bastwick, Henry Burton, and William Prynne

1 *Diary of Samuel Pepys*, ed. H. B. Wheatley, 1893–9, vol. 2, p. 244.

2 1 & 2 Philip and Mary cap. 9 (1555); 1 Elizabeth I cap. 6 (1558).

3 Dr John Williams, Bishop of Lincoln, who was fined and committed to the Tower for publishing 'false news and tales' to the scandal of the government. *Cf.* 3 *State Trials*, pp. 769–824.

4 A preliminary speech of Prynne's precedes this in 3 *State Trials*, pp. 746–9.

Six   Richard Baxter

1. 11 *State Trials*, pp. 494–6.

2 Licenser of the Press during the reigns of Charles II and James II.

Seven   Edmund Curll

1 Samuel Richardson, *Selected Letters*, ed. John Carroll, 1964, pp. 46–7.

2 *State Trials* queries whether this word should be 'formerly'.

3 The author of the report was Sir John Strange.

Eight   Henry Sampson Woodfall

1 21 *State Trials*, p. 1040.

2 *Creevey*, ed. John Gore, 1948, p. 207.

3 Talesmen were those jurors who were sworn if an insufficient number of special jurors appeared.
4 A reference to the stamping of sheets for newspapers under the provisions of the Stamp Act. Duty was payable even on those sheets which contained nothing but advertisements.
5 9 *State Trials*, pp. 1334–72.

Nine John Horne

1 Asked for a talesman to make up the number.
2 14 *State Trials*, pp. 1095–200. John Tutchin was convicted for seditious libels in the *Observator*. The libels appeared in 1702–4, and he was convicted in 1704.

Ten John Hatchard

1 R. I. and S. Wilberforce, *The Life of William Wilberforce*, 1838, vol. 3, p. 360.
2 *Ibid.*, vol. 4, p. 319.
3 *Loc. cit.*
4 *Loc. cit.*
5 *Quarterly Review*, xxviii (1822), pp. 174–5n.
6 Haiti had won its independence from France in 1804, after a struggle lasting thirteen years.